Why Intelligence Fails

A volume in the series

Cornell Studies in Security Affairs

edited by Robert J. Art, Robert Jervis, and Stephen M. Walt

A list of titles in this series is available at www.cornellpress.cornell.edu.

Why Intelligence Fails

Lessons from the Iranian Revolution and the Iraq War

Robert Jervis

Cornell University Press

Ithaca and London

First published 2010 by Cornell University Press

Printed in the United States of America

Library of Congress Cataloging-in-Publication Data

Jervis, Robert, 1940–
Why intelligence fails : lessons from the Iranian Revolution and the Iraq War / Robert Jervis.
p. cm. — (Cornell studies in security affairs)
Includes bibliographical references and index.
ISBN 978-0-8014-4785-3 (cloth : alk. paper)
1. Intelligence service—United States—Evaluation—Case studies. 2. United States. Central Intelligence Agency—Evaluation—Case studies. 3. Iran—History—Revolution, 1979. 4. Iraq War, 2003—-Military intelligence—United States—Evaluation. 5. Weapons of mass destruction—Iraq. I. Title. II. Series: Cornell studies in security affairs.

JK468.I6J48 2010
955.05'3—dc22 2009030372

Cornell University Press strives to use environmentally responsible suppliers and materials to the fullest extent possible in the publishing of its books. Such materials include vegetable-based, low-VOC inks and acid-free papers that are recycled, totally chlorine-free, or partly composed of nonwood fibers. For further information, visit our website at www.cornellpress.cornell.edu.

Cloth printing 10 9 8 7 6 5 4 3 2 1

Many intelligence reports in war are contradictory; even more are false, and most are uncertain.

—Carl von Clausewitz

The main difference between professional scholars or intelligence officers on the one hand, and all other people on the other hand, is that the former are supposed to have had more training in the techniques of guarding against their own intellectual frailties.

—Sherman Kent, chairman of Board of National Estimates, Central Intelligence Agency, 1952–1967

Contents

Acknowledgments

I would like to thank Richard Betts, Elbridge Colby, Dan Caldwell, Michael Herman, Deborah Larson, Melvyn Leffler, Rose McDermott, Paul Pillar, Marc Trachtenberg, James Wirtz, and several members of the intelligence community for ideas and comments. John Collinge was very helpful in overseeing the declassification of my Iran report and the memoranda associated with it. The staff of the Arnold A. Saltzman Institute of War and Peace Studies provided invaluable assistance throughout. An early version of Chapter 3 appeared as "Reports Politics and Intelligence Failure: The Case of Iraq," in *Journal of Strategic Studies* 29, no. 1 (2006): 3–52, http://www.informaworld.com. This book has been cleared by CIA's Publications Review Board, but nothing of substance was deleted or would have been added if I had not had to submit it.

[1]

Adventures in Intelligence

> The trouble with this world is not that people know too little, but that they know so many things that ain't so.
>
> —Mark Twain

> If it were a fact, it wouldn't be intelligence.
>
> —General Michael Hayden,
> then head of National Security Administration

> We missed the Soviet decision to put missiles into Cuba because we could not believe that Khrushchev could make such a mistake.
>
> —Sherman Kent

Failure may be an orphan, but it is often a closely observed one. This is especially true for failures of intelligence, which tend to be as misunderstood as they are berated. They clearly are important. Despite the fact that most theories of international politics assume that actors see the world fairly accurately, many wars are preceded if not caused by failures to predict what others will do, and almost by definition crises involve intelligence failures.[1] For members of the general public, intelligence failures are of course upsetting because they are often linked to costly policy failures. The public often blames intelligence agencies, a propensity that policymakers are happy to encourage because it shifts the responsibility away from them.[2]

This book examines in detail two major intelligence failures: the inability of CIA and the wider intelligence community to understand the turmoil in

The Twain quote appears in many secondary sources, but it is unclear if or where he actually said it. Hayden is quoted in Bob Woodward, *Plan of Attack* (New York: Simon & Schuster, 2004), p. 132; Kent's comment is in "A Crucial Estimate Relived," originally published in CIA's classified *Studies in Intelligence* in 1964 and reprinted in *Sherman Kent and the Board of National Estimates: Collected Essays*, ed. Donald Steury (Washington, D.C.: Center for the Study of Intelligence, Central Intelligence Agency, 1994), p. 185.

Iran leading up to the overthrow of the Shah in 1979 and the misjudgment of Iraq's programs of weapons of mass destruction (WMD) in the period preceding the 2003 war. Before saying a bit about them, I should discuss the concept of intelligence failure, which is not as unambiguous as one might expect.[3]

Meanings of Intelligence Failure

The most obvious sense of intelligence failure is a mismatch between the estimates and what later information reveals. This is simultaneously the most important and least interesting sense of the term. It is most important because to the extent that policy depends on accurate assessments, almost the only thing that matters is accuracy.

In two ways the brute fact of the intelligence failure is uninteresting, however. First, it does not take much analysis to decide that there was a failure; all that is required is the observation that subsequent events did not match the assessments. Second, the fact that intelligence often is in error does not surprise scholars and should not surprise policymakers. Although most attention has been paid to surprise attacks because these failures are so traumatic, broadening the focus reveals many more cases, starting with the report in the Bible that the spies that Moses sent to the land of Israel overestimated the strength of the enemies to be found there.[4] As I will discuss further in the concluding chapter, the existence of failures is unfortunate but not mysterious. Intelligence is a game between hiders and finders, and the former usually have the easier job. Intentions, furthermore, often exist only in a few heads and are subject to rapid change. Deception is fairly easy, and the knowledge that it is possible degrades the value of accurate information, as we will see in the Iraq case.[5]

The second sense of failure is a falling short of what we expect from good intelligence. Judgments here must be much more subjective, and we need to separate collection from analysis because what can be expected from the latter depends in part on what information is available. We also need to distinguish what could have been collected given the technical means and agents available at one point in time from what might have been within reach had different decisions been made earlier—e.g., had the United States made the recruitment of sources within Iraq a priority in the 1990s. It is particularly difficult to know what can reasonably be expected in the way of collection, however, given the limitations imposed by technology and the difficulty in recruiting informed and reliable sources. Thus while it is clear that Iraq was a case of collection failure in that the evidence collected was scattered, ambiguous, and often misleading, it is harder to say whether it was a failure in terms of what is usual and whether reforms can produce marked improvement.

The second part of judging an intelligence failure is whether the analysts made good use of the information at hand, which is the topic of much of this book. The consensus is that there were many egregious errors in both the Iran and Iraq cases and that intelligence bears a significant responsibility for the policy failures. My summary view, however, is that while there were errors and analysis could and should have been better, the result would have been to make the intelligence judgments less certain rather than to reach fundamentally different conclusions. Furthermore, better intelligence would not have led to an effective policy. This argument is psychologically disturbing and politically unacceptable because it implies that intelligence errors can never be eliminated, makes blame hard to allocate,[6] shifts more responsibility to the political leaders, and indicates that the burdens of uncertainty under which they and intelligence labor are even greater than is generally acknowledged.

I believe that the unwillingness to confront these realities helps explain why most accounts of these and other cases imply that fixing the intelligence machinery will solve the problems. Politically this makes a good deal of sense; intellectually it does not. We like to think that bad outcomes are to be explained by bad processes and that the good use of evidence will lead to the correct conclusion, but as we will see, the prevailing reasoning often is done backwards: the fact that the answers were incorrect shows that procedures and ways of thinking must have been flawed. Even after correcting the significant errors, the most warranted inference may be incorrect; intelligence failures in the first sense should not be automatically seen as failures in the second sense. Improvements are possible, however, and intelligence and postmortems on failures can benefit from using standard social science methods. As the succeeding chapters will show, in many cases both intelligence and criticisms of it have only a weak understanding of the links between evidence and inferences and the most secure routes to drawing conclusions. More specifically, they do not formulate testable hypotheses and so often rely on beliefs that cannot be falsified, leave crucial assumptions unexplicated and unexamined, fail to ask what evidence should be present if their arguments are correct, ignore the diagnostic value of absent evidence, and fail to employ the comparative method and so assert causation without looking at instances in which the supposed causal factor was absent as well as at cases in which it is present. All too often, intelligence and critics rely on intuitive ways of thinking and rhetorical forms of exposition. More careful, disciplined, and explicit reasoning will not automatically yield the right answers but will produce better analysis, do a better job of revealing where the key differences of opinion lie, and increase the chances of being correct.

The Iranian and Iraqi Cases

Although my analysis of the Iranian and Iraqi cases draws on generalizations and other cases, it cannot establish how typical they are. But I think five points are clear. First, these cases are very important in themselves, being linked to policies that have had deep and lasting impact. This is not to say that the intelligence failures directly and completely explain American policies, let alone the outcomes. In the Iran case, even if the United States had been aware of the problems earlier, it might not have had viable options because the driving dynamics within Iran were largely immune to external interventions. Furthermore, the American government was so deeply divided that forewarning might not have led to the development of a policy that was coherent, let alone effective. In Iraq, although the belief that Saddam had active programs to develop WMD was central to the arguments for his overthrow, it is unlikely that any intelligence that was true to the information available would have produced a different decision. Nevertheless, these two misjudgments are central to the way the history unfolded, and I do not think I am alone in being curious as to how they occurred.

Examining these cases is especially important because the generally accepted views of them are incorrect. The failure to see that the Shah's regime was in grave danger is often attributed to the posited fact that CIA received most of its information from SAVAK (the Shah's secret police) and the misleading estimates of Saddam's WMD programs are commonly explained by the political pressures exerted by the Bush administration. As I will show, these claims cannot be sustained. Furthermore, it is generally believed that intelligence not only was wrong but made glaring errors in that much evidence was ignored and the reasoning employed was embarrassingly deficient. In fact, although the analysts did commit significant errors, their inferences were not unreasonable, and indeed at several points actually made more sense out of the information than did the alternative conclusions that turned out to be correct.

Third, although the cases had unique aspects, they exemplify at least some of the organizational routines and ways of thinking that characterize much of political and social life. Here as elsewhere, what people saw in the evidence was strongly influenced by their expectations and needs.[7] Of course, one reply is that it is the expectations generated by my own previous work that leads me to this conclusion, but I doubt that this is the whole story. It would be surprising if intelligence organizations and the individuals who compose them were to think in ways that were radically different from everyone else, and one of the themes of this book is that political psychology is an indispensable tool for understanding how governments see the world and make decisions. Although we cannot simply carry over what we have learned from other forms of decision making, such as how people vote or how businesses decide to invest—let alone how college sophomores respond in the laboratory—we need to take full account of how politics and psychology interact. We are dealing with human beings who have to make sense of overwhelming amounts of confusing information and to do so in a realm with its own set of incentives and pressures, and its own organizational culture.

Even if these cases are similar to those of other intelligence failures, the fourth point is that these studies confront a basic methodological problem in the inferences we can draw. Looking only at failures constitutes "searching on the dependent variable," a methodological shortcoming that makes it impossible to test causal arguments because it lacks the comparisons to cases of success that are necessary to determine whether factors that seem important are unique to cases of failure. Nevertheless, analysis of failures allows us to detect how people and units went astray and often permits comparisons within each case that establish the plausibility of causal claims.

Fifth and finally, although we are not in a position to estimate the frequency of intelligence failures (and both the numerator and the denominator would be difficult to determine), it is clear that they are not rare events. There is no reason to believe that they have become less frequent over time, and their recurrence indicates that even if particular instances could have been avoided, the general phenomenon cannot. Even if intelligence officers and decision makers become better social scientists, they will continue to deal with problems more difficult than those facing scholars and to do so with much less reliable information. Even if they read the information with care and know the relevant generalizations, the latter always have exceptions. Indeed, many intelligence failures concern such exceptions,[8] and this was true for the cases of Iran and Iraq.

The plan of the book is straightforward. The rest of this chapter tells the story of how I came to the subject. Although my first two books dealt with deception and perception, topics that obviously overlapped with intelligence, I had no intention of doing any case studies until I got drawn into consulting for CIA, initially on the problem of discerning Soviet intentions, and what I saw in those months taught me much about how intelligence was and is conducted. The main part of the next chapter is the study I did on why the CIA was slow to see that the Shah might fall. Written in the spring of 1979, this is an original document that has just been declassified. I also include the memoranda written by CIA officials in response to the report. To place it in context, elucidate some ideas that I felt constrained from discussing in a government document, and say a bit about how the report was received and what scholars now think about the case, I have added an introductory section. Chapter 3 is a study of the Iraq WMD intelligence failure. This, too, grows out of work I did for the government, but thanks to the enormous amount of material declassified in official postmortems, I can present the analysis now rather than waiting thirty years.

Chapter 4 starts by discussing broader issues of the contested relations between policymakers and intelligence. The former find the weaknesses of the latter both troubling and reassuring. They are troubling for obvious reasons but are also reassuring in that they allow the policymakers to follow their own preferences and intuitions when these diverge from intelligence and give them a handy scapegoat when things go wrong. Indeed, despite the fact that decision makers always say they want better intelligence, for good political and psychological reasons they often do not, which is part of the explanation for why intelligence reforms are rarely fully implemented. I then turn to a range of reforms, both those that are overrated and those that involve greater training and infusion of social science and are worthy of more attention.

Initial Contact

My first association with CIA came, appropriately enough, surreptitiously. In the summer of 1961 I went on a student exchange to the Soviet Union (which produced my wife as well as some interesting experiences). Prior to the group's departure, we received several briefings. Only one had much political content, and it stuck in my mind because as the trip progressed it became clear that none of my colleagues had sufficient political knowledge and skills to engage in serious discussions with the Soviet citizens we met, largely in staged settings. So this was left to me, and my Soviet hosts found me sufficiently argumentative that they assumed I was a CIA agent. On my return, I wrote the organization that had briefed us complaining that we were not putting our best foot forward.

I now assume that this organization was a CIA front. Not only does this fit with what we now know about how the U.S. government waged the cold war, but the following spring, when I was a senior at Oberlin College, I got a phone call from someone who identified himself as "with an agency of the federal government," asking to meet me in front of the Oberlin Inn. Naive as I was, I knew this could only be *the* Agency. My hunch was confirmed by the fact that the gentleman was wearing a trench coat and that upon entering his room, he turned on the TV and moved it so it was facing the wall, thereby foiling any listening devices planted by Soviet agents who had penetrated the wilds of Ohio. He asked if I could do something for the U.S. government that summer (I assume this would have been attending the Helsinki youth festival). I was shocked, not because of such a request but because I had agreed to be a summer intern in the State Department and assumed that one part of the federal government would know what another part was doing. I'm afraid that my knowledge of how the government worked was excessively abstract.

One other aspect of my trip to the Soviet Union intersected with my later work for the CIA. In recent years, I have chaired its Historical Review Panel (HRP), which advises the Agency on declassifying documents of historical value. Under an executive order issued by President Clinton, materials at least twenty-five years old are to be reviewed for declassification, which is how my Iran postmortem was released. The project is an enormous one, involving the review of millions of pages a year, and starting such an enterprise from scratch was especially challenging. The officials in charge therefore decided to begin with material that would be relatively easy to declassify, including the extensive collection of photographs CIA had gotten from travelers to the Soviet Union, which were deemed useful for compiling all sorts of routine information and training agents who would be inserted into the country. Not odd, I guess, but I sat up and took notice when we were shown samples, because in 1961 I was an amateur photographer and Soviet officials had told us of all the structures we could not photograph (e.g., bridges, train stations, and police stations). I thought this was a marvelous example of paranoia, and partly for this reason I took pictures of this type. I never did find out whether any of them ended up in the collection, but it was a nice reminder that even paranoids have enemies.

Consulting for CIA

My next encounter came fifteen years later. In the interim, I had written one book about signaling and deception and another about perception and misperception, topics of obvious interest to CIA.[9] Furthermore, after Jimmy Carter's election, a former Harvard colleague, Robert Bowie, had become director of CIA's National Foreign Assessment Center (NFAC) (what before and after this period was the Directorate of Intelligence). In the spring of 1977, Bowie asked me to serve for a year as a scholar in residence. This was an intriguing opportunity, but it was not clear exactly what I would do because I was not an expert in a region or the nuts and bolts of military power. I realized that, in all immodesty, what I was an expert on was how to draw inferences about other states' intentions, which covered a great deal of NFAC's mandate. I therefore proposed that I would serve as Bowie's special assistant, reviewing major reports for their quality. Bowie liked the idea but a week later reported that his security experts objected. In retrospect, I think I know why: at this time CIA was receiving information from two extraordinarily sensitive sources. We had tapped into Soviet undersea cables that carried high-grade material on Soviet naval matters, and a Polish colonel, Ryszard Kuklinski, was providing the United States with a treasure trove of the Warsaw Pact's plans and other documents.[10] Since there didn't seem to be another assignment attractive enough to merit moving my family to Washington, Bowie and I agreed that I would become a consultant, spend a couple of weeks at the Agency, and see what developed.

Despite my participation in the student exchange to the USSR and my later role in the Free Speech Movement as a graduate student at Berkeley, the clearance procedure proceeded relatively smoothly and quickly (the latter characteristic being especially unusual). There was one hitch, however. When I appeared for my polygraph, the examiner asked whether anyone other than a member of my immediate family lived in my house, and I replied that not only did we have a live-in housekeeper/babysitter but that she was an illegal immigrant. This stopped the proceedings because the background check had missed this. The omission was striking because the officers had talked to my neighbors, who knew our arrangement, which was common in middle-class Los Angeles. Keeping to myself the lack of faith in our procedures that this lapse engendered, I had to endure a week of being cleared only through the Secret level, which not only greatly restricted the documents I could read but also meant that I had to be escorted everywhere, giving me an annoying if fortunately brief taste of what it is like to be a second-class citizen.

Once the oversight was rectified and I passed my polygraph, I was told that someone from the office of security wanted to see me. This did not seem like good news, and I was taken upstairs to see a young man who was carrying a thick file that I realized was my life's history. But instead of asking embarrassing questions, he explained that he was taking a course in which several of my writings were assigned and he simply wanted to meet me! That accomplished, I could set to work.

Soviet Analysis

Bowie and his colleagues decided that the place for me was a small group in the Office of Strategic Research (OSR) that dealt with Soviet intentions. As I learned later, it was atypical, staffed entirely by PhDs and headed by a gifted and charismatic leader, Vernon Lanphier, who tragically died of cancer ten years later. Vern had been brought into CIA from the navy, and he had previously chaired a task force on Soviet civil defense, an important component of the debate then raging about Soviet strategic capabilities and intentions. As he explained to me, it had been an arduous job to reach consensus because of the fragmented nature of the information and the high political stakes, but the group finally succeeded in producing a document that everyone could live with. The two crucial components of the estimate of how many people the Soviets could protect in case of a U.S. attack were the size of the shelters and square footage per person that was allocated (the "packing factor," as it was called). Vern explained that six months or so after the estimate was published, a defector came out who provided credible evidence that they had overestimated (or underestimated, I can't remember which) the packing factor by 50 percent. He reported this to the leaders of the departmental teams that had produced the estimate and told them, "We can either spend a year going back over all the material or we can change our estimate of the area of the shelters by 50 percent in the other direction, and so leave the bottom line unchanged." Bureaucratic politics and human nature being what they are, everyone quickly agreed to the latter alternative.

With great excitement, I started reading the finished intelligence on the Soviet Union but soon was disappointed. I had expected both better raw information and better analysis. (Remember, however, that I, like most CIA analysts, lacked access to the material from Kuklinski and the undersea cables.) What was available at the standard code-word level (i.e., drawing on overhead photography and signals intelligence) did yield a great deal of information that was vital in providing confidence that the United States would not be taken by surprise by major improvements in Soviet military posture, but our understanding of Soviet defense and foreign policy remained sharply limited. With a few exceptions, the arguments and even evidence being mustered were quite similar to those available outside the government (in part because much secret evidence is soon made public).

Because of my previous work on deception and the central role it played in debates over Soviet policy, I looked for what I assumed would be the many classified volumes on this subject. I found remarkably little. There was one long paper by David Sullivan, but it stretched the evidence, implied enormous skill on the Soviet part, reduced its credibility by its shrill tone, and, to top it off, was badly written.[11] I did think it was worth more careful scrutiny than it received, however, and Sullivan himself soon lost his security clearances because he leaked extremely sensitive information to Senator Henry Jackson's office. My hunch is that American analysts, and probably those in other countries as well, resist taking deception as seriously as they should because doing so would make their already-difficult task even more trying. They work with fragmentary and contradictory information, and they could end up paralyzed if on top of this they had to fully consider that much of what they were seeing was staged for their benefit. The possibility that some parts of the adversary's government are misinformed or are deceiving other parts (what is known as Red-on-Red deception) is likely to be ignored because it, too, can undercut the validity of what would otherwise be very valuable intelligence. On the other hand, as we will see in the case of the misjudgment of Iraq's WMD programs, deception will be credited when it is convenient to assume that crucial evidence is missing not because it does not exist but because the adversary is concealing it.

Almost by definition, finding deception is very difficult, and searching for it can be corrosive because it leads to downgrading much valid and valuable information. Furthermore, in many cases states forego opportunities for deception, perhaps because they are too complicated or could end up revealing too much valid information, in part because if deception is discovered the other side will learn what the state was trying to lead it to believe, which is likely to be untrue. Thus it now seems that although the Soviets knew about the Anglo-American tunnel tapping into Soviet military cables under East Berlin in 1955, they never used this knowledge to feed us false information. (Even more striking is the fact that it appears that the Soviets never made use of the information they gleaned when they bugged the American embassy in Moscow in the mid-1950s.)[12] Nevertheless, I was surprised by how little concerted attention CIA gave to this problem. To take just one example, about six months after the launch of the new KH-11 spy satellite, the United States learned to its horror that an Agency employee, William Kampiles, had sold the Soviets CIA's operating manual (for the paltry sum of $3,000 at that). This unfortunate turn of events would have given the United States the ability to systematically compare what the satellite saw in the period when the Soviets knew its capabilities but the United States did not realize this, and what was observed later, when the Soviets knew that we knew that the capabilities were no longer secret. In this way we might have learned about Soviet deception goals, strategies, and techniques. As far as I know, however, we did not do such a study.

In the late 1970s the Agency launched a large project on deception. (The Defense Department's Office of Net Assessment probably was involved as well because its director, Andy Marshall, was very interested in deception and had commissioned several unclassified historical studies of the subject.) I was involved on the margins and thought the project was promising. It was canceled just as it was beginning to make progress, although later the Agency did do more to track the Soviets' activities.

I learned more about the nuts and bolts of analysis of Soviet strategic programs when I did the Iran study. Because I was teaching at UCLA, I did my reading and writing at a CIA facility made famous by being the site of major espionage some years earlier, a story told by Robert Lindsey in *The Falcon and The Snowman*. As this book explains, this group was engaged in technical analysis of Soviet missile programs through overhead photography and telemetry from Soviet missile tests. I was looked on by these people as a bit odd—not only was I doing something very political, but I was writing a long paper rather than producing a briefing (even in that pre-PowerPoint era people kept asking about my slides). Nevertheless, the arrangement was convenient, and I was befriended by a veteran photographic interpreter, which meant that on my breaks I could wander into his office, hear his stories, and examine interesting photographs, which of course were hard to figure out until he told me what I was looking at.

I learned a lot about Soviet missile programs from him, and one story has wider significance. We were talking about how blast-resistant Soviet silos were, and after he explained how some of the data from overhead photography fed into the calculation, he added, "But I think the official figure is too high. From what I can tell from the pictures, Soviet construction techniques are very sloppy and the concrete in the silos often has not set properly." Although of course American calculations had to be done conservatively, I wonder how high up the bureaucratic chain this information went.

Another incident reminded me of how government works. The initial analyses of Soviet missile tests were posted on a bulletin board in the most protected vault, and one day there was a report that indicated a significant increase in accuracy. This was important in light of the fierce debates about the vulnerability of American land-based systems. Although some of the people I talked to said that our missiles were already vulnerable and that this increment in accuracy would not matter much, this still was dramatic news, and it was classified at a higher level of secrecy than I had ever seen. As I read it, I realized that when I covered this material in class, I would have to be take great care not reveal this new development. I did not have to worry; it appeared in the next morning's newspapers.

Advantages of Being a Consultant

My position as a consultant gave me an unusual perspective. Although I was based at the working level, my anomalous status, sponsorship by the head of NFAC, and academic connections allowed me access to all levels of the organization. I was able to see how information was filtered and how people at different levels misunderstood one another. At one point Arnold Horelick, National Intelligence Officer (NIO) for Soviet affairs, produced a paper arguing that the Soviets were very optimistic about their prospects, especially in the Third World.[13] I talked it over with him, and he said that while he believed the conclusions, he had not meant to be dogmatic and wanted to stimulate discussion within the Agency. When I relayed this to one of my colleagues at the working level, he laughed and said that Horelick, who was an experienced Soviet analyst but was new to CIA, did not understand how the Agency operated. "When something like that comes down from the NIO, we have to take it as established."

Another advantage of being a consultant was that I was able to talk to people in other parts of the government. I was struck by the importance of networks, which again should not have surprised me. Since I was working on questions of Soviet intentions and capabilities, it was important to talk to people in Defense, State, and the National Security Council (NSC). But

I didn't know where or how to start. So Vern sent me to those who were his professional and personal friends. Many of them had studied with William Kaufmann at MIT, as Vern had. Indeed, I found that the hawk and dove camps within the government heavily overlapped with networks of students who had studied with Albert Wohlstetter at the University of Chicago and Kaufmann, respectively. I was passed along through the Kaufmann network, and my entree was facilitated not only by Vern's sponsorship but by my own political views and the fact that I had known Kaufmann when I was at Harvard.

One specific incident proved even more profitable to me, literally as well as figuratively. One day I went to the Pentagon to see a former student who was working in Program Analysis and Evaluation, the office that carried out the systems analysis begun in the years when Robert McNamara was secretary of defense. I was particularly interested in whether the United States needed to develop a powerful successor intercontinental ballistic missile (ICBM) to the Minuteman, an issue that was part of the broad hawk-dove debate. Although my inclination was to be skeptical, I had assumed that the proponents had a good case based on classified information, and so I asked my friend to show me what he had. He gave me one paper, which I found superficial and totally unsatisfactory. When I told him this, he grumbled a bit, dug deeper into his desk, and handed me a thicker packet. After half an hour I gave it back to him and said that while this was a bit better, it still did not address the serious questions. He replied, "Bob, you have just seen the best paper in the government on this subject. In fact, it is so thorough and careful that no one outside this office will bother to read it." I really was shocked. So on the airplane back to California that evening I outlined an article that I originally thought of as "Why Minuteman Vulnerability Doesn't Matter." Thinking about it more, I realized that the topic was broader: it really was "Why Nuclear Superiority Doesn't Matter." My article with this title was published in *Political Science Quarterly* and writing it provoked me to go deeper into the subject, which led to *The Illogic of American Nuclear Strategy* and, a few years later, *The Meaning of the Nuclear Revolution*.[14] The latter won the Grawemeyer Award for the best book of the year dealing with ideas for improving world order, which provided a handsome stipend.

But these activities also carried a penalty. Although my writings did not receive a great deal of public attention, they were noticed by people engaged in disputes within Washington. Thus when I was asked to consult on an interesting nuclear strategy project in the mid-1980s, I was informed that the security officer doubted that I could be cleared (my clearances having lapsed when I stopped consulting for CIA in 1980). Given my previous clearances from CIA, the State Department, and the Department of Defense, I thought this was odd, and I asked my friend Fred Iklé, undersecretary of defense for policy, to see if he could shed any light on this. He reported that he saw no problems. My inference is that the head of the project had checked not with his security officer but with his superiors and had been told that I was politically unacceptable. Of course, my reaction may be egocentric paranoia, but Washington does encourage such a reaction, in part because it sometimes turns out to be justified.

Final Thoughts

This might be an appropriate place to say that consulting with CIA is controversial within the academy. Some people decline to consult either because doing so would hinder their own research, especially in the Third World, or because they object to U.S. foreign policy. I have some sympathy with these positions but believe that over the long run it is better for the country and the world that the American government be as competent and well informed as it can be.

The obvious reply is that improvement will just enable the United States to do greater harm to others (and, as in Iraq, to itself). Better guidance toward a bad or even evil goal is not good. This view has some logic but has to rest on a root-and-branch rejection of American foreign policy. A Marxist would argue that American policy is driven by the exploitive needs of the capitalist class and will inevitably bring misery to the world. Others with a more realist bent could argue that exploiting the rest of the world serves the interests of the entire American population, not just a class, but the result would be the same infliction of harm.

A narrower argument against consulting with CIA is that the Agency tortures prisoners, engages in covert action, immorally meddles in others' affairs, and overthrows governments. But this position makes little sense. Not only is analysis separate from interrogation and covert action, but these are matters of national policy, established by the president (and perhaps Congress). CIA carries out the policy but does not make it, and I find it surprising that people refer to CIA's undermining or overthrowing other governments, which is like calling the wars in Vietnam and Iraq actions of the army. It is particularly odd that radicals attack CIA in this way, since doing so implies that policy would be better if it were under national direction and obscures the fact that credit or blame should go to the elected leaders, if not to the broader American political system and the American people.

Although my experiences with CIA have been frustrating, they have also been educational and enjoyable. It remains unclear how much good my reports did for intelligence, but at least I trust they did no harm. In return, I gained some understanding of how the system worked and was disabused of several of my naive notions. I also came to a renewed appreciation of the substance and methods of social science, which I had come to take for granted. Although social science rarely has the answers—or at least the right answers—it does have a body of knowledge that should be used, if with some skepticism, and a disciplined approach to forming questions and using evidence. Part of the explanation for the failures in Iran and Iraq is the unwillingness or inability of the intelligence and policymaking communities to take advantage of social science methods, as the next chapters will show. Part also lies in the continuing and necessary tensions between good intelligence and policymaking, a topic discussed in the concluding chapter.

[2]

Failing to See That the Shah Was in Danger

Introduction, Postmortem, and CIA Comments

My dabbling in issues of Soviet policy described in the previous chapter contributed to my education (more about the American government and policy than about the USSR), but it did not lead to a major project. At the time when this was becoming clear, my friend Bob Bowie, director of CIA's National Foreign Assessment Center (NFAC), was testifying before Congress that the unrest in Iran, although troubling, seemed to be diminishing. A few weeks later, however, a new round of riots was so serious that the Shah installed a military government and arrested several of his regime's leaders, thereby making it obvious that the situation was indeed serious. Bowie was curious, to put it mildly, about how he and CIA could have been so wrong and so asked me to evaluate NFAC's analysis. (As far as I know, this was independent of President Carter's handwritten note to Secretary of State Cyrus Vance, National Security Adviser Zbigniew Brzezinski, and Director of Central Intelligence (DCI) Stansfield Turner telling them that he was dissatisfied with the quality of political intelligence.) Bowie paired me with a senior analyst who was about to retire (and who thus would not suffer any ill effects from what he might say). But Bowie had little faith in his ability to do the analytic work required: "Treat him as your research assistant," he told me. I was taken aback, but unfortunately this appraisal turned out to be accurate. While my colleague made helpful comments and guided me through the bureaucratic labyrinth, he wrote only one section (legitimately still classified) that did not shed much light on the central questions. The few paragraphs that say, "One of us believes…" or that preface a statement with a blank that would have revealed a name are his and draw from his previous experience in the Agency. Bowie also gave us a very competent assistant who could dig out the papers that we needed, not an easy task in the era before files were electronic.

How the Report Was Done

It was clear that the report should stop in the first week in November 1978 because that is when the U.S. government became alarmed. The start date was more arbitrary, but I picked mid-1977 because that is when some minor unrest started, albeit coming from the secular opposition rather than the forces that later overthrew the Shah. My colleague and I looked at the reports from the embassy, consulates, and CIA station and studied the various forms of finished intelligence to see what inferences had been drawn.[1] We supplemented this with interviews with analysts, office managers, and the National Intelligence Officer (NIO), Robert Ames, a rising star who was to die in the bombing of the Beirut embassy in 1983 but who did not distinguish himself in this case. The people we interviewed were helpful, although of course I do not know what they withheld. The lead analyst, having been forced into retirement in the wake of the failure, was particularly forthcoming and friendly. Several of the other analysts were more guarded, which puzzled me until I realized that their careers, already damaged, could be further impaired by my report. I was also struck by the fact that their memories were quite good on substance but were often way off on timing—they could remember their reactions and evaluations but not when they were formed. This was true even though some of the events had occurred only three or four months previously. Some of the errors were self-serving, of course, but not all were, and they were frequent even when sensitive issues of being right were not at stake, as when the analysts tried to recall when various people traveled to the region. Events had come so thick and fast that it was simply impossible to keep them straight.

Although the materials I was working with were classified, the existence of my project was not, as I insisted on being able to tell colleagues and students what I was doing. I needed to talk to academic experts to learn about Iran, and it would have been inappropriate to do so without telling them my purpose in case they felt that helping me was a form of helping the CIA, which they did not want to do. Similarly, some of my graduate students were quite radical, and although I was not going to give them a veto over my activities, I wanted to allow them to change advisers if they would feel morally tainted by continuing to work with me. In fact, none of them cared, and the most radical one simply laughed.

Writing the Report

The work was straightforward, but a few points may be of interest. First, I believed that because the Iran intelligence failure was so salient and politicized, the report was sure to leak.[2] I therefore decided—unwisely in retrospect—that although it had been commissioned by Bowie, I would maintain my independence and not give him periodic progress reports. Perhaps the report would have had more impact had I kept him informed as I went along, but my initial concern was compounded when I learned that the colleague who was helping me was a close friend of the lead Iran analyst and when I also saw that although he and his colleagues had committed a number of blunders, they were not the complete idiots portrayed in the press. So I feared that the report would be seen as biased and exculpatory, which meant that it was even more important for me to maintain complete independence.

Collection, Reporting, and Policy

Being well aware of bureaucratic power and protocol, Bowie told me to concentrate on judging the quality of the work in light of the information the analysts had at their disposal and to probe less into the quality of this information, which would have taken me into the territory of the State Department, the embassy, and CIA's Directorate of Operations (DO). Indeed, other agencies were not informed that the study was under way. Because of these restrictions there were many subjects I could not get into and many things I could not say. Most obviously, I felt I had to downplay my criticisms of the collection efforts by the embassy and CIA station in Tehran (the memos by CIA officials about my report printed below felt I should have said more). The conventional story is that to avoid antagonizing the Shah, the U.S. government had agreed not to have significant contacts with the opposition and to get its information on sensitive domestic matters from SAVAK. Indeed, these "facts" were and still are used to explain why the United States failed to understand what was happening, but they are wrong. I am sure there were extensive CIA-SAVAK communications, but I suspect that these largely dealt with the activities of the Tudeh (Communist) Party. I looked only at reports about internal Iranian politics and the activities of the opposition, and almost none came from SAVAK. This meant that CIA was under a major handicap since SAVAK collected extensive information on the protests, which it did not share. As far as I could tell, CIA never commented on this or alerted intelligence consumers to the fact that a great deal was going on of which it was unaware, but at least its perspective was not biased by SAVAK. Bowie told me he thought that one reason we went astray was that we relied on SAVAK, and so he and other top Agency officials (and policymakers) may have greatly overestimated the body of information on which the analysts were able to draw. The problem was less that SAVAK fed us misleading information than that we knew very little.

It may be correct that the need to maintain good relations with SAVAK and the Shah inhibited an aggressive program of gauging the strength and goals of the opposition (or I should say oppositions, since different factions were involved). But Agency officials and, as far as I could tell, the State Department never argued for such a program or complained that restrictions were preventing them from getting information they needed. My guess is that the U.S. government is rarely well informed about opposition forces in undemocratic countries, especially when they are as unconventional (by our standards), as those in Iran. In the first place, to have gathered good information would have required a diplomatic and covert collection corps with linguistic skills. In fact, however, almost no Americans on the scene spoke good Farsi. Even if the Shah had not wanted the Americans to be isolated, they would have been. (Of course, one can argue that without any restrictions, the United States would have trained more people in Farsi, but I doubt this.) The linguistic barriers meant that what few and late contacts U.S. officials did have were concentrated on the secular, middle-class National Front. Unfortunately for American understanding, this group, important as it had been in an earlier period, played only a small role in the revolution. Furthermore, Iranian internal politics was not on the priority list established for DO. Much more important were the security of the secret American facilities that were intercepting Soviet communications and missile telemetry (the "listening posts"),[3] the threat of communism in the region, and the danger of anti-American terrorism.

The weakness of the collection effort meant that the analysts knew little about what the revolution's leader, Ayatollah Khomeini, was saying beyond what they could read in the newspapers. Although his cassette tapes circulated freely in Iran, the embassy and station were either unable to find them or felt they were of no value. Only one tape was received even though the leading Agency analyst told the station where in the Tehran bazaar they might be found.

I did not read enough reporting from other capitals to know whether this performance was markedly below standard. But if this had been the case, I would have expected to hear complaints. My fear is that what I saw was fairly typical. I would like to believe that things have greatly improved in the subsequent years, but in fact the increased burden on embassies to carry out other chores, especially escorting congressional and business delegations, has led to a decrease in the amount of political reporting.

Corridor gossip was that the ambassador in Tehran, William Sullivan, was an intimidating figure. "He ran a tight ship," was the phrase I heard. This certainly is plausible and would explain why reports from the consulates outside Tehran were more informative and why the embassy reporting become more incisive and worried when Sullivan was away on home leave in the summer of 1978.

The idiosyncrasies of the ambassador and the limits of what was reported were striking but perhaps not crucial. As far as I know, no other country was deeply alarmed much before November 1978. In the winter of 1978–79 there were public reports that months earlier Israeli intelligence had said that things were very serious, but such cables, if they existed, did not reach the American analysts. I was later told that significant information from Israel was passed through American military channels to DO, but I was never able to confirm this. I was also not able to inquire about what oil companies believed. They had a major stake and a major presence in the country and presumably had a wider range of contacts than the U.S. government did. But my mandate excluded exploring this question, and it remains unanswered.

My mandate also excluded U.S. policy. The larger issues, such as whether it was wise to have unstintingly supported the Shah over many years, I will still leave aside. But a few specific points can be broached. First, much ink has been spilled over what the United States should have done once it realized that the Shah was in danger. Indeed, these debates raged while I was writing the report. Although not without interest, they largely miss the point that by November effective American options had almost entirely disappeared: the Shah could no longer have brokered a compromise even had the United States pushed for such a solution, and a military coup would also have been likely to fail.[4] Much as American decision makers want to believe that they can influence the course of events, in this case, by the time they had a glimpse of what was afoot, it was too late. The descriptions of the horribly contentious and fragmented American decision-making processes in the winter would be amusing if they were not so disturbing, but while they tell us a great deal about the Carter administration, there is no reason to believe that a better process would have yielded an effective policy.[5]

Even before the situation received high-level attention, the government was divided on the issue of whether the Shah should be pushed toward greater democracy. Although Brzezinski and others were skeptical, until November, day-to-day guidance was supplied by the State Department, whose officials, especially at the working level, urged reforms. It is Political Science 101 that reform from above is very difficult and often leads to disintegration, as the experience of the former Soviet president Mikhail Gorbachev reminds us. The general topic is a fascinating one, but what is relevant here is how it did—or did not—play into intelligence. As my report makes clear, CIA expected that if instability grew, the Shah would "crack down"—i.e., use massive force. Later I will discuss why this sensible judgment was in error; the point here is that although cables from the U.S. embassy made it clear that it was urging the Shah to continue liberalizing, the analysts never pointed out the discrepancy between what they expected to happen if the situation deteriorated and the advice the United States was giving.[6] The reason is that analysts are not permitted to comment on American policy. This is understandable since decision makers do not want kibitzing, but it can be a major defect when the other side's behavior is strongly influenced by what the United States is doing.[7] The Iran analysts accepted this limitation and internalized it. Indeed, when I asked them about this discrepancy, they were startled and said they had not even noticed it.

I mentioned this problem only briefly. The first draft had several pages on it, including full documentation. But as I noted above, I expected the report to be leaked and feared that this section would stand out and would be seized upon to attack the Carter administration, which I did not think needed even more bashing. So I deleted most of the detail and just left the basic point. Had I not been constrained, I would have emphasized the point, which I do think has general importance. Ironically, the Agency commentators criticized the report for lack of attention to the political context.

Even though I doubt that American policy determined the Shah's behavior, I was and still am puzzled by the State Department's position. Since Bowie did not want other parts of the government to know what I was doing, I could not talk to people at State, and nothing I have read later gives me a coherent picture of what these officials were thinking when they pushed for liberalization. This behavior would have made sense if they had believed that the regime was strong and skillful enough to carry out this policy. Instead, they seem to have believed that the regime was not only despicable but also rotten, which means they should have sounded the alarm early (and State's Bureau of Intelligence and Research (INR) did take a pessimistic position). They also should have been hesitant to push for reforms that could have brought the regime down. Perhaps they shared the impression of some nongovernmental observers that a revolution would not be disastrous for the United States, that Khomeini would be moderate and/or not seek to dominate the government, and that the liberal middle-class reformers would take power.[8] In the period covered by my study, these questions did not arise for CIA because it believed that the Shah's regime was in no real danger. It is unfortunate that there were no full and frank discussions during the spring and summer when the United States had more options.

In light of recent controversies, we should ask whether intelligence was highly politicized—i.e., whether the analysts were pressured by policymakers or, more likely, whether their knowledge of the extent to which the United States relied on the Shah generated psychological pressures against seeing that American policy was not working. I do not think either of these was the case, although some of the CIA commentators on the report have a somewhat different view. Until early fall of 1978, policymakers were not concerned enough about Iran to pay any attention to intelligence. Then, as things grew more serious, the administration was preoccupied with the Camp David negotiations with Israel's prime minister Begin and Egypt's president Sadat. My interviews did not produce any indications that intelligence analysts suppressed doubts in order to avoid disturbing their superiors or customers, although such biases, discussed in the Iraq case, can operate without the person's awareness. If the analysts did trim their sails, then journalists and other countries' diplomats who did not feel these pressures should have been much quicker to understand what was happening. Although I am sure that one could find some people who were, most journalists reported on the waxing and waning of the unrest without any greater insight than that shown in the embassy cables or the intelligence. Similarly, other countries that were not so tied to the Shah do not appear to have seen the situation any more clearly.

Substance of the Report

I hope the report speaks for itself, but before highlighting a few of the main findings and what surprised me, I want to reassure readers that the parts that are deleted ("redactions" is the term of art) do not change the story. Many classification markings, references to other documents, and names have been removed, as has some material provided by other governments or intelligence services. In a few cases, information from sensitive sources has been deleted. But everything important has been declassified. Because I wanted to make the report as complete as possible, I included large sections that quoted and summarized reports from the field and detailed what NFAC drew from them. In the interests of keeping this chapter to a manageable length I have deleted some of this material. Such cuts are indicated by ellipses, and are distinguished from redactions which are marked by angle brackets. The report also included a summary of fifteen pages (unusually long for a government paper) drawn entirely from the text. I have not printed it on the grounds that readers of this book are more willing than officials to read the entire document. The only other changes I have made are to correct typographical errors.[9]

Surprises

The first surprise was the paucity of resources dedicated to Iran. There were only two political analysts and two economic analysts in CIA; neither INR nor the Defense Intelligence Agency (DIA) had an expert on Iranian politics, although each did have a person who was nominally responsible. The CIA station in Tehran was not large and produced little political intelligence. Like many people who did not know the government from the inside, I had assumed extensive coverage of every country. In fact, this was out of reach and remains so. During the cold war, only the USSR and, to a lesser extent, the People's Republic of China (PRC) were studied by more than a handful of analysts. I was also surprised that CIA in particular and the government in general did not engage in more thorough and detailed research.[10] There probably was more work of this type on Iran than on many countries because the lead analyst liked to work in depth, which he could do because there was little pressure for comments on current happenings. Ironically, in the summer of 1978 he completed a long paper on the religious leadership. But this paper, like much else I saw, was more descriptive than analytical. It had a lot of facts but did not try to make much of them.

Until the crisis, intelligence on Iran did not receive much of an audience. This also surprised me, although it should not have. Top officials are incredibly busy, and even thirty years ago, when they probably read more than is the case now, intelligence about a country that did not require immediate decisions could not attract many readers. This not only lowered the analysts' morale but meant that their reports did not get the kind of questioning and critical scrutiny that could have helped keep them on their toes. (As the Iraq case shows, attention can be a mixed blessing, especially when policymakers know the answers they want to hear.)

I had expected, again naively, that even if policymakers did not read long intelligence papers, the members of the intelligence community would constitute a sort of intellectual community, with people probing, commenting on, and criticizing one another's work. In fact, this was not the case, and contacts among the people working on Iran were relatively infrequent. Some years earlier an enterprising State Department desk officer had organized a monthly meeting, but such interactions depended on individual initiative and so were episodic. Contact was also inhibited by CIA's physical isolation and the fact that thirty years ago secure telephones were rare and cumbersome.[11] This might not have been so bad if analysts working on different countries had formed a peer group whose members shared ideas and reviewed one other's analysis. But the orientation of the Agency was vertical, not horizontal, and despite the fact that many analysts moved from one country to another every few years, not only concerns for security but informal norms militated against these kinds of discussions.

Even more startling, there was little communication between the political analysts on Iran, located in the Office of Political Affairs (OPA; also known as Office of Regional and Political Affairs, or ORPA) and economic analysts, housed in the Office of Economic Affairs (OEA). From my perspective, one obvious source of the unrest was the unstable economic situation.[12] This obviously called for joint political and economic analysis. But little occurred as each group examined its area with little attention to the political consequences of economic changes or the way in which Iranians might use political instruments for economic purposes. Interestingly enough, when Ronald Reagan was elected president and William Casey took over as DCI, he not only replaced NFAC with the Directorate of Intelligence (DI) but changed its internal organization from a functional to a geographic one, thereby bringing economic, military, and political analysts into closer contact.[13]

I was also surprised that CIA had few contacts with academics and other outside experts. Of course the Vietnam War had generated a great deal of mistrust and hostility, and many academics strongly objected to American policies or feared that associating with CIA would hamper their foreign contacts. For their part, CIA analysts anticipated a chilly reception if they reached out to academics, and they were so accustomed to living in a highly classified world that they had difficulty talking to people without clearances. Furthermore, despite some lip service, CIA as an institution did not foster outside contacts. It is worth noting that more contact would not have been likely to lead CIA to sound the alarm much sooner than it did. Outside experts were just as blind to what was happening in Iran as were the analysts, partly because they shared the same assumptions, which I will note below. Indeed, at one point the Agency did consult Iranian experts, and while some of them had different political preferences and a greater sense of the strength of anti-Shah sentiment, in harmony with prevailing social science theories they saw the opposition in terms of a liberal, modernizing, middle class. There was little understanding of what was really happening in Iran.

Another surprise concerned a different aspect of the relations between CIA and scholars. I had expected analysts to work in a manner not unlike that of academics. Both groups are, after all, trying to make sense of the world. But in the Iranian case and many others involving the politics of a country, despite being called analysts, CIA officers writing on Iran were more like journalists than social scientists. That is, they drew heavily on their sources and tried to construct a coherent story. Use of explicit methodologies and analytical frameworks, drawing on generalizations, and posing of alternative hypotheses were foreign to most of them. They would utilize multiple kinds of information and sometimes note trends and changes, but they kept close to their sources. If the cables from the field explicitly pointed to a conclusion, the analysts would draw it, but rarely would they go much beyond, let alone against, the incoming information.

A final and related surprise was the importance of the norms, informal organizational dynamics, and incentive structure that characterized the production of intelligence. I am told that on reading my report, one CIA official said, "Jervis is an expert on misperception, so it is no wonder that he found it." He was not completely wrong, but it is this remark more than the report that illustrates the propensity for people to see what they expected. What I hope comes through in my report is not only the perceptual problems but also the general sense that the organization was not run in a way that would encourage thoughtful political analysis. Putting aside the Soviet and perhaps Chinese areas, which of course were the largest and most important to the Agency, in-depth research was unusual, and probing for alternative explanations of what was happening was very rare. The incentives were to publish in the National Intelligence Daily (NID) (now the Senior Executive Intelligence Brief, or SEIB) and the President's Daily Brief (PDB), although the latter then did not have the depth or prominence that it later achieved under President George W. Bush. These briefings are like newspaper stories, designed to tell the reader what has just happened. There is no space for background and perspective, let alone analysis of alternative possibilities, evaluation of the quality of the evidence, or a discussion of the reasoning behind the conclusions. Consistent with this culture, there was little peer review. Review there was, but it was hierarchical, as nothing went out the door of CIA without oversight by several levels of managers. It does not appear that these were analytically probing, however.

Of course my objections rest in part on the implicit model of an intelligence agency as resembling a university, but this may not be foolish. For all their faults, universities and academic disciplines do a good job of developing knowledge, and they do this in part by a rigorous system of peer review. This is why I asked CIA to allow me to present my draft at a meeting with three experienced analysts and three outsiders. Almost all postmortems have called for more peer reviewing, and indeed, major estimates now not only are scrutinized by the entire National Intelligence Council but are commented on by informed outsiders. But this cannot substitute for sustained internal peer review throughout the organization, of which there was none on Iran in 1978. Today there is more of this, but it is still not enough.

Four Major Errors

The report details the problems with the analysis that I found, and here I want to note four key factors. First, some of the central beliefs held by intelligence were disconfirmable. One major reason why the analysts did not think the situation was dangerous was that the Shah had not cracked down. If it were dangerous, they reasoned, he would do so. The very absence of a massive response then led them to conclude that the situation, although unpleasant, remained under control. This inference was not foolish. Indeed, a good social scientist would have argued that revolutions cannot succeed in the face of functioning and effective security forces, and as I will discuss below, it was not until months after the revolution that crucial facts came to light that might have explained why the Shah did not use them. But what the analysts failed to realize was that they could discover that this belief was incorrect only if the crisis became very severe. In parallel, the important belief that the opposition was such a diverse group that it would eventually split could be shown to be false only when it was too late. This meant that analysts lacked early warning indicators and, even worse, neither they nor the policymakers knew that this was the case.

Second, the analysts—and everyone else—believed that the Shah was strong and decisive and would not shy away from what he needed to do. American and other diplomats saw the Shah as a self-confident, even arrogant, leader who would not waver. As I will note below, only subsequently did scholars paint a different picture of the Shah, drawing on his youth and behavior in the 1953 coup. Had analysts gone back over this history or had they read the assessments written in the 1950s and 1960s, they would have seen a different Shah, as CIA officials noted in their comments on my report.

Third, no one in or out of the government understood the role of religion and Khomeini. The senior Iranian political analyst had a great interest in the religious establishment and had conducted thorough if descriptive research on this subject, but he did not perceive the beginnings of what we would now call radical or fundamentalist Islam. Hindsight of course is easy, but perhaps he and others should have realized that the Shah's clamping down on all other forms of opposition meant that the religious leaders could become focal points for antiregime sentiment and activities. The main difficulty was that analysts, like everyone else at the time, underestimated the potential if not existing role of religion in many societies. Although modernization theory had taken a battering by the late 1970s, it still seemed inconceivable that anything as retrograde as religion, especially fundamentalist religion, could be crucial.

Finally, the role of nationalism and its twin, anti-Americanism, was missed and misunderstood because CIA associated these forces with terrorism, a danger that was of primary concern. Analysts were aware that Khomeini had led violent protests against the status-of-forces agreement governing the small American military presence in Iran in 1964 (although when I asked to see the CIA analyses of these events, I was told it would take weeks to retrieve them from dead storage), and they took comfort from the fact that this pattern was not recurring. What they and most others missed was that Iranian nationalism had turned not against the United States directly but against the Shah because he was seen as an American puppet. Perhaps if the embassy and CIA officers had filled the analysts' requests for more of Khomeini's tapes or had been able to talk to people in the streets, bazaars, and mosques, intelligence would have detected this dynamic. But people were slow to understand how nationalism was functioning, especially because everyone in the United States knew that the Shah was anything but a puppet.

Anticipating Revolutions

As the previous points indicate, CIA was not good at determining the causes or the extent of the revolutionary impulses in Iran. Neither this nor the subsequent (and probably ineffective) call for American intelligence to be in better touch with mass opinion should be surprising. For one thing, predicting revolutions is very hard. They are not well understood by social science and almost by definition must come as a surprise to many informed observers, especially those in authority. If the latter understood what was coming, they would flee, use force, or make concessions.[14] While those who would try to make a revolution must make themselves believe that success is possible, most people must remain in doubt because revolutions arise not from a simple aggregation of desires and action but from a complex interaction among large number of individuals, groups, and centers of power. Anthony Parsons, the British ambassador at the time, gets at part of this when he says that "we were under no illusions about the popularity of the regime.... Where we went wrong was that we did not anticipate that the various rivulets of opposition, each of which had a different reason for resenting the Shah's rule, would eventually combine into a mighty stream of protest."[15] But these groups did not act independently of one another because what each did depended in part on what it thought others would do: beliefs about a revolution's prospects of success are central, volatile, and subject to self-fulfilling dynamics.[16]

Although intelligence organizations do not like to recognize it, they rarely have special advantages in understanding revolutions and general political developments. CIA and its counterparts are in the business of stealing secrets, but secrets are rarely at the heart of revolutions.[17] This is not to say that confidential information is completely irrelevant. As I will discuss later, there was a secret that helps explain the Shah's behavior, better access to the government's inner workings might have indicated that a full crackdown was unlikely, and agents or listening devices close to Khomeini could have told CIA much about the thinking and intentions of the revolutionaries. But even this information would not have predicted how the public would react, which was the crucial factor, and indeed Khomeini himself was wrong in some of his estimates.[18] Spying on the secular opposition also was possible, but any secrets gained would have been misleading because these groups were as misinformed as U.S. intelligence was.

Better nonsecret information would have helped more. Mingling with the demonstrators and talking to the rank and file in the opposition might have shown the breadth and depth of the hatred of the Shah, the power of nationalism, and the role of religious leaders as focal points. But even with the relevant linguistic and interpersonal skills, it is unclear how much any foreigner could have learned, although American diplomats serving in the consulates outside Tehran did provide better information because they mixed with people across much more of the social spectrum.

Changes

The obvious question is the extent to which the Agency has changed since the late 1970s. I cannot offer anything like a full answer because the only subsequent case I studied in detail was that of Iraqi WMD (see chapter 3), and it was of a very different type. For what it is worth, however, my impression is that there has been significant improvement. Despite all the errors discussed in chapter 3, the levels of competence and professionalism seem higher than they were in 1978. Of course, the issue of Iraqi WMD in 2002–2003 was much more important than Iranian politics was in 1978 and thus received many more resources and was subject to more in-depth research and more vigorous debate. It could be that if one were to look at intelligence today on a country with the same level of priority that Iran had in 1978, things would look much the same. Nevertheless, my sense is that there has been an improvement in the general level of training, analytical sophistication, and openness to outside views, in part as a reaction to the Iraq failure. The basic culture remains, however, and will be discussed in chapter 4.

How My Report Was Received

This section can be quite short because as far as I could tell at the time, there was no substantive reaction to my report. What I heard was nothing—literally nothing, not even a pro forma thank you, let alone a request to come and discuss the report. Even though I had become accustomed to some of the strange habits of CIA, this did seem odd. When I was back at CIA headquarters on some other business about six months later, I asked to see Helene Boatner, the head of OPA. We had a nice talk, and she said, "I know that our not having gotten back to you must confirm all your worst suspicions about our desire to change. But let me reassure you. We have taken your report very seriously and soon are going to have a retreat with top managers and will ask you to join us to talk about what we should do." That was the last I heard.

As I mentioned, I thought that if the report leaked, it would be attacked as being too soft on the Agency. Thus I was surprised to hear the rumor that DCI Turner and his deputies considered it an extremely harsh indictment. In fact, they initially refused to let anyone other than the top officials see it. Since I had written it so that it might be of value to middle-level managers and working-level analysts, I thought this was a waste. After a while, it was released and used in the new training courses that were being instituted. Some friends have said that through this channel the report eventually was widely read and had a noticeable impact.

I now know a bit more about how the report was received because I have just read the memos that are printed in this book, with a few redactions and the omission of some summaries. They can now speak for themselves, and I have only a little to add. It appears that Bowie asked for comments only from the former NIO for the area, David Blee, and the three members of the Senior Review Panel (SRP). I assume that Blee is correct in saying that I was wrong to assert that the National Intelligence Estimate (NIE) was started as part of a preset schedule, but my main point remains that it was not triggered by deep concern or an understanding that the situation was unstable. The members of the SRP had much more to say. This is not surprising since they were experienced and, while familiar with the Agency, were outsiders.

Klaus Knorr was a professor of political science at Princeton and had written an excellent postmortem on the Cuban Missile Crisis, based, I am sure, on work he did for CIA.[19] It is not surprising that I find his comments most congenial, although I may be influenced by his praise for the report. Bruce Palmer was a former army general who had held many high-level positions, including leading American troops in the Dominican Republic in 1965. He did not have much to say. This is not true for William Leonhart, a former ambassador. Although I find his tone annoying, he makes a number of good points.

They all feel that American policy had more of an impact on the estimates than I said. They may be correct, but as I noted earlier, I did not feel it was appropriate to get far into this subject. More important, I did not see any evidence for this influence. But as I have noted throughout this book, it can be hard to detect. It is perhaps true that the general sense that the United States lacked any alternative delayed a recognition of how serious the situation was, but I still doubt that this was a large part of the problem.

Bowie and Leonhart ask whether the revolution was inevitable. This is an intriguing and important question and one that is still open for discussion. It was not central to the report, however, which was commissioned in November when events had not yet unfolded, and the mandate was to explore why NFAC was slow to see that the situation was quite dangerous, something that was true whether or not it ended in revolution. For what it is worth, I do think the revolution was inevitable by the middle or end of November, especially since the Shah had decided not to use massive force.

All commentators note the limits of the report, and these stemmed from my desire not to overreach, my lack of familiarity with CIA (let alone the rest of the intelligence community), and the fact that I was not working on the project full-time. Leonhart in particular raises important issues, and he is quite correct to say that I criticized the role of managers without documenting exactly what they did or did not do. The problem here was that I worked mostly from the written record, and it contained few comments by managers. I thought it was telling that neither the NIO nor the analysts said that the intervening levels had improved analysis or asked probing questions, but Leonhart is right that this is not definitive. Since I believe that the role of these managers is important, as I will discuss in chapter 4, it would be valuable to have greater information about what they did in this and other cases.

I find it disturbing that only Knorr raises the obvious question of possible remedies for the deficiencies, and even he has no suggestions. The point of the exercise, after all, was to improve the organization. I was not asked to make recommendations; I had only a limited store of them and was quite discouraged about the possibilities for change. I now know a bit more and am a bit more optimistic, and so I address this subject in chapter 4.

A memo indicates that Bowie discussed the report with Turner, but there is no record of what they said. Both Knorr and Boatner (in a memo not reproduced here) felt it should have fairly wide distribution, but Bruce Clarke, Bowie's successor as director of NFAC, decided to send it only to branch chiefs at OPA and not to let it go outside NFAC. I would be curious to know what the branch chiefs did with it. Consistent with her memo and conversation with me, Boatner presumably would have liked more discussion of the report within the Agency and would have welcomed my participation. I have no doubt that this would have been interesting, and I like to think it would have been helpful to the government. For all I know, there were productive discussions that did not leave a paper trail, but I do see this as a missed opportunity.

The Iranian Revolution in Retrospect

When I wrote my report, the Iranian revolution was still under way, and it would have been both premature and a digression to try to analyze its causes. All that was relevant for me was the reasoning that led CIA to conclude that a revolution was unlikely. Even now, it would be a digression—and beyond my expertise—to fully analyze it.[20] But a few remarks are in order, especially concerning one crucial factor that was not known at the time.

Scholarly interest in revolutions waxes and wanes, often in synchrony with the prominence of such disturbances in current politics. Since revolutions have not been prominent recently (unless we count the disintegration of the USSR in that category), it is not surprising that the subject has become less popular as a topic of study. We still lack a general theory of revolutions, and as noted, their nature makes such a theory particularly problematic. There will always be discontent in repressive regimes, and its breadth and intensity will be hard to judge.

The Shah not only was repressive but also sought major economic and social change with his "White Revolution." A fundamental cause of the actual revolution, and one that intelligence and other observers should have grasped at the time, was that the Shah's project was a dangerous one. Losers as well as winners were created by economic change, and even individuals and groups whose misfortunes an objective observer might attribute to other causes were quick to blame the Shah. Although the power of the "revolution of rising expectations" was simplified and exaggerated by social scientists during the period when modernization theory flourished, it retains some validity, and the Shah had established expectations that would have been hard to meet. It was, then, perhaps foolish of many observers—and not only of President Carter, who coined the phrase—to see Iran as an "island of stability."

In the late 1970s the Shah instituted political reforms to supplement economic ones, and these allowed opposition to surface. More important than American pressure to liberalize (although the perception and anticipation of Carter's policy may have emboldened the secular reformers)[21] was the Shah's belief that greater popular participation, if not Western-style democracy, was a central part of development and would increase support for him and his policies. After all, these policies were for the good of the country and so would receive widespread assent. But revolutions from above are notoriously difficult to manage, and neither the Shah nor foreign observers fully took this into account.

The Shah labored under another handicap, one that is more apparent in retrospect. This was his association with American dominance. To American officials, the Shah was an important ally deserving of full support but far from a puppet. Although the United States and United Kingdom, in conjunction with a significant segment of Iranian society, had saved his throne in 1953, a generation later he was very much his own man, or so we thought. Many Iranians, however, saw him as a tool of the Americans, and this meant that nationalism could be enlisted in a revolutionary cause. Since the Americans' perspective was different, this vulnerability of the regime escaped them.

When the opposition grew, the Shah used measured force but never instituted full-scale repression. How is this to be explained? In the report I admitted to being puzzled. Until the final months of the regime the army would have carried out such orders. Why did the Shah not try to save himself? Carter's critics blame the continuing American support for liberalization. While the contradiction noted earlier of expecting the Shah to use force if he had to and urging continued political liberalization was more evident to the Shah than it was to the Americans, to attribute his behavior to American mixed messages would be to make the same error that the Shah's nationalist critics did of seeing him as a puppet. It is possible that, like foreign intelligence services, he simply misjudged the situation until it was too late. But unlike them, he could not have relied on the belief that the situation must be stable because if it had not been, he would have used force. After the fact, the Shah said that "a sovereign may not save his throne by shedding his countrymen's blood," a view he said he expressed to the British and American ambassadors in the fall and winter of 1978.[22] But this is not the entire story.

I suspect that much of the answer lies in three factors involving the Shah. The first was his personality. Although most contemporary observers believed that he was strong and decisive, this was a misreading of the man. As Marvin Zonis has shown, throughout his career he was more often vacillating and hesitant,[23] and in the year before the revolution he was further weakened by the deaths of two of his very few confidants. Intelligence had characterized him correctly in the decade following the 1953 coup, but in the subsequent years his effort to appear in charge of himself as well as the country took hold, partly because of his unwillingness to brook any opposition. Had CIA and other observers understood the Shah correctly, they would not have been so certain that he would act boldly to save his regime. The United States might also have been more careful to speak with one voice, although it is far from clear that this would have been possible or made a difference.

A second factor compounded the first: the Shah's serious illness. For some years he had been under treatment for a form of cancer, and he died shortly after the revolution. It is possible that the disease or the medicines affected his will, energy, or judgment. But even if this was not the case, the illness affected his calculations. He wanted above all to pass on not only his throne but his rule to his son. He realized, however, that his son was less experienced and skillful than he was and lacked the unswerving loyalty of the military. He knew that if he used massive force, the power of the military would inevitably grow and that in the near future when his son succeeded him, he would be more its tool than its master. Even if the military stayed in the background, his son would not be capable of running the sort of repressive regime that would be necessary for several years after a massive crackdown. Force could then save the Shah but not what he cared most about. It therefore made sense to gamble that the combination of measured force and continued liberalization would bring about conditions under which his son could play a central role.

CIA knew nothing about the Shah's illness, however. Indeed, as far as I can tell, the Shah's French doctors did not even tell their own government.[24] In retrospect, there were signs of the Shah's illness, and field reporting contained scattered comments about his appearing unwell, but this was mainly in the context of his changing moods, and no diplomat or intelligence service even entertained the hypothesis that the Shah's behavior was traceable to an ailment. Had he been healthy, he might have acted decisively and been able to prevent or at least postpone the revolution. Here as elsewhere, social scientists are prone to underestimate the influence of disease.[25] In our discussion of "fundamental causes" of phenomena like wars and revolutions we often overlook human skill and frailty.

Observers did know, but perhaps underestimated, the impact of the Shah's conspiratorial cast of mind. At the risk of indulging in national stereotypes, I must say that in this he mirrored his countrymen. In the years since the revolution, many of us have met educated Iranian émigrés who have earnestly asked why the United States put Khomeini into power. To the protest that while American policy may have blundered and failed to keep him out of power, surely the United States did not seek his victory, the reply always is that nothing happened in Iran against American wishes, and so the United States must have desired this, albeit for reasons that cannot be readily discerned. Perhaps because for much of the twentieth century Iran was strongly influenced if not controlled by first British and then American power that was exercised behind the scenes, Iranians overestimated the skill and cunning of these countries. In their memoirs Sullivan and Parsons reveal their inability to talk the Shah out of his belief that the rising unrest had to be explained by the machinations of the American and British Secret Services, a view that the Shah reiterated in his own memoirs. British and American avowals of support, meant to stiffen the Shah, may have had the opposite effect of leaving him even more convinced that he was the victim of a devious plot. Building on what must have been his puzzlement over the American urgings to simultaneously liberalize and use force if need be and perhaps influenced by his disease and the effect of medications, the Shah compounded an extremely difficult situation by constructing a mental world that was even more threatening than the one he actually faced. This was also a difficult world for observers to penetrate, especially when they thought they understood what was happening.

Note: Some elements of the following report remain classified, and many internal references were suppressed before its release. The text indicates missing text materials within angle brackets. Some background and summary materials from the report have also been omitted; such omissions are also indicated within angle brackets.

Acronyms

DIA	Defense Intelligence Agency
D/NFAC	Director of the National Foreign Assessment Center
EIWR	Economic Intelligence Weekly Report
GOI	Government of Iran
IIM	Interagency Intelligence Memorandum
INR	Bureau of Intelligence and Research at the State Department
NESA	Near East South Asia
NFAC	National Foreign Assessment Center
NID	National Intelligence Daily
NIE	National Intelligence Estimate
NIO	National Intelligence Officer
NSC	National Security Council
OER	Office of Economic Research
OPA	Office of Political Affairs
ORPA	Office of Regional and Political Analysis
SAVAK	The Shah's internal security service
SNIE	Special National Intelligence Estimate
USG	US Government

Analysis of NFAC's Performance on Iran's Domestic Crisis, Mid-1977–7 November 1978

"It has been explained to me that it would have been impossible for the Mullahs to have obtained this power to lead a large and successful protest movement had it not been for the general discontent which prevails throughout Persia which has led the people to hope that by following their advice some remedy may be found for the grievances from which they undoubtedly suffer. . . . It is evident that a severe blow has been dealt at English influence in Persia." British Ambassador to Iran, 1892.

"Either we are doing something wrong, or else [the protesters] are all crazy. But there are so many of them. Can so many all be crazy?" Shah of Iran. (Tehran 4355, 8 May 1978.)

Note

The purpose of this report is to address NFAC's performance in treating the Iranian situation from the summer of 1977 to November 1978, when it became clear that the Shah's regime might not survive. We have therefore examined only the information that was available to NFAC at the time and discussed the inferences that were or could have been drawn from it. (We have not analyzed the quality of that information or discussed what might have been done to improve it.). . . .

INTRODUCTION

1. NFAC failed to anticipate the course of events in Iran from late 1977 to late 1978. It was not alone. It was no further off the mark than its main source of information, the Embassy in Tehran. Indeed few observers expected the protest movement to be able to bring down the Shah. Some academics and journalists thought the Shah was weak, but we have seen no published articles indicating that they expected him to fall by early 1979.* By the end of August 1978 some countries were becoming more pessimistic than NFAC, but the differences were mainly of shading and tone. The State Department, and particularly the Iranian Country Director, had a more accurate view than did NFAC, but little of his view was passed on to the Agency. (For a further discussion of this point, see pp. 103–104, 134–135)

* The comparison to academies and journalists is appropriate because in this case, unlike many others, little of the important information was secret and available only to governmental analysts.

2. There was also an intelligence failure in a second sense—there was evidence available at the time which pointed to the Shah's vulnerability. With hindsight, much of it stands out and is reported below. Because this information was scattered and ambiguous and because there were good reasons to expect the Shah to survive (these are discussed below), it is much harder to say whether there was an intelligence failure in the third sense of the term—i.e., given the information available at the time, was NFAC's judgment unreasonable? Did NFAC ignore or misinterpret events in ways and to an extent that consumers can legitimately expect should not and will not occur? Although we cannot give a short and precise answer to this question, much of the discussion below addresses this point. In addition, we will try to explain why the analysts went wrong, note the ways in which the intelligence production processes inhibit good analysis, and discuss ways in which NFAC might do better in the future.

3. By looking only at a single case, many questions cannot be answered. These deal with how common some of the problems we have detected are and the importance of factors which can only be examined in a comparative context. For example, if one wanted to look with care at the question of the degree to which analysis was hampered by lack of information derived from contacts with opposition forces, one would have to compare the evidence available from Iran (and other cases in which intelligence collection was similarly restricted) with that available in countries which are roughly similar but in which intelligence did have extensive contacts. In the same way, if one wanted to explore the subtle aspects of the question of whether intelligence was influenced by policy one would have to look at the analyses made by people or governments who had different policy preferences or compare NFAC's analysis of Iran with its treatment of unrest in a country that was not supported by the United States. Similarly, one reason for the error in Iran may be that NFAC tends to overestimate the staying power of right-wing regimes. But this question could only be explored by comparing its analyses of these regimes with those it makes of radical ones. To take an issue touched on in the body of this report, if one wanted to explore the problems created by the lack of disagreement among the analysts on Iran, a comparison between this case and one in which there were major disputes within the community would be in order.

4. Comparisons could also shed light on defects in intelligence if we did post-mortems on successful cases and also examined "false alarms." As it is, the rare post-mortems that are undertaken concern failures to predict untoward events. Useful as they are, these may give a skewed view. By focusing on cases where intelligence failed to detect danger when it was present, they imply that this is the most common and important problem. But it may be that there are lots of errors of the opposite type, cases where NFAC expected a government to fall and it survived, or instances in which it expected another state to take a hostile action and the state refrained from doing so. Intelligence may not systematically err on the side of being too complacent. It would both be useful to know whether or not this is true and to learn what factors

are responsible for the false alarms. For example, does intelligence systematically underestimate the staying power of certain kinds of regimes? Do the problems in the analysis that we have detected in the Iranian case crop up in the "false alarm" cases or are the difficulties there quite different?

5. It might also be worthwhile to look at some cases where the Agency was right. The obvious point would be to try to see if there were differences in the information available or the process of analysis employed that distinguish these cases. The most useful finding would be that better intelligence is associated with certain procedures and ways of treating evidence which can be applied to a wide range of cases. But almost anything that was found to discriminate cases in which the Agency did well from those in which it did badly would be useful, even if it only reminded us of the large role played by luck, skill, and the particularities of the individual cases.

6. In a post-mortem one obviously focuses on what went wrong. This produces an unbalanced account, even if one tries to distinguish between what only could have been clear from hindsight and what people might reasonably have been expected to see given the information available at the time. We wish to at least partially redress that imbalance by noting that several potential problems were correctly downgraded by the analysts. Little attention was paid to the role of the Tudeh Party and although terrorist activities were constantly tracked, this concern did not overshadow the more important one of general political unrest. The analysts easily could have been distracted by these topics, but were not. Furthermore, the analysis of the unity and morale of the armed forces—a particularly important topic—was proven to be essentially correct. The armed forces stayed loyal to the Shah and remained willing to execute his internal security orders until very late in the year; they began to waver and defect only when he appeared to be close to quitting.

7. The extent to which a retrospective examination distorts the situation is hard to determine. The conditions under which people worked fade and become obscure even in their minds and can never be known by the reviewer. Such a person knows what the outcome of the events is, and he cannot fail to be influenced by that knowledge. Moreover, the material that he reads in order to determine what happened, what people knew, and what they wrote about it comes to him in a form much different from the way it comes to the intelligence analyst. The reviewer has the opportunity to read material through in a coherent order. For the analyst working on events as they happened, material or information must be absorbed as it comes in—sometimes in fragments, often not in a timely fashion. The necessity of meeting publication deadlines can and frequently does force the intelligence analyst to commit himself to paper with substantially less than the optimum amount of information.

8. At many points in this report we will note which analysts were closer to being correct than others. Here we should stress that those who were more accurate in this case are not necessarily better analysts than those who continued to believe that the Shah

would survive. One can be right for the wrong reasons and one can carefully examine all the relevant evidence and still reach the wrong conclusion. In this case it seems that what distinguishes those analysts in and outside of the government who, as events unfolded, thought that the Shah was in serious trouble from those who thought he would survive were general beliefs about Iran which long predated the recent protests. As a generalization, those who thought the Shah was weak and had not been a good ruler took the unrest very seriously whereas those who believed he was strong and, on balance, had done a great deal to benefit Iran thought he would have little trouble riding out the disturbances. Members of the former group were correct this time, but we suspect that if we looked at their previous predictions we would find a number of occasions in which they incorrectly expected the Shah to fall, or at least to suffer significant diminutions of power. It can be argued that even if these people were wrong on important questions of timing, at least they had a better understanding of the underlying situation than did others. But even this may not be right. The underlying situation may have changed, especially as a result of the oil boom, and so the valid grounds for pessimism may have appeared only more recently than the pessimism.

9. If what distinguished "optimists" from "pessimists" was their longstanding views of the regime, would it have been useful for these differences to have been discussed at an early date? Perhaps, but the main "pessimist" in the government was the State Department Country Director for Iran who was not a member of the intelligence community. The other "pessimists" were outside of the government. Even had such discussions taken place, it is far from certain that the participants would have learned a great deal. Judging from the differences of opinion outside the government, it appears that beliefs about the strength of the regime were related to, although not totally determined by, whether the person is liberal or conservative. When disagreements are this deeply-rooted, discussion often proves unenlightening.

10. In this case, as in most examples of intelligence failure, the problem lay less in the incorrect interpretation of specific bits of information than in a misleading analysis of the general situation which pre-dated the crisis and strongly influenced perceptions of the events. Almost everyone in the government overestimated the stability of the regime. They overestimated the Shah's strength and underestimated the number of groups and individuals who opposed him and the intensity of their feelings. The *Weekly Summary* of 18 November 1977 said, ". . . there is no serious domestic threat or political opposition to the Shah's rule. At 58 he is in good health and protected by an elaborate security apparatus; he would seem to have an excellent chance to rule into the next decade." Similar judgments were expressed in the NID of 14 November 1977 and in a memorandum of 12 October 1977, "The Political Situation in Iran." The Embassy in Tehran, which held a similar judgment, listed "several verities," two of which were that "the Shah is widely recognized as probably the only viable governor of Iran today even by many of his opponents" and that "he is firmly in control." (Tehran 11408, 27 December 1977) As the draft NIE put it: "Because the Shah still holds the reins of power, most of what Iran does, how it feels, reacts, or goes, is how the Shah wants it."

11. At bottom most observers, official and unofficial, found it hard to imagine that the Shah would fall. Although there were many specific reasons for this belief—and they are analyzed below—it is hard to escape the feeling that if those reasons had not influenced beliefs, others that supported the same conclusion would have. The idea that one of the world's most powerful monarchs could be overthrown by an unarmed mob of religiously-inspired fanatics was simply incredible. Furthermore, it probably would have been incredible even had observers grasped the depth of popular discontent in Iran.

12. Other general beliefs, some of them probably held more implicitly and explicitly, may have also been operating—e.g., that serious menaces to American-supported regimes always come from the left and that religion is not an important motivating factor. Some more specific biases or predispositions are discussed in the chapters that deal with the events in Iran and how they were perceived.*

‹Two descriptive paragraphs omitted›

INHERENT PROBLEMS

1. A number of common explanations for intelligence failures do not apply in this case. Indeed, there were many factors here which militated in favor of an understanding of the situation.

2. First, intelligence was dealing with a country with which the United States had had prolonged and close contact. Although Iran's importance to the United States has increased since the rise of oil prices, the US interest dates back to World War II. ‹2 lines redacted› and many Iranian officials travel this country, giving further opportunities for gleaning an understanding of the situation. Business contacts were also extensive.

3. Second, most of the NFAC analysts had been working on Iran for a few years. The senior political analyst, ‹name redacted› knew the language and culture of the country extremely well. ‹4 lines redacted›

4. Third, and linked to the previous point, although ethnocentricism is always a danger, the analysts' experience reduced this problem. The leading political analyst was steeped in the culture of the area and, without becoming "captured" by it, seems to have had as good a general feel for the country as can possibly be expected.

5. Fourth, prior to the late summer of 1978, the pressure for current intelligence was not so great as to squeeze out time for broader and longer-run considerations.

* Another belief explains what to some observers might seem like an odd distribution of NFAC's attention. Most people thought the main problem would come in the mid-1980s when oil production started to drop, difficulties caused by industrialization accumulated, social divisions sharpened, and the Shah began implementing a transition for his son. Thus several long NFAC papers laid the ground work for analyzing the expected trials of the regime in this period.

Indeed NFAC produced several long papers on such topics of general importance as *Elites and the Distribution of Power in Iran* and *Iran in the 1980s*. Although we have not made a thorough canvass, our impression is that on few other countries of comparable importance was there as much of this kind of in-depth analysis.

6. Fifth, the developments NFAC was trying to anticipate were not sudden ones which adversaries were trying to hide from us. A number of the problems that come up in trying to foresee coups or surprise attacks did not arise here. There was time in which to assess developments and to re-evaluate assumptions—indeed an NIE was in process during many of the months in which the crucial events were unfolding. Although the way in which NIEs are written may not provide the best possible forum for addressing important questions, it still gave NFAC an opportunity often absent in cases of intelligence failures. Furthermore, analysis did not have to contend with possible concealment and deception.

7. On the other hand, the nature of the case presented some special problems. First, and most important, the Iranian revolution was a major discontinuity. Indeed, we believe that it was unprecedented. And no one does a good job of understanding and predicting unprecedented events. We can think of no other case in recent times in which a mass uprising overthrew an entrenched regime that had the support of large, functioning, and united security forces. Similarly, we cannot think of a single other case in which very large numbers of unarmed men and women were willing to repeatedly stage mass demonstrations with the knowledge that many of them might be killed. The common pattern of unrest is that once one or two mass rallies have been broken up by gunfire, people refuse to continue this kind of protest and large unarmed demonstrations cease. The other side of this coin was also unusual if not unprecedented—the Shah did not use all the force at his disposal to quell the unrest (for a further discussion of this point, see below, Force Section). Most dictators would have done so; the Shah himself did in 1963.

8. A second problem was that of correctly estimating the intensity of the opposition to the Shah. In retrospect, it seems clear that millions of Iranians hated the Shah, yet the word "hate" never appears in official documents—except for the report that Ayatollah Shariat-Madari hated Khomeini. (Tehran Airgram A-105, 1 August 1978) Intensity of feeling, however, is difficult to determine (leaving aside the point that no concerted efforts were made to assess it). What NFAC needed to know was the lengths people would go to overthrow the regime; what costs they would bear. It is very hard to estimate this short of the actual test. Indeed the individuals themselves often do not known how far they are willing to go. On pages 115–119 below we will discuss the evidence that was available on this subject and the inferences that were drawn.

9. A third problem is linked to the second. Much of the opposition was based on religion and it is difficult for most people living in a secular culture to empathize with and fully understand religious beliefs—especially when the religion is foreign to them. Most modern analysts tend to downplay the importance of religion and to give

credence to other explanations for behavior. Moreover, Shi'ism is an unusual religion, being a variant of Islam and therefore presenting a double challenge to understanding. We cannot generalize about how people in NFAC concerned with Iran—managers and analysts—viewed the role of religion in this situation. NFAC's senior Iranian analyst was sensitive to the importance of religion as a political factor. But we suspect that many others were not so sensitized and that, had the opposition been purely secular, observers would have been quicker to detect its depth and breadth.

10. Fourth, and related to the previous problems, an understanding of this case called for the sort of political and even sociological analysis that NFAC does not usually do. NFAC had to gauge many segments of society, not just a few familiar individuals and institutions.

11. A fifth inherent difficulty was that the opposition developed gradually from the fall of 1977 on. Studies from psychology and examinations of previous cases have shown that people are almost always too slow to take account of the new information under these circumstances. Sudden and dramatic events have more impact on peoples' beliefs than do those that unfold more slowly. In the latter case, people can assimilate each small bit of information to their beliefs without being forced to reconsider the validity of their basic premises. They become accustomed to a certain amount of information which conflicts with their beliefs without appreciating the degree to which it really clashes with what they think. If an analyst had gone into a coma in the fall of 1977 and awakened the next summer, he would have been amazed by the success of the opposition and the inability of the Shah to maintain order. The discrepancy between his earlier belief in the stability of the Shah's rule and the evidence of strong and sustained opposition probably would have been enough to make him question his basic assumptions. ‹5 lines redacted› But the exposure to a steady stream of events, few terribly startling when taken one at a time, had much less impact. If the analysts had been able to step back and re-read the information that had come in over the previous six months, the cumulative impact of the discrepant information might have been greater. But the pressure to keep up with the latest events militated against this. Furthermore, the growth of the opposition was not entirely steady. Lulls were common. And many expected (and perhaps planned) demonstrations failed to occur. As a result, analysts could always believe that a current peak of opposition would subside, as earlier ones had.

12. A sixth obstacle to understanding was the history of 15 years of unbroken royal success. As ORPA's senior political analyst pointed out in early 1976, "The Shah of Iran has been on his throne 34 years, far longer than any other leader in the Middle East. He has not only outlived most of these rulers, but has outlasted the many official and unofficial observers who, two decades ago, were confidently predicting his imminent downfall." (*Elites and the Distribution of Power in Iran,* February 1976, page 14). We think it likely that the knowledge that the Shah had succeeded in the past against all odds and contrary to most analyses made observers especially hesitant to believe

that he would fall this time. The past challenges seemed greater; the Shah had seemed weaker. Indeed the NIEs of the late 1950s and early 1960s had said that the Shah probably could not survive. Intelligence underestimated the Shah many times before; it was not likely to do so again.

13. A seventh factor that inhibited an appreciation of the danger to the regime was that riots were not uncommon in Iran. Student demonstrations were frequent, and so no cause for alarm. Demonstrations by other segments of the population and linked to religion were less common, but still not unprecedented. The important opposition of this kind occurred in 1963 and forced the Shah to resort to brutal, but short and effective, repression.

Information Available

14. The information that came into NFAC was not all that could have been available on Iran, but it was what the analysts had to work with. The subject of collection is beyond the scope of our investigation but an understanding of the problems facing the analysts requires at least a brief mention of several deficiencies in the information available. First, partly because of decisions made in the 1970s, NFAC received little information about the opposition or indeed about anyone outside the elite. Further discussion of this point can be found on pp. 127–129 below. This meant that NFAC not only lacked current information during the crisis, but also had not had important background information on the earlier trends in popular attitudes that set the stage for the revolution. Second, domestic politics were deliberately given a low priority. ‹2 lines redacted› Contacts with opposition elements by official Americans were limited; in view of other important US interests in Iran, such contacts were considered to be not worth risking the Shah's ire if exposed. ‹1 page redacted›. There was an obvious circularity here. As long as domestic politics were believed to be stable, they would be given a low priority. And as long as NFAC knew little about what anyone outside of governmental and elite circles was saying and doing, there would be little reason to question the prevailing faith in the stability of the regime.

15. On Iran, as in most countries, the Embassy provided the bulk of the political reporting. The FOCUS Iran memorandum of 4 November 1976 said that "Generally speaking, reporting from the Mission on most topics is very satisfactory." (page 2) An update of 10 August 1978 stated that "Reporting on domestic political concerns has been 'first rate.'" This subject is beyond our concerns here, but we should note that the Embassy had contacts only with a narrow segment of society. Furthermore, if there were biases or inadequacies in Embassy accounts of what was happening, they would greatly hamper the analysts' job. ‹half page redacted›

19. Fifth, the analysts only had limited opportunity to debrief Embassy and station personnel who returned from the field. For example, they did not see the Ambassador when he was in the US in the summer of 1978. They had more contact with lower-level officials, but even this was chancy. It depended on the analysts hearing of returning

travelers through the grapevine. The economic analysts seem to have done somewhat better than their political counterparts in talking to returnees.

20. Sixth, only limited information was available from other countries' Embassies ‹9 lines redacted› If the Embassy exchanged views with others on the scene, the analysts were not told what was learned. ‹1 page redacted›

24. Four general observations about the information available to NFAC are in order. First, the analysts feel they have little influence over the information they receive. Although they participated in the FOCUS review and have some input into the determination of collection priorities, this does not have great impact on the depth or breadth of reporting that results. Of course the decisions on what information to collect must involve many factors, but it seems to us that the analysts should have a stronger voice.

25. Second, the availability of some information from other agencies is strongly influenced by informal arrangements. Information obtained or perceptions formed by persons in agencies outside the intelligence community may not reach NFAC analysts. (For further discussion, see pp. 103–104.)

26. Third, with the exception of a few reports from the consulates (which were in touch in their districts with a broader slice of Iranian society), official sources yielded no information about non-elite segments of the population.‹4 lines redacted› An occasional newspaper report provided a scrap of information, but by and large the analysts could only rely on their a priori assumptions of how various kinds of people would react to the situation. This meant, for example, that there was no information about the organization and makeup of the protest demonstrations. No one talked to a single rank-and-file dissident to try to find out what his grievances were, what leaders he respected, and what his hopes were. Of course given the Shah's sensitivities and beliefs about American instigation of the opposition, gathering such might have been prohibitively risky. But without it the analysts were at a major disadvantage. Even when Embassy and Agency personnel met opponents of the Shah, these people almost always were members of the Westernized elite. Many of them shared the Western views about the role of religion in society. They did not share, and could not convey the feelings of those who went into the streets to bring down the regime. (The general topic of information derived from contacts with the opposition is discussed below.)

27. Fourth, there were some untapped sources that could have led to a better understanding of the opposition. One was the opposition press, published in this country and France. Of course this would have been mining low-grade ore. Before the summer of 1978 it might have seemed not worth the effort because the opposition was unimportant; after then the analysts had no extra time. It might have been more efficient to have been in contact with those Americans who had good relations with the opposition. Of course only that information which the opposition wanted the US Government to know would have been available through these channels. There were a number of

Americans, often academics, who had good relations with the opposition. ‹5 lines redacted›

28. Fifth, although it would have been difficult, the analysts might have tried to probe the differences in views on the domestic situation they knew to exist among members of the US Mission in Iran ‹2 pages redacted›.

PROCESS

Introduction

1. Many of the problems in this case can be traced to the ways in which finished intelligence is produced. NFAC tracked specific events and the flow of field reports quite well. Given the preexisting beliefs about Iran, the Shah, and the opposition; given the paucity and ambiguity of the information from the field; given the normal NFAC procedure; and given the inherent difficulty of predicting a very unusual series of events, it is not surprising that the full dimensions of the problem were not recognized until early November.

2. In the case of Iran, the system produced a steady stream of summaries of recent events with a minimal degree of commentary, analysis, and prediction. This mode of analysis may work adequately in ordinary situations; it cannot cope with the unusual. It seems to work when the information from the field is good. It cannot do as well when much of the information is in unofficial channels (i.e. through nongovernment experts) and, more importantly, when what is needed is a real reworking of the information, a stepping back from the flow of day-to-day events, an in-depth analysis of selected, important questions, a presentation of alternative interpretations, and an attempt to go beyond the specific information that is coming in. This is not what the system appears to have been designed to do and if it is to be done, the working level analysts cannot be expected to take the initiative in shifting from the normal mode of analysis to one that is more appropriate to the situation. Indeed when events come most rapidly the greatest pressures are for short reports—i.e. NID items. If more than reporting and superficial analysis is to be done, NFAC management must take the burden of reordering the priorities and ordering that selected in-depth studies be undertaken. Of course this is a gamble, since it is difficult to determine at a given time which questions are most important and what alternatives need to be examined. Furthermore, there will have to be a cost in terms of NFAC's ability to follow in detail more recent events. These problems and costs need more careful examination than we can give them here. But it is our impression that at least in this case no one would have greatly suffered if fewer NID items had been produced.

Nature of the Production System

3. What was needed was sustained and thorough evaluation of the most important questions—e.g. the Shah's ability and willingness to follow a coherent course,

the nature and depth of the opposition, the ability of the opposition groups to work together. Such analysis should have examined alternative interpretations of events and mustered all the evidence that could be found. Instead, the format of NFAC production and the informal norms of the intelligence community led to intelligence that focused on the latest events and reports, that presented one view, and that adduced little evidence.

4. The NFAC product can rarely be faulted for failure to convey the information in the latest field reports. But there was much less discussion of the forces that were affecting events and that would influence whether the latest lull was merely a temporary respite or something more lasting; whether the latest cable saying that the moderates were afraid that the protests were getting out of control indicated that an agreement with the government was likely. The analysts' pre-existing belief that the regime was very strong and that the opposition was weak and divided did not prevent them from seeing and passing on the disturbing reports from the Embassy and the station. But the belief may have been reinforced by the requirements of current intelligence and made it more difficult for them to get beyond the specific events and see what patterns were emerging.

5. *The Daily Publication.* The problems are greatest with the NID, which concentrates on telling what has happened and only rarely contains analysis or forecasts of political trends and developments. This publication absorbs a great deal of the analysts' time, accounts for a high proportion of the intelligence that NFAC produces, and is considered by most ORPA analysts to be the most important NFAC publication after the PDB. (OER analysts are rewarded not so much for NID items as for publishing in the EIWR.) Even on days when NID items are not being prepared, analysts must take quite a bit of time to be ready to write for it in case they are asked to do so. Almost all articles are short, since no more than two longer and more analytical articles are run in each issue (e.g. the two-part feature carried on 12 and 14 November 1977 on the occasion of the Shah's visit to Washington.) Most NID items that are more than a couple of paragraphs long cover several topics. The result is not only that none of the topics can receive in-depth treatment, but often that the items lack emphasis. For example, a long NID article on 14 September 1978, "Iran: Prospects for the Shah," covered the following subjects: one summary paragraph, two general introductory paragraphs, three paragraphs on the Shah's mood, four paragraphs on the loyalty and morale of the armed forces, and five paragraphs on the opposition. Each paragraph is about two or three sentences long. This format is not compatible with any but the most superficial analysis. Furthermore, stories in the NID, like those in the newspapers which the NID so strongly resembles, generally do not assume that the reader has been closely following events. They therefore do not build on what the analysts have said before, steadily producing a better understanding of the underlying forces or the dynamics that are believed to be at work. Thus none of the subjects that are touched on in successive NID items are ever examined in much detail.

6. This type of intelligence production is necessary for tracking a rapidly changing situation. If the premises on which the discussion is based are correct and remain so throughout the period, this mode of analysis will serve the community and the consumers well. But given the fragility of observers' understanding of most other countries, it is rarely wise to assume that discussing the most recent developments without reflecting on the more basic questions will be sufficient; questions that do not lend themselves to treatment in terms of the latest demonstration, the latest lull, or the most recent event.

7. NID items often draw conclusions, but do not explain how the conclusion was reached or what alternatives have been rejected. In addition, because the system requires that political NID items be tied directly to reporting, analysis often stops short of stating the full implications of the information presented. For example several stories in the NID in mid-September 1978 implied that the Shah's efforts to win over the moderates would not succeed. This is especially true if one takes all the stories together rather than reading just one of them. But of course they did come to readers one at a time and the pessimistic inferences had to be drawn from the stories rather than being presented bluntly. Similarly, in late September and October there were frequent articles about the strikes and continuing unrest. But each event was treated in relative isolation and explicit judgments about whether the regime could survive these strains were eschewed. ‹footnote redacted›

‹paragraph 8 and part of paragraph 9 declassified but omitted›

9. . . . One of the [longer papers] treated the religious bases of opposition, and we have discussed it at several places in this report. The others were "The Situation in Iran" (an evaluation of the first ten days of Sharif-Emami's government (7 September 1978; "Iran: The Prospects of Responsible Government" (the outlook in late October (20 October 1978)); and "Iran: Roots of Discontent," (the underlying causes, particularly rapid modernization (20 October 1978). "The Situation in Iran" and "Iran: The Prospects of Responsible Government," were like NID stories in their approach of summarizing recent events and looking into the immediate future. They were valuable in telling their readers what was happening, but did little to develop evidence and arguments about the central issues. Only two articles fit this description: "Iran: Some Observations on the Bases of Religious Opposition (10 February 1978, and "Iran: Roots of Discontent." The former was an excellent start, but was not followed up, and the latter would have been more useful had it appeared earlier and been more thorough.

10. NFAC produces some longer analytical papers. Two on Iran appeared during the period under review. One, *Iran in the 1980s* (August 1977),—and its executive summary (October 1977)—are discussed at several places in this report. The other, *Iran After the Shah* (August 1978) was an assessment of the prospects for an orderly succession to the Shah under certain specified assumptions. Completed in early summer, it was not designed to deal with the developments of 1978. Three sentences in its preface said: "Iran is not in a revolutionary or even a 'prerevolutionary' situation. There are

substantial problems in all phases of Iranian life, but the economy is not stagnant and social mobility is a fact of life. There is dissatisfaction with the Shah's tight control of the political process, but this does not at present threaten the government." (These were widely quoted in the press and attributed to the prospective NIE.) Apparently there was no questioning at any level as to whether it was appropriate as of late August to issue this paper.

11. These papers, and an earlier one on *Elites and the Distribution of Power in Iran* (February 1976) are more descriptive than analytical. They pulled together a large amount of data that was not known to most readers. *Elites* was particularly successful in this regard. They may have served their purposes but they did not train either analysts or the consumers to think carefully about the sorts of issues that arose in 1978.

12. *Selection of Issues to be Treated.* It seems to us that there was a failure at management levels to see that proper attention was paid to those topics which bore most directly on whether the Shah would survive. Indeed it is striking that throughout the period no papers were produced which had as their main focus the question of whether the regime could be overthrown. Part of the explanation may be that opinions shifted fairly suddenly—until mid-October almost everyone thought the Shah would survive and by early November almost everyone thought he was in very serious trouble—and part may be the lack of a suitable procedure and format. But whatever the cause, we think it is not only hindsight that leads to the conclusion that as the protests grew, the analysts and managers should have sat down and tried to locate and analyze the important questions, many of which were not pegged to the latest events. In retrospect, it is obvious that it would have been extremely valuable to have had discussions of such topics as: when and whether the Shah would crack down; the conditions under which the opposition would split; the depth of the feelings against the Shah; and the possibilities and dangers of liberalization.

13. Such questions deserved special attention because the answers to them were closely linked to predictions about the future of the regime. As it was, these topics were mentioned in passing, but never were examined in depth. Presumably, this could not have been done without either adding analysts or diverting some of their efforts away from the current reporting. The obvious question is whether it is so important for NFAC to provide as much coverage of the latest events, and this subject is beyond the scope of this report. In the absence of such an increase or diversion of resources, however, most finished intelligence on Iran was strongly driven by the latest events.

14. As NFAC operated in this case, we wonder if papers like these would have been produced even had the analysts had more time. First, they would have required someone to determine what subjects needed close examination. The analysts of course can and should have a hand in this, but they are likely to be too close to the daily events to do this on their own. Furthermore, the selection of topics must be guided in part by the problems that are of concern to decisionmakers and the chains of reasoning that decisionmakers are employing. People who are aware of what these

people are thinking must be involved in the process. Second, the analysts may lack the training and experience in this kind of work, because most of what they are called on to do in the normal course of events is largely description and summarization. When people are not used to writing analytical papers one cannot expect them to be able to do so when the need arises. Frequent experience is necessary to develop the needed skills. Third, such papers would probably not have been as good as they could have unless there was a community of analysts—both Iranian experts and good political generalists—to provide suggestions and criticisms. As we will discuss below (pp. 101–102), in the case of Iran there was no such community.

15. In the case of Iran, there was also a failure of what can be called intellectual or analytical management in the absence of substantive review of what the analysts were writing. Others in NFAC did not go over the political analysts' arguments with them, probing for weak spots and searching for alternative interpretations that needed to be aired.*

Correctives

16. *Evidence.* From reading most NFAC documents one cannot tell how the analysts reached their judgments or what evidence they thought was particularly important. One does not get a sense for why the analysts thought as they did or what chains of reasoning or evidence might lead one to a different conclusion. At any number of points in NFAC products one can find unqualified assertions without supporting evidence presented. Space limitations explain the paucity of evidence in the NID and reader impatience is an important factor in preparing the other publications as well, but the result is unfortunate.

17. To put this point a slightly different way, if one started with the belief that the Shah's position was weak, there was almost nothing in the finished intelligence that would have, or should have, led one to change one's mind. Reading NFAC production would show that other people had a different view, but not why this view was valid. Most often one finds assertions, not arguments supported by evidence. Often it is only their inherent plausibility that would lead one to accept the conclusions.

18. Of course the consumers do not have time to read a full account of the evidence on which judgments are based. But such a development and presentation would still serve important functions within the intelligence community. Individual analysts may not fully realize how much—or how little—evidence supports a given position unless they work through it systematically. And doing so can yield new insights. Analysts in other agencies can read fuller versions and so both be better informed and be in a better position to offer criticisms and conflicting views. Middle-level NFAC managers could also work with papers that had fuller evidence and would be able to see what judgments seemed questionable, where the arguments were weak, and where

* For part of the explanation, see subsection, Discussion and Review (pp. 32–37) below.

alternative explanations needed presentation and exploration. Here, as in other areas, we recognize that available resources set limits to what can be done, and that other equities have claims on those resources. But time spent on a systematic exposition of the evidence for and against a particular belief may well be more valuable than an equal amount spent on reporting the latest events.

19. *Alternative Explanations.* In addition to producing evidence, or rather as part of the same process of demonstrating why a conclusion is valid, discussions will often be of greatest value when they include explicit consideration of alternative interpretations. Most NFAC analysis on Iran did not do this. At times, it admitted puzzlement. But usually it gave a single, quite coherent, explanation.* What is most important is not that many of those explanations turned out to be incorrect—since the evidence was often skimpy and ambiguous—but that a range of interpretations was not presented. We think this should be done on a regular basis, with evidence present for and against each of the alternatives.

20. The number of questions on which this can be done and the number of alternatives that could be developed are theoretically limitless, but it is often possible to find a relatively small number of crucial ones, which, if answered differently, would most alter one's understanding of the situation and the predictions one would make. The availability of feedback from policymakers would help in choosing the questions.

21. The point of this exercise is three-fold. First, it would encourage the analysts to be more explicit about their reasoning processes by making them contrast their views with the ones they have rejected. Second, it would lead them to marshall their evidence in a systematic way. Third, the process of working through the alternatives should encourage the analysts to think more thoroughly about some of their important beliefs. Some of the problems we located in the dominant interpretations could have been addressed at the time if the analysts had proceeded in the manner we are suggesting. For example, it might have become clear that the belief that the Shah would crack down if the situation became very serious was impervious to almost all evidence short of that which would appear at the last minute. Similarly, a thorough analysis of what was believed and why might have shown the importance of what Khomeini stood for and thus led to systematic efforts to gather more evidence on this question or at least to a more detailed examination of the information NFAC had and the inferences that were being made about him.

22. One obvious difficulty is that seeing things from a different perspective or discussing possibilities that others have not seen or have rejected is not likely to occur unless it is rewarded by the organization. This would involve a recognition that in many cases the effort will not have direct benefits. Usually the dominant view is correct,

* ‹Name redacted›notes that the single coherent explanation has long been the preferred analytical style in NFAC and its predecessors. Alternative explanations have been employed from time to time, usually at the expenditure of great effort and with senior management support.

or at least closer to the truth than many of the alternatives. It is now easy to see that alternatives should have been raised about Iran, but the case must rest not on the claim that the dominant view was wrong, but on the argument that examining several alternatives will lead to better analysis. But unless this mode of argumentation is valued and rewarded by NFAC, it is not likely to thrive because it asks analysts to discuss positions that they disagree with and which they know are not likely to be accepted.

23. *Predictions as an Analytical Tool.* As Richards Heuer has pointed out,* studies in psychology show that people tend to maintain their beliefs and images in the face of what in retrospect is an impressively large amount of discrepant information. We all tend to see the world as we expect to see it and so are slow to change our minds. As the open literature has discussed at length, this tendency is not always pathological since much evidence is so ambiguous that we could not make any sense out of our world unless we allowed our interpretations to be strongly guided by our expectations.** But there is an ever-present danger that the analyst will fail to properly interpret, or even detect, evidence that contradicts his beliefs and so will maintain his views—perhaps even failing to see the alternative—in the face of mounting evidence that is incorrect.

24. The case of Iran reveals a need for analysts to make sharp and explicit predictions as a partial corrective for this danger. The point of this is not to exaggerate how much we know or to develop a scorecard, but to encourage the analysts to think about the implication of their beliefs and to have them set up some indicators of what events should not occur if their views are correct. This can sensitize them to discrepant information which they would otherwise ignore. Of course having a prediction disconfirmed does not mean that one should automatically alter the most basic elements of one's beliefs. The fact that demonstrations grew larger than most analysts thought they would does not mean that they should have jumped to the conclusion that the Shah was about to fall. But since most people correct their beliefs too little rather than too much as new information appears, paying special heed to events that do not turn out as expected can be a useful corrective.

25. Explicit predictions would have been especially helpful in the Iranian case because, as we discussed in other sections, much of the discrepant information arrived bit by bit over an extended period of time. Under these conditions it is very easy to fail to notice that events are occurring which would have been unthinkable a year before. Systematic procedures are needed to make analysts reflect on the gaps that may be developing between the events and the implications of their basic beliefs. Thus it might have been useful if shortly after Sharif-Emami was appointed Prime Minister and made significant concessions to the opposition, the analysts had made explicit predictions about their impact. Without this, it was too easy to overlook the degree

* "Cognitive Biases in the Evaluation of Intelligence Estimates," "Analytical Methods Review," October 1978.
** Robert Jervis, *Perception and Misperception in International Politics*, Chapter 4.

to which the developing events did not fit easily with an optimistic assessment. Similarly, analysts could have tried to clarify what level of intimidation they thought would be effective in discouraging the opposition and the size of protest marches and demonstrations that they thought the dissidents could muster. We think that one reason why the analysts did not see the full significance of the number, intensity, and nature of the demonstrations was that they became too accustomed to them. The size of the demonstrations and the number of casualties were implicitly compared to what had occurred in the last weeks or months rather than being matched against expectations generated by beliefs about how serious the situation was. Thus as the scope of protests increased, the amount of unrest that the analysts implicitly accepted as being consistent with their belief that the Shah could survive also increased. Had they made explicit predictions at various points in the spring and summer, they might have been quicker to reevaluate their position.

26. The belief that the Shah would crack down if it became necessary might also have been subject to great doubt if explicit predictions had been made about the level of disorder they thought the Shah would permit. Since the initial statements about a possible crackdown occurred in December 1977, it appears that when the unrest started many observers thought that this level was fairly low. Throughout 1978 NFAC received and occasionally made similar statements. No one noted that they had been made before, when the protests had been much milder. If analysts had been pushed to say not only that a crackdown would occur if things got serious enough, but how much protest would be required to trigger repression, their predictions would have been disconfirmed and they would have been more likely to re-examine their underlying beliefs.*

27. Not only predictions, but some ways of reminding people of them, are necessary. To use an example from the Embassy, it argued that the moderates might be satisfied if Prime Minister Amuzegar and some of his leading cabinet members were replaced and if a serious anti-corruption campaign were undertaken. "Concessions of this nature might at least bring the moderates into the political process and permit the GOI to direct its police and intelligence efforts against extremists..." (Tehran 7882, 17 August 1978). Within a few weeks the new cabinet of Sharif-Emami had gone much further than this and yet the moderates remained un-appeased. Recalling the earlier analysis might have stimulated a closer examination of the belief that the moderates could be conciliated, thus separating them from the extremists and permitting a compromise that the bulk of the politically relevant groups could accept.

28. These predictions need not be made in official papers and would not be for the purpose of attempting to foresee the future. Rather the process of making the

* The Embassy came close to doing this when it noted that the "initial...GOI reaction to the Tabriz riots is surprising and somewhat cheering. GOI has not gone into repressive mode...as many feared." (Tehran 1879, 23 February 1978) But because everyone was focused on the possibility of the Shah's "overreacting" and the possibility that things might get out of control was remote, the disconfirming of a prediction had little impact.

predictions would help the analysts understand the full implications of their beliefs, and the predictions themselves could serve as benchmarks which could help the analysts avoid the common trap of seeing too many events as consistent with their beliefs.

29. *Simplistic Terms.* Intelligence publications have a long history of using shorthand terms. They have the advantages of brevity and of conveying understanding to a readership not necessarily familiar with the country or subject being discussed. But there are traps in such usage. Shorthand terms such as "left-wing" or "right-wing," derived from Western political processes, are usually not applicable to authoritarian LDCs. "Extremist" and "moderate" are troublesome in that they may reflect more of the attitude of the user than of the person or institution described. Very often such an outmoded or incorrect term is so deeply embedded in the lexicon that only heroic efforts by strong-minded people will root it out. Usually it is succeeded by a new term that becomes equally resistant to change.

30. Happily NFAC production on Iran did not err grievously in this area. In describing the religious opposition to the Shah, NFAC publications used "fundamentalist," "conservative," and occasionally "dissident" as adjectives. When an analyst was not constricted by length requirements, he has attempted to define the terms he used. ‹citations redacted› Nonetheless, there were unclarities; the "moderate" religious opposition would have been more properly characterized as a group prepared to acknowledge a role, albeit limited, for the Shah and desiring greatly enhanced powers of their own.

31. The possibilities for conveying misleading information to consumers through the use of shorthand terms are many. We think that all those involved in the production process—managers, analysts, and editors—need constantly to keep in mind the prospective readership of the document they are working on and to question whether a given term will give a reader a correct, and not just a brief, understanding of the phenomenon it purports to characterize.

32. *Discussion and Review.* A basic problem with the process by which finished intelligence was produced in the case of Iran was that there was little sharp and critical discussion among the analysts. NFAC does not have any institutions that provide the functions of both evaluating and stimulating the analysts that are performed in the academic world by peer review. Analysts are then not challenged and confronted with conflicting views and counterarguments as much as they could be. In practice, coordination of finished intelligence rarely leads to discussion of fundamental judgments. Peer review is certainly no panacea, but it can both help evaluate the quality of work in instances where consumers are not experts and can help the analysts by leading them to see where their arguments might be altered or strengthened. It is hard to do good work in the absence of mechanisms for performing these functions. NFAC has all the requirements for peer review except appreciation of its value. Most analysts and managers appear to consider it threatening rather than helping. The

reception of NFAC's long papers on Iran is an illustration of the problem. Although the State Department's Country Director for Iran said that *Elites and the Distribution of Power in Iran* "should be required reading for newcomers to the Iranian scene" (the Iranian analyst in INR and a senior Pentagon official were equally laudatory), almost no one offered substantive comments and criticisms. Without claiming that criticism automatically leads to better analysis, we think that its absence renders learning and improvement very difficult. The analyst is operating in something of a vacuum. He cannot easily see alternatives to his own perspective. He does not have colleagues to point out information he may have missed or interpretations he should consider.

33. The lack of a "community" of analysts dealing with a problem, a subject, or a country is noteworthy. The division of NFAC and its predecessor by discipline contributes to this. So do the small number of analysts ‹line redacted› and the infrequent communication across disciplinary lines. An additional factor is the tradition in ORPA's predecessor office of analysts working on "their" country, building a psychological fence that others won't cross.

34. The effective size of the community was even smaller than these numbers indicate. Within NFAC, the senior political analyst was generally deferred to because of his long experience in and deep knowledge of Iran. The consequence was not only that one voice carried great weight, but that this analyst did not have the opportunity to test out his ideas on others who might disagree with his conclusions or make him fully articulate his assumptions and reasoning processes.

35. ‹Name redacted› who has seen finished intelligence produced by a variety of organizational forms, notes the importance of the current absence of institutional competition and the supportive criticism it can provide. The mechanism that once existed where a current office and an estimate office looked at issues from their different perspectives was not a cure-all, but it did offer on a regular basis opportunity for different approaches to surface. The exchange involved sharpened argument and caused people to examine assumptions. No such opportunity existed during the period we are reviewing. Its demise is a considerable loss.

36. The size of the relevant community was further reduced by the isolation of the ORPA analysts.[*] They had few close contacts with academics or other informed experts outside the government; they had few conversations with people in State or NSC; even during the fall they were not involved in any of the inter-agency meetings that considered the Iranian problem, except for ones involving the NIE. (NFAC was represented by

* OER analysts were not as isolated because OER is the largest, and probably the most important, of the government groups working on other countries' economies and is plugged into a network of economic analysts in other agencies. The establishment of the Iran Analytic Center (mid-November) may have alleviated some of the problems of analysts' isolation which are discussed below.

the NIO or his deputy.) The problem is not only in the lack of discussions between NFAC analysts and those from other agencies—ORPA and OER analysts rarely had thorough talks about what was happening in Iran.

37. The senior political analyst knew several outside experts fairly well, but not so well as to be in close touch with them during the crisis. This is especially striking because many of his concerns were "academic." But, until only a few years ago, close contacts were encouraged by only a few offices in the DDI (NFAC's predecessor); most analysts were not urged to meet outside experts or given travel money to go to meet them—and old attitudes die hard. Many people outside the government are of course hesitant to talk to anyone from the CIA, and the expectation of being rebuffed further inhibits trying to develop such contacts.

38. Relations with people at State were not close. Several years ago the Iranian desk officer had weekly meetings of Iranian specialists throughout the government concerned with policy and with intelligence, but when a new desk officer was appointed this pattern was broken. Once broken, it was hard to re-establish. The NFAC analysts felt they could not re-establish it, in part because of the obvious difficulty of getting people to come out to Langley, in part because meetings sponsored by NFAC would be of limited interest to many potential participants because they would not deal with US policy. The OER analysts frequently talked to their opposite number on the Iran desk in State and they have told us that these exchanges were very beneficial, both for the information and the ideas that were gained. There were few conversations between the ORPA analysts and the desk officer, however. This was especially unfortunate because the latter was probably the most pessimistic official in the government. The analysts had fairly frequent discussions with George Griffin, Chief of INR/RNA, South Asia Division, but these almost always concerned specific pressing questions and did not lead to a general exchange of views on such topics as whether the opposition would split or whether the Shah would act decisively. Furthermore, most conversations were carried out via regular telephone lines (INR offices do not have secure phones at hand) and so had to be very restrained.

39. Thus the differences between ORPA and INR were never argued out. Griffin (and presumably Precht) read the NID (and several long NID items in the fall of 1978 were concurred in by INR), NFAC analysts read INR's dissenting footnote of 11 September and its slightly pessimistic IIM of 29 September. But they never sat down together to learn exactly where they differed and why.

40. There was no contact between the analysts and people from the NSC. Again the analysts felt they could not take the initiative, and since they almost never saw the relevant NSC staffer there was no opportunity for them to develop habits of exchanging views.

41. As the crisis developed, inter-agency meetings were devoted to Iran. As noted above, NFAC was represented by the NIO or his deputy and the "working level"

analysts were not present. Furthermore, the NIO did not tell the analysts of what was said at these meetings, what people in other agencies were thinking, where the arguments they were making in the NID might be revised in light of other opinions, or what assumptions others held.

42. As the NIO became more pessimistic during October, he understandably lost faith in the political analysts' judgment. As a result, he did not engage in full exchanges of opinion with them. The analysts suffered by missing the knowledge that others in NFAC and outside disagreed with them and losing opportunities to have their arguments challenged and rebutted; the NIO suffered by losing some of the information and insights held by the analysts and by not being able to develop his arguments by testing them out on an expert who disagreed.

43. Several NFAC analysts mentioned that throughout most of the period of growing unrest, they reinforced each other in their beliefs that the Shah could survive. They were not wrong to draw added confidence from the fact that there was a high degree of consensus, but given the fairly small number of analysts involved and the difficulties in predicting what would happen, it might have been helpful to have sought wider views. There was one such meeting with outside experts in late October 1978 sponsored by State, and several of the analysts later remarked on the range of information and contacts which the academics had and were struck by the latter's general pessimism.* Without resorting to the artificial device of devil's advocates, the bringing in of a wider circle of analysts might serve the function of challenging assumptions and increasing the sensitivity to information that does not fit the prevailing views.

44. Because so much of the analysts' time and attention must be focused on summarizing and simplifying the confusion and complexity in the area of their specialization so that it can be understood by harried generalists, there are few incentives and opportunities for the analysts to develop more fully their views in as much sophistication and depth as they are able. In calm times, the kinds of papers we think were needed in the summer and fall of 1978 probably will be of little use to consumers. The audience will have to be others in the intelligence community and perhaps FSO's on the country desk in the State Department. But without greater incentives for the analysts to write for their colleagues as well as for their superiors, we wonder if they can be prepared to foresee crises and deal with them when they arise. (For a related point, see above, p. 27.)

45. Especially when the number of NFAC analysts working in an area is small, we think it is important for them to have as extensive contacts as possible with outside experts. Without this the analysts may not come to grips with the range of possible interpretations of events and may end up presenting facts and interpretations that are far

* Other participants detected no substantial difference between government and outside discussants.

removed from what other knowledgeable observers believe. This problem is especially great when one deals with countries which consumers know relatively little about. Any number of important facts could be mis-stated or omitted and very questionable interpretations could be asserted as though they were universally agreed-to without consumers being able to detect the problem. For example, *Iran in the 1980s,* (August 1977) reaches quite favorable judgments about the GOI's programs in such areas as family planning, education, and the economy. It claims that "Iran will probably come close to the Shah's goal of a per capita GNP equal to that of Western Europe by the mid-1980s." (p. 30) *Iran After the Shah,* (August 1978, states that "There is little in the Shah's overall reform program that would be objectionable except to the most reactionary and conservative groups.... The reforms have generally been a success because the Shah has had enough authority to push them in the face of the usual bureaucratic inefficiency and lethargy." (p. 21; also see NIE draft of 6 September 1978, p. 1–14.) These judgments may be correct and may even be shared by all experts in the field. But without drawing on a wider circle of experts there is no way of assuring that this is the case. In our judgment, NFAC should make strenuous efforts to assure that its understanding of various countries; i.e. the crucial background beliefs against which the interpretation of specific events is done, is as deep as possible. As with employing alternative arguments (above), the activity that can build such understanding must be valued and rewarded by NFAC; results will appear in the long-term, not in immediate production.

46. Although contacts with outside experts may be of some assistance if made during a crisis, they will be most fruitful if the analysts have developed working relations with them over an extended period of time. Of course this is difficult when the turnover of analysts is high and in any event requires NFAC management support for travel and conferences and a milieu which encourages such contacts.

47. In addition to maintaining close contacts with outside experts, NFAC could have involved some people within the Agency who had not been deeply involved with Iran. Such persons, even if they shared the basic predisposition that the Shah was strong and the opposition weak and divided, might have been quicker to notice the discrepancy between their views and the evidence of growing demonstrations. Having no stake in the previous predictions, they could have found it psychologically easier to take a new look at things. And because they would not have been experts on Iran, they would have been more likely to focus on some of the basic questions which the more experienced analysts by now took for granted. It may have been no accident that by early October the NIO was relatively pessimistic, and he was new to his job.

The Estimative Mechanism

48. While unrest was building in Iran, a proposed NIE on the future of that country was being drafted. The process had started early in 1978 because it had been several years since the last NIE was completed; it was not a response to specific events. ‹half-page redacted›

49. The drafting of the NIE did not lead to a fruitful discussion of important issues, perhaps because there was a great deal of agreement among the participants.* The last draft of the paper does not reveal tighter arguments, more and sharper alternative perspectives, or more carefully developed evidence than does the first draft. The scheme of organization changed, some topics were added and some were deleted, and minor alterations allowed individual positions to become community-wide ones. But by and large, all that happened was that separate parts of the drafts were paper-clipped together rather than integrated (e.g. the political and the economic sections). The NIE suffers from a rambling style which lacks tight organization and well-crafted arguments. In many places the paragraphs often seem to be placed at random; even paragraphs themselves lack any clear line of march. The document is hard to read and harder to remember. Partly for these reasons, the NIE did not focus the reader's attention on major judgments.

50. The reports of the analysts confirm the impression produced by reading the drafts: they did not learn much from putting the paper together. Their ideas were not challenged by others in the community; they did not have to probe their own pre-existing beliefs or the evidence they had felt was significant; no flaws in what they had thought were brought to the surface; no one made critical and penetrating comments on anyone else's analysis; no one was led to see things in a different light.

51. Judging from the changes in the successive drafts of the abortive NIE, most of the energy of this process went into subtle wording changes that would be apparent only to someone who had seen several versions. To show this, we have reproduced a paragraph from the 21 July and 6 September drafts, underscoring the changes.

> The Shah is supported sometimes without great enthusiasm, by all significant elements of the current power structure. The cabinet, parliament, the bureaucracy, the security forces and most of the business and commercial community are all on his side. Although many might abstractly prefer a more democratic system, even those who are lukewarm about the monarchy, the Pahlavi dynasty or both are uneasy when they consider the uncertainties about the character of a government without a strong Shah.
>
> The Shah is supported, *often* without great enthusiasm, by *most* significant elements of the current power structure. *Influential persons* in the cabinet, parliament, the bureaucracy, the security forces and the business and commercial community are *generally* on his side. Although many would prefer a more democratic system, even those who are lukewarm about the monarchy, the Pahlavi dynasty, or both, are uneasy when they consider the uncertainties about a government without a strong *monarch.*

* INR was more pessimistic, as is most clearly shown by its footnote of 11 September 1978. INR's differences apparently first surfaced at the initial coordination meeting of 28 July, but not in strong enough form to have an impact on the NIE, and were repeated more vigorously at the 30 August meeting.

52. Part of the reason why the important issues of who supported the Shah, and with what intensity, did not get analytical treatment in this forum may have been that the participants do not see the NIE, and especially the body of the paper, as opposed to its principal judgments, as particularly important because they doubt whether it would be read, let alone absorbed, by the policy-makers.

53. In retrospect, it is apparent that the government would have been better served by a paper that did address the shorter-term questions. To have asked for such a paper, however, would have required a recognition that the Shah was in serious trouble, and given the prevailing beliefs, that could not have occurred until the end of August at the very earliest. Indeed, INR called for such a paper on 12 September. But it took a week for NFAC to decide that such a paper should be produced and another ten days for the State Department to draft it. Apparently influenced by the mid-September lull, the paper concluded that "The Shah no longer appears to be in immediate danger of being overthrown. There is considerable question, however, of his ability to survive in power over the next 18 to 24 months." The paper was much more sharply focused than the NIE, but still failed to address several of the questions mentioned in other sections of this report which would strongly influence the Shah's fate. Whether this IIM would have served a useful purpose is difficult to determine. In any event, D/NFAC decided not to pursue it "on the grounds that it considers too immediate a time frame; what is needed is a new draft NIE that... considers both near and long-term problems." (Chronology of Iran NIE, page 4, enclosure (2) to NIO/NESA memo to DCI, 17 November 1978.) Such a draft was prepared by the NIO's office at the end of October, but by this time it was no longer relevant.

54. It is obvious that a lot of time and energy was expended in these efforts, with little to show in terms of results. We think that managers could have done a better job of focusing NFAC resources on the timely analysis of the most important questions.

55. At the risk of appearing parochial, one of the authors of this report wishes to point out that the intelligence community once had an estimative mechanism which could and did produce analytical papers (SNIEs) on issues such as that of the Shah's position and short-term prospects in a few days or a week. Such production forced analytical attention on what management and policy-makers (if they asked for a paper) considered to be the important issues. The present lack of an institution with such capacities may have contributed to the difficulties in this case.

REPORTING AND ANALYSIS—GENERAL

1. This section presents a general survey of the way in which NFAC intelligence production used the information available to it on Iran. Issues which are discussed at length in separate sections below are noted only briefly here.... ‹16-paragraph summary of events omitted›

18. The events which ultimately brought down the Shah began with demonstrations in Qom on 9 January 1978 which resulted in a number of dead. The government's initial explanation was that rioters had attacked a police station. Later information indicated that the police had panicked and fired into a crowd nowhere near a police station. The Embassy described this event as the worst of its kind in years. (Tehran 0389, 11 January 1978 and Tehran 0548, 16 January 1978). NFAC covered this event on 20 January, noting that there had been greater loss of life than the government had indicated and judging that "religious dissidents would be considered a more serious threat if they were thought to be allied" with other opposition elements. The item notes that such an alliance is possible but that information is scarce. (NID, 20 January 1978).

19. As is now well known, demonstrations and rioting followed a 40-day cycle during 1978. Prior to the first repetition at Tabriz on 18 February, ORPA's periodical publication carried an analytical piece explaining the bases of religious opposition to the monarchy. It noted the dilemma that the Shah faced; i.e., if he permitted his basic programs to be challenged demonstrations would continue and probably intensify; if he crushed demonstrations he would be accused of suppressing liberties. After explaining the antipathy between government and Shia clergy and referring to a decision by Khomeini in 1975 that participation by Muslims in the Shah's newly formed Resurgence Party was evil and therefore forbidden, the article concluded by saying "it seems likely that tension will continue between secular authority and the religious community with violence breaking out from time to time. Neither side will prevail completely but neither side can afford to capitulate." ‹source redacted› 10 February 1978.

20. Rioting in Tabriz on 18 February was extensive. Tehran 1710 (18 February 1978) ‹name redacted› said that the "level of violence is surprising." The Consul in Tabriz took a particularly gloomy view of the situation saying that the door that had swung open for religious and social forces would not be easily closed. The "Embassy believes situation not that difficult." (Tehran 1879, 23 February 1978). The Tabriz events were reported in the NID (21 February 1978), and the possibility that they might presage a rise in Azerbaijani nationalism was explored in ‹source redacted› (3 March 1978).

21. Some disturbances occurred at the end of March and early April and a divergence in field reporting on them is noticeable. ‹1 line redacted› give an impression that the violence in a large number of Iranian cities and towns was fairly serious. Embassy reporting (Tehran 3146, 3 April 1978) gives a more reassuring picture of "low level violence" with small groups attacking banks, public buildings, movie houses, etc. NFAC covered these events reporting that they grew from widespread dissatisfaction on the part of conservative religious elements. It judged that "the riots, demonstrations and sabotage in many cities and towns in recent weeks are no threat to government stability." 7 April 1978. In this judgment it was in agreement with the *Financial Times* of 14 May and was not far different from an article in the New York Times of 18 May. ‹5 lines redacted› Both the NID of 5 May and the Human Rights Review of 4 May noted that the Shah was going to take a hard line with dissidents and troublemakers.

22. In anticipation of a new outburst on the 40th day following the early May troubles the NID (17 June ‹name redacted›) noted that the Shah was trying to improve relations with the religious leadership but that there were many obstacles on the way to a durable compromise. ‹5 lines redacted› As it happened, events quieted down in Iran after mid-May. The 40th day commemorations in June were peaceful stay-at-home events, and it was not until late July that matters began to heat up again, the occasion being the death in a road accident of a Shia clergyman. There was no NID coverage from mid-June until early August when the Shah's promise of free elections was analyzed. The analysis noted that this promise was part of his timetable for developing the Iran he wanted, that there never had been free elections, and that the Shah would have continuing problems with the National Front and the religious opposition. His success would depend greatly on "the willingness of a generally irresponsible opposition" to forgo violence in favor of politics. (NID, 10 August 1978).

23. After some two months of relative quiet, the Iranian scene had begun to heat up in late July and early August; disturbances individually were not very serious, save in Isfahan, which was put under martial law on 11 August, but they came to occur on a daily basis as the month went on. The anti-regime repercussions from a movie-theater fire in Abadan a few days later, which killed some 400 people were strong. The regime tried to pin blame on elements allied with religious opposition; the latter with considerable success in the public mind put the blame on the regime. The repercussions showed the Shah that religious elements needed to be placated. His decision was to appoint an elder politician with reputedly good connection with religious leader, Sharif-Emami. NFAC noted that this appointment showed how seriously the Shah viewed the situation, but also that the appointment might be taken by Muslim leaders as a capitulation. (NID, 28 August). There is reason to believe that some of them did. At any event, religious leaders organized a massive, peaceful protest on 4 September (a religious holiday) and in defiance of government orders forbidding such demonstrations, a second on 7 September. These demonstrations led to the imposition of martial law in Tehran and 11 other cities on 8 September and the killing of a large number (c. 300) demonstrators in Tehran by troops later that day.

24. The events of late August and early September, as we now know, constituted a major turning point. The possibility of a compromise was probably lost then, although there was no way of knowing it at the time. Just prior to the imposition of martial law the Embassy, summing up the situation in Tehran 8485 (6 September 1978) ‹name redacted› noted the very strong anti-regime stands of the religous leadership and the less important National Front which reject compromise or negotiation. The NID (30 August 1978) ‹name redacted› reported the new cabinet, stressing that it was trying to reach accommodation with religious leaders. Political affairs in Iran were given fuller treatment in "Iran: Prospects for the Shah," (NID, 14 September 1978), which laid out the difficulties that the Shah and his associates would have in trying to cope with various opposition pressures. It made the point that given the limitations on how far the Shah was willing to liberalize, opposition leaders would need to show a greater

willingness to cooperate if a resolution of Iran's problems were to be reached. It noted that such cooperation was alien to the society and would not come easily. This element was repeated in other intelligence publications in the next couple of months, carrying the implication that such cooperation will not, in fact, be forthcoming. They do not, however, go on and draw the conclusion that efforts to effect a compromise acceptable to the Shah and his opponents would almost certainly fail.

Comments

25. The conventional wisdom concerning the staying power of the Shah's regime is mentioned elsewhere in this report and need not be repeated here in detail. The reasons for holding it were his proven record of survival, the loyalty of armed forces, weakness of political (secular) forces, belief that the Shah was ready and willing to use the force necessary to suppress opposition. The Shah intended, as part of his plan to secure a dynasty, to construct a political edifice that would function after his demise. He had not, however, let anyone know when and how he intended to do this, and his actions of loosening and tightening the political reins confused participants and observers and led some of them to conclude that he was losing his grip.

26. The demonstrations and deaths in January and February, were not in themselves cause for alarm. The continuance of the cycle in late March and early May was, and concern was reflected in the NID article of 17 June, when 40th day violence was due to take place. But the commemoration was peaceful. When trouble began again in the latter part of July it happened piecemeal, and was not well reported according to the documents we have. During August, anti-regime momentum built up, coming to a head on 8 September with the imposition of martial law and the killing of some 300 protesters.

27. One can argue that those observing Iran should have taken a good, hard look at the way events were shaping up as of early September 1978 and reached a judgment that the Shah was in serious trouble, perhaps in danger of being overthrown. The NIE then in progress offered such an opportunity, and State/INR did express a dissenting view even though it was fairly mild. Within NFAC people did consider the situation and, no doubt influenced by their judgment of the army's loyalty and by the "he's down, he's up, but he's more up than down" tenor of field reports on the Shah's moods, considered that he would stay in power. The relative peace that prevailed for a month after 6 September helped in maintaining this optimistic outlook. And so did the relative paucity of arguments to the contrary; ‹6 lines redacted›

28. The language used in NFAC publications, however, is different than that of a few months earlier. Both the political and economic intelligence talk of problems and difficulties. There is no sense that the Shah will have everything his way. But the overall impression is still that he will probably be able to outmaneuver his opposition. Only with the definitive failure of the regime's efforts to publicly divide Khomeini from the less extreme ayatollahs at the end of October, and the subsequent establishment of

a military government does NFAC conclude that “the Shah has delayed so long in taking decisive action that he has reduced substantially his earlier good chance of preserving the Pahlavi dynasty with powers like those of the past.”‹4 lines redacted›

WHITE REVOLUTION

1. In retrospect, the analysis of the difficulties of staging a “white revolution” was a bit superficial and over-optimistic. Perhaps the analysts, like many non-governmental observers, were misled by the Shah’s many successes—real and apparent—and so lost sight of how hard it was to modernize, liberalize, and yet maintain control. History provides few examples of leaders who have been able to do this over an extended period of time. That the Shah was able to do as much as he did is a testimony to his resourcefulness. Without suggesting that one could have predicted with certainty that he would eventually fail, we think that the problem was serious enough to merit more careful and sustained analysis of the situation he was in and the problems he faced. Our conclusions and evaluation are on pp. 65–67.

A Politico-Economic Problem

2. Three aspects of the issue are apparent, and we do not think that it is only hindsight that makes them stand out. One is the impact of the huge influx of oil money on the country. On this point NFAC’s product suffered badly from the separation of political from economic analysis (a subject to which we will return). The deficiency is a common one and exists outside of government as well as in it. Analysts are trained in either politics or economics, and institutional barriers inhibit joint work, with the result that topics that combine both subjects do not receive sufficient attention. Thus it is disturbing but not surprising that NFAC papers gave the facts and figures on economic growth and change, talked about the rates of inflation and the bottlenecks and inefficiencies in the economy, but never explained what this was doing to the political system. More specifically, little was said about the changes in power that were occurring and the resulting grievances among those who were losing out economically—at least in relative terms and losing political influence—even in absolute terms. Brief mentions are sometimes made. Thus a short part of the economics section of the draft NIE of 6 September 1978 was headed “Basis for Popular Unrest,” and began:

> “Most Iranians have gained little in terms of standards of living from the oil and construction booms, and discontent with the Shah’s economic and military priorities could add to labor unrest in the years ahead. . . . The gap between rich and poor has widened, and the poor have been particularly hard hit by inflation. . . . The small-scale artisans, retailers and providers of services and simple manufactured products that constitute the private sector have languished for lack of credit and because of high taxes. . . . As in the past, programs to expand housing and social welfare will be carried out slowly. The Shah’s development program seems likely to lead to growing discontent among the urban poor.”* ‹footnote redacted›

Some of this analysis also appears in the NID for 18 September 1978 and similar analyses are presented in CIA ER 14 September 1978, ‹citation redacted› Although a bit bland, this analysis was better than that found in the section of the NIE dealing with the "Power Structure":

> "The Shah has deliberately aimed his program at the common man, hoping to build mass support, make easier the building of Iran into a modern industrial state, and assure a peaceful transition and reign for his son. At this point, however, it is not clear whether the Shah has achieved positive mass support or simply avoided mass discontent."

3. Further analyses were needed, especially of the political implications of these economic changes. Not only did intelligence need to try to find out whether the Shah's support was eroding among the working classes which were generally thought to have benefitted from his rule, but there was a need for analysis of the changing position and attitudes of bazaaris and other segments of the middle class. The political impact of the cooling off of the economy after mid-1977 should have been examined. The common belief, mentioned in many NFAC publications, that the greatest dangers would arise in the mid-1980s when oil revenues decreased, social problems accumulated, and the Shah tried to arrange the transition to his son's rule helped to distract attention from the present problems. Had this belief been borne out, NFAC would undoubtedly have been congratulated on its foresight. That it was not does not mean that such attempts to see problems long before they arise should be discouraged.

4. These economic changes produced several effects. First, the quality of life was actually lowered for some people, especially those who were hard hit by inflation. Second, many important groups lost power and influence as new entrepreneurs made their fortunes, often through connections with the regime. Thus it is not surprising that the bazaaris strongly supported the opposition. Third, foreigners had a large role in the economic changes—and were probably seen as even more important than they actually were—thus increasing nationalism. Furthermore, since the Shah was closely identified with foreign interests, he was the target of much of this feeling. Fourth, the dislocations and rapid changes led in Iran, as they usually do, to a resurgence of traditional values, in this case religious values. Hindsight makes these patterns clearer, but they are common ones in societies undergoing rapid economic growth and we think that both analysts and management in NFAC should have known that they called for close attention.

5. The second aspect was the peculiar nature of the oil boom, which posed special problems. Not only was the increase in government revenue both terribly rapid and terribly large, but the government did not have to develop efficient state machinery for mobilizing or extracting resources from the general public. This enabled the government to avoid unpopular measures, but it also had two unfortunate side-effects which were hot treated in the NFAC papers. First, the government could avoid heavily taxing the rich. While this had some political benefits, it allowed the income disparities to increase markedly and fed resentment among the rest of the society. Second,

it allowed the government to forgo ties to the grassroots—either repressive or mobilizing. It was thus easy for the government to lose touch with mass opinion. It lacked the organizations and cadres which could have channeled demands, transmitted information and coopted local leaders, and exerted control through means less intrusive than SAVAK. These efforts are difficult and often fail, but in most cases states that do not have some success along these lines simply cannot bring about great social change because they lack the instruments for doing so. In sum, the oil boom allowed the government to foster large-scale social change, with the resulting disruption of much of society, without having to develop the instruments that could help ameliorate some of the problems and channel and control the dissent. The GOI apparently realized this and tried to develop the official political party and several auxiliary organs (Tehran Airgrams A-124, 23 July 1977, and A-157, 19 September 1977, PR AME 77–054, 14 September 1977), but these efforts failed. The government was then more fragile than it seemed.

The Shah's Liberalization Program

6. The third aspect of the Shah's general dilemma that received insufficient NFAC analysis was the problem of liberalizing a repressive regime. This problem was mentioned with some frequency, but there was no detailed and careful discussion of how great the problem was or how the Shah might cope with it. This question was of obvious importance after the fall of 1977 when the Shah started to liberalize and when the USG had to decide how much to push the Shah to liberalize, but at no time in the succeeding year was there an NFAC discussion that was more than a few sentences long. In early August 1978 when the Shah pledged that the forthcoming Majles election would be completely free and when Sharif-Emami introduced a number of wide-ranging reforms a month later, the question of the ability of the government to carry out this policy, without losing control of the country should have been sharply raised. These measures and this problem were of course overtaken by events, but since this was not known at the time we do find it surprising that they did not receive more attention. By early September the new political parties were allowed to form, the government sponsored Resurgence Party was allowed to collapse, free debate was permitted in the Majles and the press was allowed to print what it wanted. These were enormous changes.

7. *Field reporting* was skimpy on these questions. The Embassy's reporting did not express concern that the Shah was moving too fast or unleasing forces he could not control,* and it provided little information on which the opportunities and dangers of

* on 1 June the Embassy noted that "There is little reason for us to doubt the Shah's commitment to liberalization.... It is obvious, however, that he is having trouble keeping Pandora's box only partly open." (Tehran A-80, 1 June. 1978) Similarly, in mid-August the Embassy pointed out that "The Shah is on a tight rope—trying to minimize violence while channeling political conflict into electoral realm." (Tehran 7882, 17 August 1978) While this set the general problem well, the rest of the cable, which offered acute comments on a number of topics, which are quoted in other sections of this report, did not add much information or analysis. ‹1 line redacted›

the program could be evaluated. It occasionally worried that the Shah's inexperience with this kind of endeavor would lead him to commit tactical errors and appear indecisive (Tehran 4836, 21 May 1978), and as the unrest and reforms picked up speed in mid-September it felt the "Critical question ... is how fast GOI can move to implement [Sharif-Emami's] program and convince fence-sitters and oppositionists that GOI is serious about political freedom and social justice," (Tehran 8659, 11 September 1978, also see Tehran 9157, 21 September 1978). Thus the Embassy felt both that the way out of the difficulties lay in the Shah's pushing ahead and that halting the liberalization would incur high domestic and foreign costs. But partly because of its lack of contacts with non-elite groups, it could say little about how the program would be received. It seemed to assume that the Shah had broad support throughout the country and that many of those who had doubts about the regime would be won over by a degree of liberalization which would show them the Shah was moving in the right direction. ‹footnote redacted›

8. In 1977 Embassy reporting had been skeptical about how much the Shah would liberalize because it thought "this could only be done if it is perceived that [greater] opposition is safely manageable in security terms, and that the system is stable enough to afford what the Shah calls the 'luxury of dissent.'" (Tehran Airgram A-124, 25 July 1977). As the Shah moved much further and much faster than anyone had expected, no one returned to this common-sense analysis. The Shah had previously felt that much milder reforms were incompatible with the security of his regime. Why would they not be terribly dangerous now? How could the Shah reconcile a high degree of liberty with the maintenance of much of his power? The Embassy's reports did not address the question of whether the Shah could win out in a free political struggle, although the sections quoted above imply an affirmative answer. Similarly, the Embassy reported former Prime Minister Hoveyda's prediction that "nearly two-thirds of current Majles [of 268 members] could be re-elected in an honestly free election." (Tehran 9689, 5 October 1978) ‹1 page of historical summary omitted›

11. The Station provided only two reports on the liberalization issue, but they are quite informative ones. In one, ‹source redacted› said that the combination of martial law and political liberalization had been very effective in "shifting the venue of dissent away from the streets" and into normal channels. The willingness of the government to permit dissent in the Majles and mass media "has done much to prove the government's sincerity, and acts as an important 'saftey valve.' ... [M]uch of the sense of crisis built up over the past months has abated. There is a valid prospect for a stable but generally orderly society moving toward significant political and economic reform."* The second report, ‹source redacted› was much more pessimistic. Whereas the first saw martial law and liberalization as working together to curb violence and

* A milder version of this argument was voiced by the Embassy during an earlier period that tried to combine liberalization with a firm hand—see Tehran 4526, 12 May 1978, and Tehran 4583, 14 May 1978.

promote legitimate dissent, the second saw them as posing "an intricate dilemma" which would bring down the government. To proceed further with the anti-corruption program, for example, would be to implicate many high officials. But to curb it would be to show that the reforms were hollow. ‹1 line redacted›

12. *NFAC analysis* was alert to the general problems posed by liberalization quite early and generally not only did a good job of summarizing the reports from the field but also adopted a slightly more pessimistic—and more accurate—view than the Embassy. But NFAC production was not thorough, penetrating, or sustained. It stayed too much on the surface of events, in part because of the pressure to report the latest developments, and did not come to grips with the basic problem of whether the Shah's dictatorial regime could safely permit a high level of political freedom. Part of the explanation is that the pace of liberalization was fastest after late August and by this time so many things were happening that the analysts had to carefully ration their attention. The demonstrations, strikes, and riots were more pressing and had to be reported.

13. As early as 10 February 1978, ‹name redacted› noted an aspect of the problem when he analyzed the protests of the month before:

> Such demonstrations have been encouraged by the recent worldwide interest in human rights and by the somewhat more lenient policies the government has been attempting to follow as a result of foreign criticism. The government—and therefore the Shah—is in something of a dilemma. If it permits its most basic programs to be challenged, demonstrations will continue and probably intensify; if it meets such demonstrations with force, it can be accused of suppression of civil and religious liberties. Short of capitulation there is probably little that the government can do to mollify most of its opponents. 10 February 1978. Also see "Iran: The Shah's 'Hundred Flowers' Campaign," 14 September 1977.

14. When the Shah continued the new policy of allowing public criticism of his regime and tried to cope with the winter and spring riots with as little bloodshed as possible, ‹name redacted› noted that "The new line of tolerance of dissent adopted by the Shah presents the security forces with the problem of how to control public disorder without resort to the harsh measures of suppression that have been common—and effective—for the last 15 years." ‹source redacted› 7 April 1978. After the announcement that the Majles elections would be free, ‹name redacted› pointed out that:

> The Shah is taking a calculated risk. Just as his more liberal approach to dissent in the last two years has resulted in violent demonstrations by those hoping to force more concessions from him, so the promise of free elections is likely to produce new political ferment.... His success will ultimately depend on the willingness of a generally irresponsible opposition to forego violence in exchange for a legal political role... The next year in Iran could, like 1906, 1941, and 1953, be a turning point in Iranian history. Sinbad, the Persian who let the genie out of the bottle, was never the same afterwards. ‹Source redacted› (9 August 1978)

A shortened version of this memo which ran in the NID the next day omitted the last two sentences. ‹10 lines redacted›

15. But after this, NFAC production said little about the consequences of liberalization. On 11 September 1978 the NID reported that the imposition of law had not weakened the Shah's commitment to liberalization and on 14 September the analysts made the important point that "The radicals are portraying both the Shah's liberalization program and his recent concessions to the religious community... as a reflection of his weakness. They argue that they must now exploit this by demanding further and more extensive concessions." (15 September 1978) This paralleled the observation in the NID two weeks earlier that "The Shah's appointment of a new cabinet [headed by Sharif-Emami] could be interpreted by some Muslim clergymen as a capitulation to their demands. This could encourage Muslim leaders to push for further political concessions, such as the right of the Muslim clergy to veto Parliamentary legislation—something the Shah is certain to reject." (NID, 28 August 1978. ‹citation redacted› These articles pointed to a dynamic process which the Shah would not be able to control and indicated why limited liberalization was not likely to succeed. But this was never stressed or treated in more detail and depth. The strength of these forces was not compared with those that were conducive to a peaceful solution and the potential clash between the Shah's desire to liberalize and his willingness to use force if the protests got out of hand (see below, pp. 72–74) was not noted.*

16. On 16 September the NID argued that the combination of martial law and political liberalization might be effective when it presented a cautious version of the first of the two station reports discussed above, and included the important reservation that the clergy still showed no willingness to negotiate. (16 September 1978) ‹1-1/2 pages redacted›

18. Little attention was paid to the ability of the radical opposition to create sufficient unrest to make it difficult for the Shah to avoid halting liberalization and establishing a military government, as he eventually did in early November. The desire to prevent this outcome was mentioned in a field report as one reason why the moderates opposed large demonstrations during Muharram (the especially important religious month beginning in early December), and an Embassy cable in October noted the danger that even if the religious groups reached an agreement with the government, other elements might continue the unrest. "The government would [then] have to face up to continuing disturbances whose forceful repression might involve bloodshed—and thus force the religious leaders back on the warpath to preserve their position with the population." (Tehran 10061, 16 October 1978)

* In this same period, INR's proposed footnote to the draft HIE put the problem more sharply: "The conflict between the liberalization program and the need to limit violent opposition raises serious questions about the Shah's ability to share power and to maintain a steady course in his drive to modernize Iran." (11 September 1978)

19. When NFAC analysts returned to the dilemmas of liberalization in late October, they sounded the same themes they had a month earlier: "The political liberalization [the Shah] once thought would mark the final stage of his labor now seems instead to signal the beginning of a greater task." 20 October "The Shah believes he must demonstrate to moderate opponents and politically aware Iranians that he has abandoned one-man rule and intends to build a liberalized government based on consent. At the same time, his critics must be persuaded that the Shah has no intention of stepping down and that further civil disturbances would serve no useful purpose." (NID 23 October 1978). The problem with these statements is not that they are wrong, but that they should have been made earlier and formed the beginning of the analysis, not its end. The question of whether the Shah could survive, let alone prevail, in a relatively free political climate was never addressed. Indeed it was never even posed sharply enough to alert others to its importance.* Similarly, the possibility that the Shah's commitment to continued liberalization might either make it harder for him to crack down or indicate a frame of mind which would not turn to repression was not noted.

Conclusions and Evaluation

20. *It seems in retrospect that had the situation not developed into a crisis in October and November, the attempts to carry out the announced liberalization would have led to the development of greater domestic opposition. For the Shah to have cracked down would have become increasingly difficult and costly; for him to have allowed the process to continue would have undermined his power to rule and even to reign. Even without hindsight the problem was great enough to have called for much more attention and analysis. The 1961 NIE, "Prospects for Iran" ‹5 lines redacted›*

21. *Five factors seem to account for the deficiency. First, information from the field was not particularly good. The analysts had little to go on. Second, there was great pressure to report the latest events and, especially in the fall, many things were happening that had nothing to do with this issue. From mid-year on the analysts had to deal with a steadily growing volume of traffic and increasing demands for articles for the NID for memoranda, and for briefings. Furthermore the analysts felt that it would serve no purpose to discuss a problem that would not demand the consumers'*

* The proposed NIE did not help much. One of the principal judgments of the final draft of the long version was that "Popular reaction to the Shah's liberalization policies . . . will provoke greater dissident activity and attacks on him." Its five-page section on "The Shah's Liberalization" can be faulted less for its optimistic conclusion ("His program of liberalization is not likely to be derailed by the protestors . . .") as for its lack of sustained argument. (6 September) The IIM pointed out that in order to survive, the Shah must expand "public participation in the political process" and "exercise sufficient authority to discourage those who . . . attempt to challenge the regime" and noted that "The dilemma facing the Shah is that these two courses of action conflict to a great extent," but drew no conclusions. (29 September 78) The thrust of the draft of a shorter NIE was similar. (22 October 1978) In another section the IIM stated that "Iranians have a generally negative attitude toward government and tend to yield to the political will of others only when greater authority is manifested. Thus, lenience by the government can be more destabilizing in Iran than a show of force."

immediate attention for several months. In their view, a month or two before the elections would have been the time to treat the issues. Third, many of the dilemmas of liberalization were not unique to Iran but could have been well approached by an appreciation of the process as it was attempted in other autocratic states. The analysts, however, were not experts in such general problems. Their expertise was on Iran and similar countries. Yet there was little in the detailed facts of what was happening to provide adequate guidance. Analysts or scholars who were familiar with other countries' attempts to liberalize might have been able to help identify the crucial issues and note indicators that would show whether the Shah was succeeding, but they were not called in because this was seen as an Iranian problem and because such consultations were not customary. (See further discussion in Process, p. 37)

22. Those working on Iran may have shared the broadly held American view of liberalization as desirable. It is possible that this had an influence on analysis. If there was such an influence it was a subtle and unconscious one.

23. The final, and probably most important, factor is highlighted by the reception of the optimistic station report of mid-September. This led not only to a report in the NID, but also ‹phrase redacted› and was reflected in D/NFAC's testimony before the Senate Foreign Relations Committee on 27 September 1978 in which he argued that much of the explanation for the apparent abatement of the crisis was the combination of martial law and new freedom of press and parliament. This argument was not only plausible, it was also consistent with the belief that most politically relevant Iranians wanted to modify the system, not overthrow it. It made sense against the background belief that the differences within the country were not so great as to preclude compromise. Part of the reason for the expectation that the opposition would split, discussed on pp. 79ff, was the belief that important actors wanted to preserve the Shah as a bulwark against radicalism. A similar consideration seems to have been at work here. The Shah, most Western observers felt, had done a lot of good for his country, and many of his countrymen recognized this. Thus, as late as 25 October, the Embassy was referring to the "silent majority" that favored his retention, albeit perhaps with reduced powers. (Tehran 10421, 25 October 1978). Since it was clear that the Shah was willing to grant many of the protestors' demands, it made eminent sense for a compromise to be struck on a major program of liberalization. This was, we think, a typically American view. (The authors differ on the extent to which such ethnocentrism may have affected intelligence production.)

24. There is another possible explanation, and it hinges on the premise that Iranians do not compromise in the give-and-take sense, but rather that they compromise by submitting to superior power. Given the belief that the Shah was strong and that he retained the support of the military and security services, analysts may have reasoned that enough opposition figures feared that the Shah's superior power would be loosed on them so that they would opt to accept what they had already won. With hindsight, it is fairly clear that many Iranians saw power flowing away from the once all-powerful

Shah and that they were more heavily influenced than observers knew by the ultimate noncompromiser, Ayatollah Khomeini.

THE ISSUE OF THE SHAH'S WILLINGNESS TO USE FORCE

1. One of the crucial beliefs that underpinned the optimistic analysis of developments in Iran was the view—from which there were few dissents*—that the Shah would be able to exercise control of the situation. In 1977, ‹name redacted› noted that opponents of the regime placed undue faith in student and religious protest because they looked back to relatively successful protests in the early 1960s without realizing that the Shah was now in a much stronger position. ‹source redacted› 27 July 1977. The events of most of the next year did not shake this confidence. The Embassy and the analysts thought that if there were a real and immediate danger to the Shah's regime he would clamp down effectively, even though doing so would have been costly. This view was shared by many newsmen—"Most diplomatic observers and dissidents agree that the Shah has more than enough resources to crush any serious challenge to his regime" (William Branigan in the *Washington Post,* 7 April 1978); "even [the Shah's] political foes agree that he still has the power to crush any major threat to his rule," (*An-Nahar Arab Report,* 17 April 1978). Even a Marxist opponent of the regime agreed; he argued in a recent book that the Iranian terrorists "underestimate the degree to which the repression and post-1963 boom have placed new weapons in the hands of the regime." (Fred Halliday, *Iran: Dictatorship and Development,* p. 243).**

2. As the final draft of the proposed NIE put it: "The government has the ability to use as much force as it needs to control violence, and the chances that the recently widespread urban riots will grow out of control is [sic] relatively small. The limiting factors are the Shah's expressed desire to permit some liberalization and the possible fallout abroad from harsh measures. These limitations may encourage further demonstrations, but the threat of the force that the Shah has available if he is pushed too far will deter all but the most virulent opposition." (6 September 1978, PP. I-14—I-15) This merely formalized and restated what had been said often over the past year. As early as December 1977 the Embassy said that if student protests continued "we have no doubt the authorities are prepared to reimpose order forcefully." (Tehran 10777, 6 December 1977). After the Tabriz riots, the Embassy explained that it did not share the gloomy views of the US Consul because "GOI has until now refrained from using full range of social controls." (Tehran 1879 23 Feb). On 8 August 1978 the Embassy argued that the Shah "is thus far unwilling to wield a heavy hand unless there is no other way

* Henry Precht, the State Department Country Director for Iran, apparently disagreed. But his views reached the NIO/NESA only in September and were not directly expressed to the other analysts.

** The inherent plausibility of this view was reinforced in the minds of at least some of the analysts by the analogy to 1963 when the Shah put down protest demonstrations by force.

to proceed. This does not mean that he will not or cannot put the lid on again, because he can do so, although he would be faced with even greater problems than in 1963." ‹citation redacted› Ten days later it argued that "At some point, the Shah may be forced to repress an outbreak with the iron fist and not the velvet glove if Iran is to retain any order at all. We have no doubt that he will do so if that becomes essential.... He is mindful of what vacillation brought Ayub Khan and Bhutto in Pakistan."* (Tehran 7882, 17 August 1978). Even the relatively pessimistic draft Interagency Intelligence Memorandum drafted by INR in late September declared: "Possessing a monopoly of coercive force in the country, [the armed and security] forces have the ultimate say about whether the Shah stays in power." (29 Sept., p. 9)

3. NFAC analysts took a similar position. On 11 May 1978 the NID concluded that "The Shah is gambling that his program of modernization has enough political support to allow him to take stern measures, if necessary, against the conservative Muslims." ‹Name redacted› also repeated in the NID for 17 June 1978, ‹text redacted› On 14 September 1978, NFAC reported that "The Shah is not minimizing the current challenge to his rule in Iran, but he seems determined to weather the storm and to keep a firm hand on the levers of power." (NID, ‹redacted›)

4. Those further removed from day-to-day events shared this assumption. The NIO/NESA and his assistant reported that until well into the crisis they expected the Shah to be willing and able to use as much force as was necessary to re-establish his control. The DCI noted in retrospect: "I persisted, personally, in believing... well into October, that the Shah had the horsepower to take care of [the opposition]. At the right time, before it got out of control, [I thought] he would step in with enough power to handle it...." (*Los Angeles Times*, 17 March 1979)

5. The problem with this line of argument is not that it turned out to be incorrect, but that almost no evidence, short of the most massive and disruptive of protests, could have disconfirmed it. And by the time such protests occurred, they might signal the end of the Shah's regime. The Shah's failure to crack down at one point did not show that he would not use force in the near future. Thus the first nine months of 1978 did not show that the Shah could be forced out, and indeed it is hard to see what events could have shown this, given the basic belief in the Shah's as-yet unused power. Furthermore, this view fed an underestimate of the significance of the protests of the spring and summer, since the corollary to the belief that if matters were really serious the Shah would clamp down was the inference that if the Shah had not clamped down, matters could not be that serious. (Indeed this inference may have supported the belief that liberalization would strengthen, rather than weaken, the regime.)

6. Just because a belief is impervious to a great deal of evidence does not mean that it is wrong. This belief, furthermore, was not only inherently plausible, but had

* The inherent plausibility of this view was reinforced in the minds of at least some of the analysts by the analogy to 1963 when the Shah put down protest demonstrations by force.

been supported both by the Shah's general history of behavior and his use of force to break up a dissident meeting in November 1977. But if an analyst does hold such a belief, special precautions should be taken. Not only should especially strenuous efforts be made to probe whatever evidence is available, but consumers should be alerted to the danger that information that could disprove the belief is not likely to become available until the situation has gravely deteriorated. Furthermore, analysts and consumers who are aware of these problems might reduce the confidence with which they held their belief. No matter how plausible it seemed, the fact that the belief could not be readily disconfirmed provided an inherent limit to confidence that should have been placed in it.

Missed Warning Signs

7. There were at least a few signs that the Shah was extremely hesitant to crack down that could have been noted. They stand out only in retrospect and even had the analysts singled them out for attention at the time it would have been impossible to have said exactly how significant they were. But we think that they could have been noted if the analysts had been fully aware that their important belief that the Shah would use force when he needed to was not amenable to much direct evidence. Throughout the crisis, the Shah vacillated and used less force than most people expected. In early November 1977 the Embassy noted that peaceful protests had not incurred the "crackdown expected by many." (Tehran 9692, 4 November 1977) At the end of the month the Shah signaled the limits of dissent by sending a goon squad to break up a large, but peaceful, protest meeting. But restrictions were soon put on SAVAK again. Similarly, in the spring the Shah first exercised restraint, then launched "private" violence against the dissident leaders (much to the dismay of US officials), and then halted the campaign even though the unrest did not diminish. Again later in the summer the Shah showed that he was very hesitant to use force. He had to be persuaded by his generals to institute martial law in a dozen cities in September. None of this proved that he would not crack down at a later stage, but it could have been seen as a warning sign. ‹footnote redacted›

8. Vacillation not only cast some doubt on the expectation that the Shah would crack down, but may have been an important cause of the growing unrest. On the one hand, the repressive incidents further alienated large segments of Iranian society and probably made people even more skeptical of the Shah's professed desires to liberalize. On the other hand the concessions to the protestors and the restraints on SAVAK weakened one of the main pillars supporting the regime and, more importantly, led people to see the Shah as vulnerable. Finished intelligence noted the Shah's swings from repression to concessions, but did not point out that they might have the effect of greatly increasing the strength of the opposition. Here, as on other subjects discussed elsewhere in this report, NFAC did a better job of reporting events than of analyzing their probable causes and effects.

9. Similarly, tension between the Shah's sustained commitment to liberalization and his ability and will to crack down could have been noted. The two are not

completely contradictory since the Shah could have planned on liberalization as his first line of defense and repression as his instrument of last resort, but in many ways the two policies did not sit well together. The Shah's willingness to continue liberalization and indeed speed up its pace in the face of increasing unrest might have thrown doubt on his willingness to use massive force.

10. Another kind of evidence might have disturbed the belief that the Shah would crack down. The analysts knew that it was the policy of the US Government to strongly urge the Shah not to resort to repression. This theme appeared at the beginning of the unrest in the fall of 1977 and remained, and indeed was strongest, in late October 1978 even as NFAC analysts were concluding that the Shah's survival was problematical. Throughout the period of this study, the United States had believed it possible and necessary for the Shah to liberalize. In late 1977 and early 1978 this meant a curbing of abuses by the security forces; in the middle of 1978 it meant a continuation of the trend toward more political freedom which it was expected would culminate in free elections; in the fall this meant urging the Shah to view martial law as only a temporary set-back on the road to a more open regime and strongly opposing the imposition of a military government. Although a firm hand with the violent demonstrators might have been compatible with aspects of the liberalization program (and this was often the Embassy's analysis; e.g., Tehran 4526, 14 May 1978, and Tehran 4583, 15 May 1978), there was always tension between these two policies (recognized in Tehran 7882, 17 August 1978), a tension that increased with the size of the unrest. By the late summer it is hard to see how a crack down widespread enough to have been effective could have co-existed with liberalization. (This view was not universally shared, as can be seen by the reports discussed in White Revolution, above.)

11. In the earlier periods it could be argued that while the United States was urging restraint, this did not contradict the belief that the Shah would crack down if he needed to because the situation was not that serious and the main danger was that the Shah would overreact. But this was not true in September and October. Although it was still believed that the Shah could survive, his margin was seen as quite thin. If he were ever to crack down, it would have to be now.

12. Of course it was not the job of the analysts to second-guess the policy-makers. But the knowledge of the policy should have led them to question whether the Shah would crack down. He might not take the American advice. Indeed, analysts may have come to believe over the years that the Shah was not greatly moved by what American ambassadors told him about Iranian domestic affairs, and US representations did not seem to have much impact in the late winter and early spring. But given the vehemence of the American position the analysts should have noted two things. First, there was strong pressure on the Shah to avoid repression even when the situation became extremely tense. Of course the Shah might crack down anyway. But everyone agreed that the Shah shared the Iranian view that nothing of significance happened in his country that the US was not involved with. The Embassy noted his frequent claims that

"some people" thought the United States was behind the protests. The analysts presumably understood that much of the American role in the 1953 coup was to give the Shah courage by stressing how much we supported him. The obvious danger, then, was that the strong American representations would interact with the Shah's distorted outlook and lead him to entertain real doubts as to whether the United States was still wholeheartedly on his side and fear that he would be deserted if he used force.* Second, the Ambassador and the State Department seemed to have a very different view than that held by the NFAC analysts—the former seem to have thought that a crack down would be neither effective nor necessary. The belief that it would not be effective contradicted the basic assumption of NFAC. The belief that it wasn't necessary indicated that NFAC's assumption was irrelevant, because the contingency it assumed would not arise. NFAC analysts could have tried to find out why the State Department disagreed with them and weighed the evidence and arguments that led to a contrary conclusion.

Events That Changed Minds

13. Two streams of events finally undermined the belief that the Shah would reassert control if and when he had to. First, the unrest grew to such proportions that the analysts came to doubt whether repression would be possible. This did not appear in finished intelligence until November, but it seems to have been developing in people's minds from mid-October, with different people coming to this conclusion at slightly different dates.** For some, the strikes which started in early October and soon spread to the oil workers were most important. Force might be used to scatter demonstrators, but it could not produce oil. For others, the continued unrest throughout the country was at least as important, for it indicated that people would go into the streets in larger numbers, and over a longer period of time, than had been true before and sharply raised the question of whether the amount of force needed might be more than the Army could supply.

14. The second stream of events contradicted the belief that the Shah *would* crack down. We have discussed this at greater length in our treatment of NFAC's analysis of the Shah's changing moods, but here should note that for some analysts, events were taken as showing that the Shah lacked the will to use what power he had. In early October the Shah was giving in to almost all the economic demands of the various striking groups and later martial law was being widely disregarded. For these analysts

* The ORPA analysts have explained to us that although they did not pay much attention to this aspect of US policy, they would mention this factor in finished intelligence only in the context of reports concerning the Shah's reaction to American pressure.

** on 11 September 1978 INR submitted a footnote to the draft NIE which said in part: "We are dubious that the Shah, in the near term, can suppress urban violence without substantial use of force. That, in turn, would further aggravate his difficulties by enlarging the circle of opposition against him and possibly calling into question the loyalty of the armed forces and security services." But this position does not seem to have been stressed or developed, at least not in material which reached NFAC. ‹6 lines redacted› the crucial evidence came in a bit before that which showed that they could not reassert control even if he tried, but this still was relatively late. ‹Line redacted› the Shah which told them that he would not crack down. For unless something in the Shah's past behavior told them that he would not be firm and decisive, they had to await direct evidence of a failure of will in his handling of the current crisis. Field reports had paid attention to the Shah's moods from the late spring on, and many of them appeared in the finished intelligence, but they were read against the background of the basic belief in the Shah's strength of character and decisiveness. Although these reports indicated that the Shah was frequently depressed (but not wildly beyond reason, given the situation he was facing), they did not unambiguously point to the conclusion that he would not ask decisively if he had to. Analysts who started with the view that the Shah was weak, on the other hand, did not need the direct evidence of his unwillingness to move against the strikes and protests of October to conclude that he would not meet the test. The NIO remembers a meeting at which the State Department desk officer said: "you've got to remember, the Shah is a coward. He ran away in 1953."* This, the NIO reports, was an unusual perception, and once he was convinced of its validity he no longer expected the Shah to survive. But if one started from the more common perception of the Shah as all the CIA analysts did, one could not be expected to change one's mind until sometime in October. ‹1 page redacted›

Conclusions and Evaluation

17. *In conclusion, while the belief that the Shah would reassert control if he had to was certainly plausible, at least until the fall of 1978, NFAC did not do as good a job as it could have in carefully analyzing the evidence or in alerting consumers to the fact that clearly disconfirming information would not arrive in time to give them warning that the Shah was in deep trouble. NFAC produced no papers which dealt with this question. While the Shah's moods were commented on, the possible implications for his deciding to use force were not drawn. The Shah's swings from leniency to repression and back again were not probed for patterns and clues to the future. Although much attention was given to whether the Shah could use force (e.g., the analyses of the army's morale), little was said about his willingness to do so. NFAC did not explore either the impact of US policy, which may have been magnified by the Shah's exaggeration of American power, or the apparent discrepancy between NFAC's analysis and that of the State Department and Embassy.*

18. *We think the primary explanation for these failings was two-fold. First, the belief was shared by all NFAC analysts (at least until the early fall), was very plausible, fitted with the pre-existing view of the Shah, and so became an article of faith. Most observers outside the government also shared this view and even in retrospect it is hard to say*

* This statement is pithy but probably not accurate. In retrospect it appears more likely that the Shah's fundamental lack of self-confidence, noted in several NFAC papers, came to the surface again.

why he did not crack down. The incentives to challenge this belief were slight. Second, it did not need to figure in the reporting or analysis of most day-to-day events. When the Shah cracked down it would be news; until then the possibility still remained open. Only when the unrest grew to enormous proportions did his restraint seem important in explaining what was happening. So the analysts' main task of dealing with the latest events did not make them look more carefully at this crucial belief.

SPLITS IN THE OPPOSITION

1. Another crucial belief was that the opposition would split. Before examining the evidence that was available and the inferences that were drawn, we should note that this belief was subject to the same problem as the expectation that the Shah would exercise control if things got really serious—i.e., definitive negative evidence could not appear until the Shah was on his last legs. At any previous point all that could be known was that the split had not yet occurred. Given the obvious tensions within the opposition, one could never be sure that it would continue to hold together. Indeed, expectations of such a bargain were very high in the last days of October. The point is not that these beliefs were silly or automatically wrong. Even in retrospect, we cannot tell how close the opposition came to splitting. But NFAC should have realized that the belief that a split was possible was not easily disconfirmable and alerted the consumers to the problem.

2. Furthermore, the belief that the opposition would split did not sit too well with the companion belief that the Shah could clamp down when he needed to. Granted that one reason the moderates might split from the more extreme opposition was fear that if they did not strike a bargain with the Shah, he would resort to force (this was noted in several of October's cables), but in other ways the two beliefs pulled in different directions. Repression would presumably unite the opposition and the longer the Shah waited for the opposition to split, the harder it would be for him to repress because the unrest was growing stronger. If the Shah were torn between these two possible solutions, he might well end up with the worst of both worlds. While one could believe that the Shah would first try to split the opposition and then crack down if he could not do so, this assumes that the failure would become obvious before the Shah lost too much power or nerve.

3. The belief that the opposition would split was widespread throughout the period under consideration. As the proposed NIE put it:

> The Iranian Freedom Seekers Liberation Movement would like to become the spokesman for all oppositionists, but the disparity in basic views and personalities among the several groups makes this difficult and unlikely. Any cooperation probably will be limited to paper pronouncements and minimal joint activity. There is virtually no chance that the opposition can develop a joint program that is meaningful and capable of attracting popular support. (p. 1–15, 23 August 1978)

The IIM drafted by the State Department on 29 September on "The Near Term Political Prospects for Iran", which generally had a more pessimistic tone than the draft NIE, took a slightly different view: "Far from a disciplined coalition, [IFSLM] nevertheless provides a modicum of coordination among the opponents of the regime. There is a perceived need on the part of each faction in the coalition to cooperate with the others." (p. 7)

4. This view was shared by the Embassy and all levels of NFAC. ‹1 line redacted› the common belief in NFAC was that the opposition would split, D/NFAC stressed the heterogeneous nature of the opposition in his testimony before the Senate Foreign Relations Committee on 27 September 1978 (Briefing Notes, *Situation in Iran*) and the DCI has said that he did not think the opposition could remain united. (*LA Times,* 18 March 1979; *Director's Notes* No. 39, 7 February 1979)

5. There were several ways in which the opposition might have split—e.g., among factions in IFSLM (an umbrella group for all 'political' opposition), between political and religious opposition, between moderates and extremists in the religious establishment. While the first two are not unimportant—one major opposition political figure became PM in December 1978—the 'political' opposition did not have the numbers or the strength to affect the Shah's position on its own. The following discussion concentrates on what became the key issue, i.e., the split that the Shah wanted to bring about in the religious leadership and, consequently, in its following. Such splits were, as we understand it, not uncommon in modern Iranian history.

6. The Embassy's basic rationale for the expectation of a split was put in a cable of late May:

> The majority of religious leaders... have found it useful, or necessary, to join the extremists managed... by Ayatollah Khomeini, but their motivation is different from his. Unlike Khomeini, who makes no secret that his intention is to overthrow the Shah..., these leaders have more limited aims in mind. Chiefly, they wish to call attention to their grievances. As long as the government was paying little attention to them, they had no reason to withhold support for Khomeini. Now there are indications that the government is beginning to listen.... Since many of these religious leaders see the monarchy as a necessary institution which helps protect Islam against communist challenges, and no alternative to the Shah is apparent to anyone, they probably are prepared to be reasonable and settle for a rational, responsible attitude on the part of the government without any major changes in institutions. Rather, they hope for a more understanding application of laws and regulations and a greater, more public recognition of the continuing importance of religion in Iranian life. (Tehran 5131, 20 May 1978)

An airgram of 1 June made a similar point:

> The Embassy's soundings among religious leaders suggest an underlying basis of loyalty to the Monarchy and to the independence of Iran as the Shah envisions it, but increasing unhappiness at the breakdown of communications between the religious leadership and

> the Shah...He is attempting, therefore, to open better channels to the religious leadership and will doubtless act on some of their complaints. If done deftly, this should go a long way to assuage them and lead to a break-down of opposition unity. (Tehran A-80, 1 June 1978)

Slight variants of this analysis were to be central to the Embassy's views until the end of October. This view was certainly plausible and probably contained a large measure of truth, but because of the scarcity of contacts with the religious-based opposition, it had to strongly rest on indirect inferences and second-hand reports and so should have limited the confidence that was placed in the conclusions.

7. NFAC's basic analysis of the religious community, conducted before the current crisis, is compatible with the Embassy's perception but put much more emphasis on their opposition, stressing that "the Moslem clergy are among some of the Shah's fiercest critics." (*Elites,* February 1976, p.43)

> Probably no more than 10 percent of the clergy...can be counted as outright supporters of the Shah. They are probably the least influential of the clergy....Probably 50 percent are in outright opposition of the government and are wholly dependent on their popular following for support; this includes nearly every religious leader of any stature. The remaining 40 percent qualify as fence-sitters, maintaining a popular following but avoiding overt attacks on the government.

The religious leaders have "their roots...in traditional Islam, and their constituency and support are found in the lower classes, the traditional middle classes, and portions of the modern middle class. They represent the *din-e-mellat,* the religion of the people as contrasted with the *din-e-dowlat,* the religion of the government." (*Iran in the 1980s,* August 1977, S, p. 35)

8. For the sake of convenience, field reports and finished intelligence on the question of whether the opposition would split can be divided into four periods: spring and summer; late August to mid-September (the Sharif-Emami reforms and the reactions to the imposition of martial law); late September; October (the final attempt to split the opposition). Readers who wish to skip the detailed treatment of these materials can turn to page 93, for our conclusions.

Field Reporting and NFAC Analysis

Spring and Summer

‹2 pages of description omitted›

13. The occasional warnings culminated in an Embassy cable of mid-August which deserves to be quoted at length:

> Moderates such as Ayatollah Shariatmadari do not at this time feel capable of opposing Khomeini openly, though they reportedly still work for moderation within the religious movement and would doubtlessly welcome a chance to participate in an electoral process which might not leave them wholly subservient to Khomeini, who remains outside the

> country. In Shia Islam there is no institutionalized hierarchy: A religious-leader attains his prominence by consensus within his parish. Some of the violence we are witnessing here results from a fervid competition for eminence by the ayatollahs, moderation apparently does not beget followers from the workers, small shop keepers and artisans at this time. A tradition of throne/opposition dialogue does not exist in Iran, and neither temperament nor tradition favor western concepts of political conciliation and brokerage.
>
> .... [material omitted in the original]
>
> The earlier efforts to establish a dialogue with the more moderate leaders were not pursued with much vigor and the objective of splitting the religious leadership has simply not worked so far. Part of the reason for this latter failure has been the threats and harassment of the moderates by the well-organized Khomeini fanatics; also, as noted earlier, no ayatollah wishes to lose his followers by appearing soft. Furthermore, the Amouzegar government (as opposed to the Shah and the court) has proved surprisingly inept at dealing with religious elements on anything other than a take it or leave it basis.
>
> If our general assessment is valid, the shah has to find a way to pen serious give and take with the so-called religious (and some political) moderates (this will be hard to swallow because of his utter disdain for "the priests"). We should realize at the outset that this may ultimately prove impossible because of their ultimate demands (as opposed to what they might accept as a part of an on-going process) would mean religious control of the government and reduction of the Shah to a constitutional monarch. The Shah would never accept the first and would see the latter emerging only in the context of rule passing to his son. (Tehran 7882, 17 August 1978).

These comments, both on the moderates' goals and on their power, were never refuted by later Embassy reporting. The evidence provided was not conclusive, of course, and later events might lead the moderates to be willing or able to play a more independent role. But by mid-August they had not done so, and there appeared to be good reasons why they would be very cautious about breaking with Khomeini.

14. Throughout this period, NFAC analysis made few comments on these questions. Although ‹identification redacted› paper on the religious-based opposition on 10 February talked of the differences within the religious community, the government at that time was not working to divide the religious leaders and so it did not address the possibility later envisaged by the Embassy. In early June, ‹identification redacted› briefly returned to this subject, implying that a split was possible: "Too little is known of factionalism among the clergy to be certain, but it is likely that a considerable number of them, while unenthusiastic about the regime, would prefer not to confront it and risk greater losses in position and power than ahs already been the case." (2 June 1978), The Embassy and station reports summarized in the last paragraphs were not covered in finished intelligence and there was no discussion of whether the opposition could be split, what the moderates' goal were, and how independent they could afford to be. With the exceptions cited above NFAC products in the spring and summer referred to

the religious community as though it were united. In some cases this may have been done in the need to keep the analysis brief (e.g. NID, 10 Aug.), although even a longer NID report on 17 June, "Iran: Increase in Religious Dissidence," does not mention any split between Shariat-Madari and Khomeini.

Late August—mid-September

15. When Sharif-Emami took office as the Prime Minister in late August, he made a number of concessions to the religious groups (e.g., returning to the Moslem calendar, closing gambling casinos, removing Bahais from positions of power). But instead of being conciliated, the religious leaders issued a string of demands. The Embassy's comment was the "clergy have been slow to react positively, but historical background of their ties with GOI would not encourage optimism under best of circumstances. . . . Competition among local religious leaders . . . is not conducive to cooperative posture with GOI." (Tehran 8351, 31 August 1978) Other lists of religious demands are in Tehran 8548, 7 September 1978, and Tehran 8485, 6 September 1978. This, however, did not really address the question or whether the earlier expectation that the opposition would eventually split still held.

16. Events in early September, before the imposition of martial law, continued to provide both encouraging and discouraging signs although, at least in retrospect, the latter predominated. The report that the moderates could not exercise restraint, partly because the Shah had made so many concessions "as the result of mob terrorist activity" was consistent with the refusal of Shariat-Madari to negotiate with the new Sharif-Emami government. (Tehran 8485, 6 September 1978) But both these reports also carried some optimistic news. Tehran 8485 noted that while Shariat-Madari publicly said he and Khomeini were in complete agreement, "in other contacts Shariat-Madari is much more cautious and leaves room for eventual differences of opinion." And the source which said that the moderates could not now exercise restraint also noted that "Moderate opposition leaders are afraid that the temper of the country is such that further violence . . . threatens the entire course of the movement toward representative government."

17. At this point finished intelligence began referring to the religious moderates and implied that the Shah's strategy was to separate them from the extremists by making reasonable concessions. (See the NID for 28 August 1978 and 3D August and the Weekly Summary of 1 September.) But it also pointed out that previous attempts to do so had failed (NID 30 Aug.) and concluded that while "some moderates may be satisfied with the Shah's recognition of their importance, the more militant of his religious critics . . . will be mollified by nothing short of his abdication." (Weekly Summary, 1 Sept.) A few days later ‹name redacted› argued that although "the new prime minister is optimistic about his main task—to try to find a modus vivendi with the clergy . . .—the only clerical reaction has been to demand more concessions. (‹citation redacted› 7 September 1978) The implications of this perceptive remark were not noted and the moderates ability to break with Khomeini if they wanted to was not discussed,

a serious omission in view of the fact that the purpose of the Shah's appointing Sharif-Emami's reform cabinet was to strike a bargain with them.

18. The imposition of martial law and the killings of 8 September turned attention away from relations within the opposition, although when Sharif-Emami announced his program to the Majles, the Embassy implied that, while the moderates had not yet been won over, this remained a real possibility if the GOI carried out an effective liberalization program. (Tehran 8659, 11 September 1978) This seemed to be the view at every stage. As we noted earlier, almost no evidence could disconfirm it. Furthermore, neither the Embassy nor the analysts noted that the government concessions, although not sufficient to win over any of the opposition, were massive by standards of only a few months earlier. In the spring, no one would have thought that the Shah would have gone as far as he did and, more importantly, most observers probably would have predicted that the sort of concessions which were made in August and September would have satisfied a large segment of the opposition and brought about the split which observers were anticipating. Thus the relatively luke-warm response to the concessions should have suggested either that the moderates would not be won over by anything the Shah could be expected to do or that they had little power and could not afford to be seen as opposed to Khomeini, a conclusion suggested by the reports quoted earlier. In either case, doubt would be cast on the belief that the opposition would split.

19. In this period the finished intelligence had more to say on the issue than it had previously. But the analysis was a bit thin in both quantity and quality. On 14 September the NID discussed the issue more fully than it had in the past, and for that reason we shall quote all the relevant sections:

> Responsible opposition leaders, religious and political, will have to show a greater willingness than they have thus far if they are to accommodate the Shah's efforts to reconcile critics who want a greater voice in setting the pace and direction of national policies. The bloody events in Tehran on Friday will make it more difficult for moderate opposition figures to rein in demonstrators and forestall radicals who call for the Shah's ouster....
>
> The divisions within the religious and political factions of the opposition will hamper the efforts of Prime Minister Sharif-Emami to begin negotiations with more responsible critics of the government. Moderate opponents who may be inclined to open a dialogue with the Prime Minister will be anxious not to be outflanked by radicals who will denounce their "capitulation" to the Shah.

The Weekly Review added that cooperation from the moderates would be extremely important—"cooperation that, thus far, the moderates have refused to provide." (15 September 1978) Similarly the NID of 16 September pointed out that "muslim clergymen... still show no sign of interest in negotiating a political compromise that would give the Muslim leadership a greater voice in government policy affecting religion but would leave the Shah's ultimate authority intact." Two days later the NID noted that

"A leading religious figure, who has been urging the people to avoid violence, vowed that he will not cooperate with Sharif-Emami, who he said is 'unfit to govern.'"

20. In *late September* the relations between the moderates and the extremists received more attention from the field. In a relatively pessimistic cable, the Embassy reiterated that in the past months "the Shariatmadari clergy did not dare to let itself be outflanked on the left and lose mass supporters to the extremists," but also stressed that "the nature of the opposition is not as unified as it might appear." (Tehran 9158, 21 Sept. 78) The Embassy did not, however, explain why the same pressures which forced the moderates to keep up with the extremists would cease operating. But a week later station reports came in which indicated that the Embassy might have been correct; Shariatmadari and other moderates:

> Have privately stated that they are very concerned by the increasingly radical nature of opposition to the Shah and his government. These religious leaders fear that this might result in 'political chaos and complete disorder,' which could prompt a Communist take-over or a military dictatorship. As a result of these concerns, these Ayatollahs are urging moderation on their followers and are actively seeking to enter into effective negotiations with the Shah....

Another report ‹citation redacted› ran parallel. But both these reports also struck pessimistic notes. The first said that "Negotiations have so far been hampered by the religious leaders' lack of confidence in emissaries who have already come to them from the Shah." A field comment in the second underscored the moderates' mistrust not only of the emissaries, but also of the Shah himself, noted the power of Khomeini over the moderates, and concluded that "Some of the moderate religious leaders' demands are in all probability unacceptable to the Shah... [I]t is uncertain what actions by the government would constitute an acceptable program for the religious leadership."

21. These reports were summarized in NID ‹citation redacted› of 29 September, which, partly because of the order in which the paragraphs were placed, emphasized the optimism. The bold-faced lead paragraph in the NID stated: "Important religious leaders in Iran are anxious for an accommodation with the government in order to solve the political crisis." Later on came some pessimism—"the two sides are still far apart."‹3 lines redacted› Of course it had appeared, although without emphasis or elaboration, in the NID of 14 September quoted above, but since these reports, if true, would remove many of the grounds for optimism, they deserved more thorough analysis. At minimum, the consumers should have been warned that the moderates' desires for a settlement might be irrelevant. Given the paucity of the information available, perhaps this was all that could have been done.

22. In *mid-October* hope for reconciliation between the government and the moderates increased. It rested on three not entirely consistent considerations. First, National Front leaders were reported to be increasingly anxious for a settlement and offered to try to bring religious leaders, including Khomeini, along if the Shah made suitable

concessions. Second, there were some indications that Khomeini might sanction the moderates' attempts to deal with the government (although the Embassy noted that "our reading of the Khomeini published interviews out of Paris does not lead us to fully share [National Front] source's optimism that Khomeini may be willing to go along with local leaders." (Tehran 10281, 22 October 1978) Third, shortly after the Embassy reported that "Source close to moderates had told us there would probably be public evidence of break between Shariat-Madari and Khomeini within next week," (Tehran 10059, 16 October 1978) complex talks between Khomeini and the moderates and the government seemed to be starting. On 22 October the Embassy made the important point that the moderates "have begun to lower their apparent ambitions. While two or three weeks ago, many of these politicians were openly calling for the dismissal of the Shah, most of them now quietly state that they accept the need for the Shah's continued leadership, albeit within the framework of a democratic, constitutional society. These same figures have also begun discreetly to disassociate themselves from Khomeini and to urge restraint upon the mullahs." The reasons were the growing fear that a military government would take power if the unrest continued and the "greater sense of self-confidence" on the part of the religious moderates, who "are in the process of negotiating an understanding with the government, which would entail their allegiance to the Shah." Furthermore, the moderates had more room to maneuver because "the Khomeini star seems to be waning." (Tehran 10267, 22 October 1978) This report was consistent with the earlier conversation with a representative of Shariat-Madari in which he "confirmed what we had been told previously by others: moderate religious leadership respects Sharif-Emami and appears ready to work with him despite problems engendered by martial law.... We have somewhat more doubts about moderate leaders' ability to bring Khomeini aboard, but suspect merely muted opposition which would give moderates a breathing space would be satisfactory." (Tehran 9904, 11 October 1978) This seemed also to be Sharif-Emami's view, since he said he was close to a deal with the moderates and that Khomeini was going to "remain quiet." (Tehran 9990, 15 October 1978)

23. The one discouraging note was supplied by a SAVAK official who stressed that the negotiations "cannot reach a successful conclusion as long as religious leaders fear the adverse reaction of Ayatollah Khomeini to any agreement which permits the retention of the Pahlevi dynasty.... SAVAK is convinced that moderate Ayatollahs desire an accommodation with the government which will defuse the present tense situation. However, these Ayatollahs know that they will be deserted by their followers, if after an agreement is reached Ayatollah Khomeini condemns it." (‹Citation redacted›; also see Washington Post, 29 October.) ‹6 lines redacted›

24. The NID generally mirrored these reports. On 14 October ‹name redacted› said that Sharif-Emami was "making some progress in his negotiations with moderate religious leaders." The "moderate opponents now realize that the radical actions to which they had contributed might trigger a complete collapse of governmental authority." (Also see ‹redacted›, 20 October) A week later the NID reported that "The Prime

Minister seems confident that he can reach a modus vivendi with moderate clergymen that will isolate extremists led by Ayatollah Khomeini," an expectation it neither endorsed nor contradicted. (23 October) A few days later the NID told of a tentative agreement between Sharif-Emami and the moderates, although it pointed out that "a number of pitfalls...could wreck chances for restoring stability." The report concluded cautiously: "Emissaries of the moderate opposition are trying to persuade extremist religious leader Khomeini...to drop his demand for the Shah's overthrow and accede to the accord. The chances seem bleak in view of Khomeini's implacable opposition to any compromise with the Shah. The moderate opponents therefore will probably be forced either to formalize a split with the extremists or to repudiate the fragile accord with the government." (26 October) On 31 October, the NID reported that the latter course of action had been chosen.

Conclusions and Evaluation

25. *We do not think this issue was treated well in the finished intelligence. At best it summarized the reports from the field and did so—to its credit—often with a slightly pessimistic tone. But until mid-September it did not even do this very well. As early as May the belief that the Shah could split the opposition was one of the main pillars supporting the conclusion that he could weather the storm. Yet NFAC finished intelligence said almost nothing about this until September. The Embassy cable of 17 August which questions the ability of the moderates to break with Khomeini did not make its way into finished intelligence.*

26. *In the spring this subject received little attention because the analysts concentrated on explaining the general causes of the unrest, reporting the disturbances as they occurred, and discussing the danger that the Shah might use excessive brutality in an "overreaction." Furthermore, no finished political intelligence was produced in July, although work continued on the proposed NID. To the extent that relations among opposition groups seemed important, analysts drew attention to the improbable "alliance of convenience" between the moderate left (National Front) and the religious right. (NID, 17 June 1978) The question of whether the latter community itself would split took on most significance only after it became clear, first of all, that it was supplying the bulk of the support for the protests, and, second, that the Shah felt the situation serious enough to require concessions to the religious moderates. Nevertheless, NFAC was a bit slow to see the importance of this question. The analysts have explained to us that they wrote the items as they did because the moderates and Khomeini were in fact working together during this period. This strikes us as an example of the unfortunate tendency (noted in the Process section) for NFAC product to report on specific events at the expense of in-depth and analytical treatment of the questions which are believed likely to strongly influence future developments.*

27. *After late August finished intelligence not only summarized the latest reports, but was more pessimistic and more accurate than most other observers. Nevertheless, problems remained. The articles left important parts of their messages implicit.*

They did not point out that much of their reasoning undercut the common optimistic assessments, conclude that an agreement between the government and the clergy was unlikely, or point out that the Shah might soon face the choice of repression or abdication. This was, perhaps, a matter of style and norms—analysts have been conditioned over the years to keep as close as possible to the facts rather than draw out the implications which consumers can do for themselves. Furthermore, the analysts were aware of the relatively optimistic reports from the field and understandably felt restrained by the possibility that the field was correct. NFAC products can be faulted for not clarifying the lines of argument, noting any inconsistencies, or pulling together the existing evidence (which here, as on so many other points, was not extensive). The issues were not posed sharply enough or treated in sufficient depth. It did not take hindsight to see that what was crucial was both the desires and the independence of the moderates. Neither point was singled out for special attention. For example, the reports that the moderates had responded to the Shah's concessions by making greater demands were noted, but their significance was not probed. The validity of the reports that the moderates felt that they could not agree to anything that Khomeini opposed were never denied, but neither did the analysts explain how, if they were true, conciliation was possible. These reports seem to have had little impact. ‹7 lines redacted› *Similar reports had been received since mid-August and even, in muted tones, in the spring. This is not to say that the evidence was so overwhelming that the analysts should have automatically accepted it. But there should have been a probing of the reports that the moderates could not move on their own and a discussion of why and under what conditions the moderates might break with Khomeini and whether they could maintain their power if they did.*

28. *Furthermore, there was no analysis to support the implicit assumption that if the moderates did break with the extremists, the latter would not be willing and able to continue violent protests, thus probably making the government respond with force and putting the moderates in an untenable position. (A variant of this danger is noted in Tehran 10081, 16 October 1978.) Indeed little was said to substantiate the belief that the moderates were numerous enough to be an important force on their own. In the spring and early summer this view seemed quite plausible, but by late summer and early fall as the protest grew in size and intensity a good deal more evidence should have been required before the analysts accepted the conclusion that an agreement with the moderates, even if possible, could have saved the situation. D/NFAC implicitly questioned this belief in his testimony before the Senate Foreign Relations Committee of 27 September when he noted that the religious moderates were much less numerous than the extremists. But the NID item of 29 Sept. and much of the discussion of the negotiations between the moderates and the Shah in mid and late October implied that the actions of the moderates could be decisive.*

29. *It was also unfortunate that finished intelligence did not address the question of whether the shah could survive if the opposition remained united. If the answer had been that he could not have, more attention might have been focused on the relations*

within the opposition. An additional benefit would have been to illuminate the relationship between the expectation that the opposition would split and the belief that the Shah would crack down if he had to.

30. *No definitive answers were possible, but a more thorough weighing of the evidence and a more penetrating analysis of the problems were. Here as at other points the felt need to report daily events seems to have distracted NFAC from analyzing the fundamental problems.*

THE RELIGIOUS OPPOSITION

1. It is ironic that a misreading of the appeal of the religious opposition was one of the major problems with NFAC's analysis. The person who placed the greatest stress on the importance of the religious groups was NFAC's senior Iranian political analyst. He had an extensive knowledge of Islam, had included analysis of the influence of religion and religious leaders in his writings, and consistently called for more information. His efforts over the years to stimulate the collection of more data were strenuous ‹line redacted› and his awareness of the information deficiencies is recorded most recently in *Elites in Iran,* p. 75. Without this background of concern, he could not have produced the paper, "Iran: Some Observations on the Bases of Religious Opposition" 10 February 1978, which set forth the importance of the religious movement, which we shall draw on later.

Information Available

2. Despite these efforts, the amounts of information available to NFAC on the religious establishment was slight. Non-governmental experts who may have had information were not sought out by NFAC (and it is not certain that these people would have responded). More importantly, until late summer 1978, the field paid little attention to this subject; nor had it for many years. Thus, although it was known that Khomeini was one of the most important opposition religious leaders until February 1978 the US did not know that his son had died the previous October ‹citation redacted› and not until May that he blamed the regime for the death (*Manchester Guardian,* 21 May 1978), and that he had decided to make his opposition more strident and urgent. Only after the Shah fell was it reported (in public sources) that the Shah had heavily cut the subsidies to the religious groups. Similarly, it was 2 1/2 weeks before field reporting attributed the Qom riots to a newspaper attack on Khomeini, published at the instance of the GOI.*

* The first Embassy report, apparently derived from the official news agency, said that the "incident occurred on anniversary of land reform legislation passed in 1963." (Tehran 389, 11 January 1978) A week later the Embassy said the occasion had been the "anniversary of banning of veil." (Tehran 548, 17 January 1978) Even when the Embassy received a copy of the newspaper article, it did not know enough about the context to properly appreciate the depth of the insults that it contained. (Tehran Airgram A-27, 12 February 1978) The *Washington Post* story on 11 January 1978 reported the cause accurately.

3. NFAC had a pretty clear idea of what it knew and where data was lacking—specifically information on the relative influence of the religious leaders. (See *Elites,* 1976, pp. 43–47, 75) Little if anything was added in the succeeding two years. NEAC knew that Khomeini, and other ayatollahs, received financial support from bazaaris, and that he supported one terrorist group financially. But his power and influence relative to other religious leaders—made progressively apparent from late summer 1978 and abundantly clear in January 1979—was not well understood by NFAC in the early stages of the crisis. Indeed, in retrospect, we still don't know how or when he achieved dominance or whether the other ayatollahs followed his lead because they agreed with him or because they feared that to do otherwise would be to lose their followings. Khomeini had been exiled in 1964 for opposing certain of the Shah's reforms, had lived in the Shia center of Najaf, lecturing in theology and jurisprudence, and had attracted a following. Khomeini consistently advocated the overthrow of the Pahlavis; the other leaders did not go so far.

4. It can also be argued that Khomeini had achieved a position of dominance over his fellow ayatollahs long before 1978. This has been asserted in one scholarly article published in 1972* and is suggested in an Embassy Airgram as far back as 1963 (A-708 of 17 June 1964) before Khomeini was exiled. But information about him and about religion in general, virtually ceased from the mid-1960s on. ‹footnote redacted› Analysts had no way, given the paucity of data, to estimate the amount of his support relative to other religious leaders. Khomeini was mentioned in the field reporting no more often than his fellow ayatollah, Shariat-Madari. A number of scholars believed that Khomeini was politically the most important of the religious leaders; we have not tried to determine whether their belief was supported by significant evidence that academics, but not NFAC, had.

5. The field reported little about the articulated beliefs of the religious protesters. NFAC analysts had little to rely on in trying to determine the strength of religious protest; there was no data that indicated the extent to which tapes and pamphlets containing Khomeini's speeches were circulating in Iran. Analysts didn't have any information on what religious leaders were saying to their congregations. One of the cassettes Khomeini sent into Iran was obtained and transcribed, and a few of the opposition leaflets were translated, but this was not nearly enough to provide a full picture of what Khomeini and other religious leaders were advocating. Of course such information would not have told us how the leaders would behave or how many people would follow them, but without it, it was even more difficult to understand the motives, beliefs, and values of these people. This was especially important because, as we noted earlier, the religious movement was inherently difficult for Western observers to understand.

* Hamid Algar "The Oppositional Role of the Ulama in Twentieth-Century Iran," in N. Keddie, *Scholars, Saints, and Sufis* (U. of California Press, 1978).

6. Similarly, although the field had noted the growth of the religious opposition long before the riots occurred (Tehran Airgram A-124, "Straws in the Wind: Intellectual and Religious Opposition in Iran," 25 July 1977), the information it provided was not detailed. Occasionally, an observation such as "we have heard... that religious leaders in Qom have been coordinating much religious dissident activity by messenger and telephone" (Tehran 4583, 14 May 1978) appears in the reporting. But, NFAC did not know—and still does not know—what sort of structure and organization it had. How did people get the word of whether to demonstrate, whether to be belligerent or to treat the soldiers as brothers? When riots ensued, were the targets picked in advance? What were the relations between the religious leaders and the bazaaris?

7. The paucity of field reporting is consistent with the basic predisposition, shared by almost every one in and outside of government, that the religious groups were no longer central to Iranian society and politics. In part this grew out of an optimistic view of modernization, discussed in a later section of this report, and in part was probably the product of the general Western secular bias. Even those outside the government who saw the Shah as weaker than NFAC analysts did not believe that the religious groups would be instrumental in bringing him down.*

Underestimated Factors

8. In retrospect, we can identify four elements in the religious-based opposition movement that contributed to its appeal to a wide range of the public and that were not well covered in finished intelligence.

These were:

a) attacks on the Shah for the way he was changing Iran: ignoring the mullahs, flouting many Islamic customs, denying important parts of Iran's past, and aiding the rich more than the poor;

b) nationalism, i.e., attacks on the Shah for being a foreign (US) puppet;

c) the "populist" tradition of Shi'ism whereby religious leaders gain and retain their authority by becoming recognized by followers as men of wisdom and piety, a circumstance that encourages them to articulate the desires of their people;

d) the traditional role of the Shi'ite clergy as spokesmen for political protests.

9. *Attacks on the Shah for the way he was "modernizing"* appealed to a wide segment of the population. This element was described in the analysis as deriving from the view of religious leaders that modernization was undermining the hold of Islam on

* For example James Bill, "Monarchy in Crisis," a paper done for a State Department seminar on 10 March 1978, forecast serious trouble for the Shah, but did not mention religion. And two books completed in 1978, Robert Graham, *Iran: The Illusion of Power* and Fred Halliday, *Iran, Dictatorship and Development,* each give religious opposition no more than two pages.

the people. In fact, it was more directed at how he was changing Iran. Under the Shah, and especially since the start of the "oil boom" in 1973, the income gap had increased significantly; the quality of life in Tehran had deteriorated; corruption and government favors had boosted the power and income of new groups as opposed to small merchants and bazaaris. (For a further discussion, see pp. 120–123). How much the failure to make this distinction stems from institutional pressures to use short-hand terms (see p. 169) and how much from the analysts not understanding it is unclear. Certainly, they got no help from reporting sources; the Embassy ‹three words redacted› didn't make it either.

10. This view of the religious leaders played a large role in the belief that the Shah could weather the storm since it was felt that many important sectors of society found their views repellent. Under this belief, even those who, like the students and the National Front, opposed the Shah would find it difficult to join with Khomeini because they differed so much in their basic political orientation. In fact, Iranians could favor modernization and still strongly oppose the Shah, as many of Khomeini's followers did. Students and many members of the middle class, without endorsing all that he stood for, could find important elements in common with Khomeini. Shared opposition to the perceived gains of the newly-rich and the impoverishment of the lower ranks of society formed an important common bond between Khomeini and the political left and between Khomeini and a wider constituency. (This was noted by Professor Richard Cottam in a letter to the editor of the *Washington Post* on 3 October 1978 and mentioned by the Embassy in Tehran 9157, 20 September 1978.) Given the prevailing view and paucity of data, it is not surprising that even after the Embassy had mentioned that the Qom riots had been sparked by a newspaper attack on Khomeini, finished intelligence continued to report that the demonstrators had been "protesting against the 1963 land reform and the 1936 ban of the veil" 10 February 1978, or, more generally, "against the shah's modernization program." (NID, 21 February 1978)

11. Although we think the view presented here has been borne out by hindsight—and indeed partly derived from it—there is still room for disagreement. We do not fault the analysts for not having accepted this view at the time when the evidence was even more ambiguous. But we do think they should have indicated the existence of an alternative perception of what the religious leaders stood for. Even Khomeini and his followers were not claiming to be totally opposed to modernization and, while their statements need not have been accepted at face value, they at least showed what this group thought was popular and, more importantly, believed by large numbers of Iranians. Khomeini had for fifteen years centered his attacks on the Pahlavi dynasty and its evil ways. If this view was widely believed, the analysts' stress on the religious opposition as anti-modern greatly exaggerated the degree to which it would be cut off from the wider society.

12. The *second element* is the possible role of nationalism. ‹footnote redacted› This factor is not mentioned in any of the official reporting or NFAC analysis and only

received occasional mention in the mass media. It could be that this was not a motivating force. But we suspect otherwise. Some of the slogans painted on walls called for the death of the "American Shah." A leaflet distributed during the Tabriz riots spoke of the "anti-Islamic regime of the Shah and the usurping American overlords." Khomeini's recorded speeches which circulated in Iran strongly attacked the United States in nationalist terms. The text of the one NFAC had said: "The Americans... have helped impose upon the Iranian people a ruler who... has turned Iran into an official colony of the United States." It ridiculed the Shah's claim that he had brought Iran "into the ranks of the most advanced industrial countries" by saying: "In large areas of the capital people live in hovels and dungeons and have to go a long way to get a bucket of water from some public tap. People know that Iran is a potentially rich country with a huge variety of natural resources. But they see that foreigners have installed an agent at the top of the government to make sure that this wealth does not go to the poor masses." (Tehran Airgram A-60, 17 April 1978)

13. The American role in the 1953 coup was known—probably in an exaggerated version—by all Iranians, and American support for the regime has been prominent, especially in the past several years. The Embassy frequently pointed out that all circles in Iran saw an American hand in everything that happened. Supporters and opponents of the regime alike greatly exaggerated US influence. Thus it is reasonable to believe that a wide segment of the populace saw the Shah as an American puppet. To many, he was not only a despised leader, but a foreign one. This handicap was compounded by the process of rapid social mobilization which almost inevitably increases nationalism. We think it likely that Khomeini was seen as a nationalist leader. He frequently criticized the United States and repeatedly called for a greatly reduced role of foreigners in Iran.*

14. If this argument is correct, it would account for a good deal of the support Khomeini received from the secular parts of Iranian society. Of course we cannot be sure we are correct, but the complete absence of any mention of nationalism in NFAC analysis still strikes us as unfortunate. While the analysts knew that everyone in Iran believed that the United States was largely responsible for most events in that country, neither this fact nor the implications of it were discussed in 1978's finished intelligence. Part of the explanation may be the understandable hesitancy to engage in discussion which would have had to have been speculative. Second, nationalism was associated in the analysts' minds with terrorist attacks on Americans, which were rare until October 1978. Third, the analysts knew that the United States did not in fact dominate Iran and that the Shah was very much his own man. It was hard to empathize with people who had what most Americans felt was a distorted view of the world.

* Much data on Khomeini's anti-foreign statements became available in late 1978; very little appears in official or other reporting prior to, say, November.

15. The *third element* involves the sparse comment on the "populist" tradition of Shi'ism, growing in part out of the fact that the Shi'ites do not have a recognized hierarchy within the sect. Instead of being appointed by a superior, mullahs and ayatollahs gain their authority by becoming recognized by followers as men of wisdom and piety. This encourages current and aspiring leaders to articulate what they think are the grievances and desires of their people. It gives them incentives to be in the forefront of popular movements. The Embassy noted this on 17 August: "In Shia Islam there is no institutionalized hierarchy: a religious leader attains his prominence by consensus within his parish. Some of the violence we are witnessing here results from a fervid competition for eminence by the Ayatollahs; moderation apparently does not beget followers from the workers, small shop keepers and artisans at this time." (Tehran 7882) Obviously they will not always lead, especially if these movements conflict with their basic values and interests. But these incentives mean that there is a greater chance that the religious leaders will try to articulate popular demands. Furthermore, the fact that this has often occurred in the past means that large segments of the population—even those who are not deeply religious—look to the religious leaders to play this role.

16. The propensity for religious leaders to act as spokesmen for wider groups and to voice general political concerns was reinforced by the Shah's suppression of most other forms of opposition. Given the support they had from their committed followers, the religious leaders could speak out more freely than others because they knew it would have been very costly for the Shah to silence them. They became salient rallying points. People would follow them because they were the only identifiable source of opposition and they gained strength as they became the symbol for opposition. (This was noted by Ambassador Robert Neumann in his comments on the draft NIE p. 6). It seems to have been the case that many people who disagreed with Khomeini on many points joined his movement because it was the only vehicle for trying to bring down the government. The NID pointed to this phenomenon in the spring when it said: "The politicized clergy, who oppose the Shah on religious grounds, have been able to exploit other popular grievances—inflation, poor housing, and the inadequate distribution of basic commodities—that are chronic problems in urban working class areas." (17 June 1978). Also see Tehran 9157, 21 September 1978. Although the separation of political and secular grounds may be a bit artificial, the basic point was important. Unfortunately, this perspective did not reappear in finished intelligence.

17. The *fourth element* that could feed the power of the religious-based opposition received more attention from the analysts, although here there was a problem of emphasis and follow-up. As the analysts noted, for the Shi'ites "every government is illegitimate" (78–006, 10 February 1978; also see Tehran Airgram A-19, 1 February 1978, and *Elites,* February 1976, p. 43) and there is a fusion between what Western thought would call the secular and the religious realms. For the Shi'ites, it was perfectly natural for the clergy to become the spokesmen for political protests, and indeed they would hardly recognize the line between politics and religion that is so

clear to us. In the most thorough discussion of the religious-based opposition that NFAC produced, the leading analyst made the following point: "Since religious, social, political, and economic affairs are considered inseparable, the mujtahed [religious scholar] can dispense guidance on political matters and oppose the will of the state, becoming a leader of the opposition." ‹citation redacted› Unfortunately this theme, and others in the paper on the religious-based opposition, were not elaborated or built on in the spring and summer. If the consumers had been fully aware of the Shi'ite tradition, stress and elaboration would not have been necessary. But given the problems for non-experts in understanding the strange people the United States was dealing with, a fuller treatment was called for. These factors were not mentioned in most papers—perhaps because they do not change and the analysts assume the consumers remember them—and did not appear in the NIB that was being drafted in the summer of 1978.

Conclusions and Evaluation

18. *In summary, although NFAC was alert to the importance of the religious groups for years before the start of the current crisis, retrospect has allowed us to detect aspects of the religious-based opposition that strongly contributed to its powerful role in the overthrow of the Shah and that were not adequately covered in NFAC production. The problem was not the missing of one or two vital clues to the nature of the religious groups; rather it appears to have been a general outlook which did not give credence to the links between the religious leaders and the grievance of wide ranges of the general population. This outlook powerfully influenced the interpretation of incoming information (as any established belief will do) and specifically led the analysts to be insensitive to the possibility that the opposition could unite behind Khomeini.*

19. *The factors and the related argument we have discussed in paragraphs 9–18 can, of course be disputed. This treatment benefits from hindsight, and at the time NFAC analysts certainly could have rejected these elements. Data was skimpy; several lines of analysis were possible. But what is disturbing is that they were not refuted, but ignored. (At least some of these factors figured in the thinking of several academic experts.) Of course analysts cannot comment on every possible view, but these factors should have been examined with care because if they were present there would be greater support for the religious groups, greater unity of the opposition, and greater problems for the Shah.*

20. *Had this general outlook noted above been held by some of the analysts, they would have been more sensitive to a number of indicators that were in fact glossed over. First, many of the students and student groups supported Khomeini's protests. Field reports sometimes noticed the seemingly odd facts that students were making "ultra-conservative demands" ‹citation redacted› or that they were cooperating with the religious leaders. In June, the NID noted that "Militant students... added their weight to religious demonstrations this year," 17 June 1978), but by and large these joint efforts received little attention. They deserved more not so much because the students were*

*powerful but because many of them did not favor a reactionary program. Their support for Khomeini indicated either that what he stood for was not as repugnant to the students as most US officials thought or that the students were willing to back someone with whom they disagreed on many issues in order to bolster the strongest opponent of the Shah. Similarly, there were scattered reports that Khomeini "is widely respected among diverse opponents of the Shah who do not necessarily share his religious beliefs, specifically leftist students.... Among the devout bazaar merchants of the country, large sums of money are still collected in his name. These collections are voluntary, not by duress." <citation redacted> This was consistent with the reports that many women had begun wearing the chador, not because they had suddenly adopted conservative religious views, but because adopting traditional dress was a way of joining the protests.**

21. *In the same vein, the analysts could have explored—although it was late in the game—the implications of the report (which were never disputed) that Shariat-Madari and Khomeini were "above arrest" (Tehran 9157, 29 September 1978) and that Khomeini's return would pose grave difficulties for the GOI. On 3 October, the Embassy reported Sharif-Emami's belief that if Khomeini were to return, "GOI would be faced with grim alternatives of (A) arresting him, immediately and precipitating 'civil war al la Lebanon' or (B) letting him run loose and becoming the head of the anti-Shah forces." (Tehran 9555, 3 October 1978). If this were so, it indicated severe and lasting restraints on the Shah's power and implied a depth and breadth of support for Khomeini which was not easily reconciled with much of the analysis,*

22. *Finally, the reports that many people in Iran believed that SAVAK, not religious extremists, set the disastrous fire in Abadan movie theater (Washington Post, 26 August 1978) indicated both that the latter groups were not seen as ruthless and inhumane and that the Shah was.*

23. *To conclude, the view expressed in NFAC production, that the religious opposition to the Shah was essentially driven by dislike of modernization, made analysts insensitive to the bits and pieces of evidence indicating that the bases of opposition were far wider. This evidence made most sense when viewed from the perspective that Khomeini was, or was seen by Iranians as, a nationalist populist leader who opposed the Shah in large part because his regime was serving foreign and rich interests. But unless one used that perspective, the evidence would not stand out as especially significant.*

THE SHAH'S POSITION AND HOW IT WAS PERCEIVED

1. In the course of 1978 a number of reports on the Shah's mood as events unfolded in his country were received. Some of these were personal observations by the

* See the *New York Times*, 17 May 1978 and Morton Kondrake, "Iran's Queasy Modernization," *New Republic*, 18 June 1978, p. 22. This apparently started in mid-1977. See Tehran A-124, 25 July 1977.

American and ‹word redacted› Ambassadors and others who met him; some reflected how Iranians saw the Shah and interpreted his behavior. In retrospect they assume considerable importance, because, when removed from the background noise of other voluminous data, they begin to show a pattern,

Reports From the Field

• *The Economist* of 4 March 1978 in a generally good article said that foreigners were reporting that the Shah was troubled and disillusioned by events.

• Ambassador Sullivan on 8 May (Tehran 4355) reported that in a conversation the Shah had seemed "tired and depressed, almost listless." He had considered that perhaps something was wrong with his system and his game plan. The Ambassador noted that this was the first occasion in the ten months he had been there that he had seen the Shah in such a mood, but he stressed that he found it striking.

• In mid-May, just after some very serious demonstrations the Shah held a meeting with representatives of the Iranian media. In commenting on this and other events Tehran 4742 (17 May 1978) said that "People, including many in the establishment, are trying to figure out exactly what GOI policy is toward demonstrators." Tehran 4836, (21 May 1978) reported that people are concerned by what is seen as the Shah's display of "indecisiveness, nervousness and imprecision" in the way he conducted the above-mentioned interview. The normal conclusion that many Iranians draw is that "he is losing his touch." The Embassy noted that some of the Shah's imprecision derived from his efforts to follow an unfamiliar policy—liberalization—and that he gets insufficient feedback to be aware that this is the image he is projecting. (‹Name redacted› recalls that the Shah had given the same sort of impression to the press when he announced the formation of the Resurgence Party in 1975.)

• Many of those in the establishment found that the Shah was not sending a consistent signal as to whether they should take a hard or soft line. (Tehran 4836, 21 May 1978) Instructions to the police on handling of demonstrations and to the Ministry of Information on press guidance concerning demonstrations caused similar confusion. ‹Citation redacted›

• The US Embassy in Pakistan reported (Islamabad 5380, 1 June 1978) that senior Pakistani officers who had seen the Shah on 26 May "said that he appeared 'frightened and upset' and 'no longer exuded confidence.' The Shah was described as unable to understand why people were turning against him."

• The Embassy reported (Tehran 6557, 10 July 1978) that the Shah had told the Ambassador that he felt he had no choice but to continue liberalization. The latter noted that the Shah appeared to be over his earlier indecision.

• *US News and World Report* of 7 August 1978 in an article which was generally bullish on the Shah's prospects but acknowledged problems of lack of business confidence and flight of money abroad also said that his "experiment with democracy . . . worries many Iranians."

• Three items received around the end of the second week of August pull together scattered earlier evidence of popular concerns at corruption, of the belief that "the Shah is losing his grip" and of a sense of uncertainty among the people in the country. Tehran Airgram A-105 (1 August 1978) quotes a well connected source who advised the Embassy to start thinking about the Shah's leaving Iran, saying that he was "down" mentally as of 22 July although he was physically fit. (The Embassy commented that "The actual situation is not as bad as pessimists say.") ‹Line redacted› said "Perhaps the single most important concern is that [many Iranians believe that] the Shah may be losing control" and ". . . his present uncertain behavior could lead to chaos." (It is worth noting that ‹name redacted› reported on 15 September that he thought the Shah was out of danger; see p. 113.) Tehran 7882 (17 August 1978) noted that "many Iranians of the middle and wealthy classes believe that the Shah is not acting forcefully enough, that he is weak and indecisive."

• The charge d'affairs met with the Shah on 13 August (Tehran 7700, 14 August 1978) and reported that he looked very fit. Ambassador Sullivan, who returned from leave at the end of the month, reported finding the Shah thin, tense and dispirited on 28 August (Tehran 8187).

• By September the press was beginning to concern itself with the Shah's appearance and attitude. *Newsweek* of 4 September reported that the Shah had been ill early in July and disappeared from view for six weeks. (There is no other reporting that substantiates an imperial illness; he had been seen by US Undersecretary Newsom on 9 July and by Iranians in late July (Tehran A 105) and spoke publicly on 5 August. Tehran 8607 (9 September 1978) reports a *Time* correspondent as saying that the Shah "looked awful," as if he were on the brink of a nervous collapse, and that his entire tone was very negative.

• The Ambassador met the Shah on 10 September and "found him tired and unhappy, but considerably more spirited than he was a week ago. . . . The Shah, in the past few weeks, has played a Hamlet-like role, without asserting his influence in either direction. He seems, as of today, to have recovered some of his former confidence. . . ." (Tehran 8614, 10 September 1978).

2. The Shah's attitude continued to be a subject of interest, up to the time of the establishment of the military government. ‹11 lines redacted› The American Embassy reported that the Shah was "down in the dumps again" on 3 October. (Tehran 9743, 5 October 1978) Ambassador Sullivan portrayed him as "drawn-looking and tense" but animated in conversation on 10 October in a meeting which had the purpose of trying "to snap him out of his current funk and to focus his attention on problems requiring

his leadership." (Tehran 9872) The Shah was "sober, but not depressed" in a meeting with the US Ambassadors on 24 October. (Tehran 10383) ‹2 lines redacted›

3. ‹paragraph redacted›

4. These reports contain two themes. First, over a period of several months, persons who saw the Shah found him more often than not behaving differently than usual. Instead of being forceful, authoritarian, and taking charge, he was depressed, nervous, dispirited, uncertain. Second, his efforts to liberalize the political system without surrendering his essential authority (discussed on pp. 123–131) sowed confusion in the minds of his supporters, who were accustomed to firm direction. In addition, his behavior led them and many other Iranians to believe that he was losing his grip. With the image of imperial power diminishing, people would be more inclined to take the risks of open opposition.

5. We do not intend to analyze the Shah's personality in this report. It is sufficient to note that "the vacillation and indecisiveness which he displayed during the first third of his reign" (*Elites,* p. 17) had been replaced by growing confidence after the overthrow of Mossadeq in 1953. The indications of indecisiveness in 1978 came after a quarter century of vigorous exercise of authority. A long NID article (12 November 1977) assessed his position as very strong but did note that "Although he appears extremely self-confident, he has underlying doubts about his worth."

6. NFAC production took note of the Shah's changed mood at the end of the summer. Thus: "The Shah, described by the US Ambassador as dispirited by recent events. . . ." (NID 30 August 1978); "The Shah was described by the Ambassador yesterday as 'tired and unhappy but considerably more spirited' than he had been a week earlier." (NID, 11 September 1978) ". . . the Shah displayed some of his former resilience under pressure and appeared to have recovered his self-confidence, which was evidently badly shaken last month . . . [when] he seemed unsure about the clarity of his vision as to how Iran should develop politically. . . ." (NID, 14 September 1978) and "Foreign observers who have met with the Shah in the last month agree that this year's cycle of violence has visibly shaken him." 20 September 1978

7. NFAC's treatment of the Shah's mood and attitude in the fall reflected field reporting about his ups and downs and tended toward the optimistic. In a generally gloomy assessment of the situation in Iran the NID wrote, "The Shah has brief episodes of depression, but these have not materially affected his leadership capabilities. . . ." (23 October 1978) An article, "Iran: the Prospects of Responsible Government" 20 October 1978, put it this way:

> "The Shah has had periods of depression as he contemplates the ruins of his carefully constructed, if ineptly handled, programs which he once hoped would produce by the end of the 1980s a country that would compare favorably with Western Europe. These moods have alternated with periods when he has appeared confident and prepared to tackle his many problems." ‹8 lines redacted›

8. The second theme, that many Iranians perceived the Shah as losing his grip, first received NFAC attention in the NID on 16 September:

> "There are signs of cautious optimism among influential Iranians in government, business, and press circles that the Shah may have pulled the country back from the brink of chaos, ‹line redacted› noted a marked shift in opinion since early August, when there was widespread concern that the Shah's inability to put an end to countrywide rioting meant he was losing his grip." ‹citation redacted› The judgment was part of a general appreciation that martial law and political concessions had stabilized the situation. Not until 23 October was the subject touched on again:
>
> "Among the Shah's supporters, especially the military, his initial indecisive response to civil disorders and his opposition has produced an uneasy sense that he is losing his grip. Some of his supporters have begun for the first time to contemplate an Iran without the Shah." (NID)

Conclusions and Evaluation

9. *In retrospect, there were enough signs over a sufficient period of time for NFAC to have raised a warning flag. Not that it could have known what was wrong with him; but the reasons for his behavior were less important than the consequences of it. NFAC production, beginning in late August, reflected the reporting on the Shah's mood, which seemed to improve in September and October, in the view of the two Ambassadors who saw him frequently. It did not, however, discuss what his untypical failure to exercise leadership might do to the morale of his supporters (which, we should note, stayed remarkably high until well into the fall) or to the opposition.*

10. *One might speculate that as the summer wore on the opposition was beginning to smell success because of his appearance of indecisiveness, while the Shah himself, stubbornly determined to liberalize and arrange a transition to his son, may not have been able to "crack down" on the opposition as the Embassy and NFAC production judged he could do successfully if he chose to do so. But the issue is not what was the right assessment. Rather, as on other questions, it is that the subject was not raised analytically. Readers of NFAC publications would have learned in September that the Shah was showing signs of indecisiveness and in late October that some of his supporters were losing faith. They did not receive any assessments of what his indecisiveness might mean for political developments in Iran, for the perseverance of his supporters, or for the attitudes of his opposition. We are not sure why the issue did not receive more prominence, but the belief that the Shah was strong and able to crack down if he judged it necessary, the format of publications that militated against speculation, and the press of events in the fall are among the likely reasons.*

INTENSITY OF ANTI-SHAH FEELING

1. Judging the breadth and depth of sentiment supporting and opposing the Shah was extremely difficult. In the period we are concerned with, almost no direct

information was available.* Neither the Embassy nor the station nor the media reported on the one kind of obvious objective information that might have been useful—the size and composition of the protest demonstrations. Were there 10,000 or 100,000 people in the streets? Were the demonstrations growing? Were they so large that the amount of force required to disperse them probably would be very great? What sorts of people were participating? Were new groups being drawn in? Field reporting did not address these questions. Thus all NFAC had from the field were occasional impressions, such as the Embassy's assessment that the "silent majority" supported retention of the Shah, although perhaps with reduced powers (Tehran 10421, 25 October 1978), and its view that "we assume vast majority of middle class . . . generally pleased" by the imposition of martial law (Tehran 8563, 9 September 1978), although the next day it spoke of a "sullen population chafing at the imposition of martial law." (Tehran 8614, 10 September 1968) The Consuls were more pessimistic, although again did not provide a great deal of information. Consul Shiraz observed that "Anti-Shah sentiment runs deep and broad in Iranian society" (Airgram A-15, 14 May 1978) and Consul Isfahan reported that "public discontent remains strong and widespread" and that members of the middle and upper classes had begun publicly criticizing the Shah. (Airgram A-007, 3 August 1978) But mostly the analysts had to rely on inferences. Very little was known about many important groups—e.g., the bazaaris, the oil workers, factory workers, even the professional middle classes, but we think that there were some possible bases for inference that remained untapped.

2. First, the analysts could have commented on the government's unsuccessful attempts to stage pro-Shah rallies (see the *Washington Post*, 20 August 1978). As early as 27 December 1977, the Embassy recognized that "there is a concerted effort to get out the 'silent majority' with the assistance of the Rastakhiz party militants so that government and party workers, professors, students, parents and other identifiable groups may be led into positive demonstrations and other shows of loyalty to overwhelm the dissenters. . . ." (Tehran 11408) This could have alerted the Embassy and analysts to the utility of tracing the fate of these attempts since they were seen as important to the GOI and presumably would be pursued with some energy. It is our understanding that over the years Iranians had shown no great enthusiasm for demonstrating in support of the government. Nonetheless, the failure of government efforts in 1978 to generate manifestations of support would therefore indicate some problems with the existence or intensity of feeling of the "silent majority." Similarly, the Embassy's report a month later that "Initial soundings indicate that GOI has not been able to mobilize middle class around slogans depicting religious demonstrators at Qom as hopeless reactionaries" was worthy of greater attention and of attempts to gather more information. As the Embassy noted, "Workers and peasants, plus businessmen, government employees, students and some intellectuals turned

* For general impressions of this topic before the crisis, see INR's "The Future of Iran," 28 January 1977, p. 3 and *Iran in the 1980s*, August 1977, Section V.

out dutifully for government demonstrations, but this has not bound middle class more closely to government." (Tehran 961, 26 January 1978) Similarly, after the Tabriz riots the Embassy noted that "Some professors and businessmen of our acquaintance feel things reached the point . . . where their own important values are beginning to be threatened. Many who have thus far tacitly supported moderate oppositionist heckling of GOI may be having second thoughts." (Tehran 1814, 21 February 1978, also see Tehran 4455, 10 May 1978)* But these people did not seem to rally to the Shah even though the opposition grew in a way that should have challenged their values and interests even more.

3. In retrospect, the intensity of feeling in the opposition can be seen as one of the critical factors in the overthrow of the regime. At the time it should have been seen that intensity would be important because it would play a large role in determining how people would react to the Shah's attempts to maintain order. If people were not willing to run considerable risks of being shot, the demonstrations could be put down with an amount of force that was easily within the regime's capabilities. If fairly large numbers were willing to sacrifice themselves, on the other hand, the Army would be forced to engage in quite extensive killing and, as many reports and papers noted, this could severely strain morale, perhaps to the point where it could not be relied on. Unfortunately, the intensity question was rarely addressed. A consultant, ‹name redacted› made a passing reference to it in his comments (p. 9) on the 21 July 1978 draft of the proposed NIE, but that was about all.

4. Two other categories of events might have yielded information on the strength of the opposition to the government. First, the frequent and lengthy closures of the bazaars could have been more closely monitored in NFAC. Even if many merchants were coerced into closing their shops (this was asserted by the Embassy and certainly is plausible, although little evidence was produced to substantiate the claim), the closures were a warning sign. They showed that the opponents of the regime had quite a bit of power and the regime was either unwilling or unable to thwart them. Assuming that keeping the bazaars closed was an important part of the protest movement and that the Iranian Government for this reason if for no other wanted to keep them open, the government's failure was noteworthy. If the closures were a genuine gesture of support for the opposition and if the bazaaris were paying a price for their actions, this was an indication of the intensity of feeling involved. Furthermore, if those inconvenienced by the closing did not blame the protesters—there were no signs that they did—this was an indication of the degree to which at least potential support for the opposition was widespread. The reports from the field were not full and detailed, but the frequent mentions of shops and bazaars closing could have

* For a report of the fairly successful pro-government rally, see Tehran 665, 18 January 1978. Khomeini noted the contrasting sizes of the pro- and anti-government demonstrations (Tehran Airgram A-60, 17 April 1978). While he is of course biased, his basic point was correct.

been collected and analyzed as a group.* (For some of these reports see Tehran 548, 16 January 1978, ‹6 lines redacted›

5. Second, even if the field could not talk to any demonstrators and thereby provide some information on their motives and strength of commitment, the very fact of repeated protests with significant casualties told us something about the intensity of opposition to the Shah. ‹3 lines redacted› This should have been apparent both to the Shah and observers a good deal earlier. The draft NIE argued that "the threat of the force that the Shah has available if he is pushed too far will deter all but the most virulent opposition." (6 September 1978, pp. I-14—I-15) This might have been turned around. Because the demonstrators continued their activities in the face of the Shah's credible threat, the intensity of feeling that was firing them must have been great indeed. As we noted earlier, Iran was a rare and perhaps unique case in which unarmed people were willing to repeatedly take to the streets in the face of a united Army that frequently inflicted significant casualties. Of course the fact that people come into the streets five times under these conditions does not automatically mean they will come back the sixth time. All people and groups have their breaking points, and these are sometimes reached without much prior warning. Even with hindsight we cannot be sure what would have happened if the Shah had been less restrained and ordered the Army to shoot more people. But the analysts should have derived more information about the intensity of feeling from the unusual willingness of demonstrators to run high risks.

6. Reports based on observations of demonstrations also supported this conclusion:

> "According to dissidents with whom the journalist has spoken, the police are trying every means possible to control crowds before firing on them. These less drastic means include tear gas, fire hoses, and firing over the heads of the crowd. The rioters, however, appear to be almost in a frenzy, and these measures sometimes have little effect on them. Even when the firing starts, they have been seen to charge directly at the police guns." ‹citation redacted›

Before the soldiers fired into the crowd on 8 September they gave a warning and then fired into the air. But the protestors would not disperse. (Tehran 8563, 9 September 1978) Part of the explanation for the lack of discussion of this point may have been that after the first couple of incidents, the analysts became used to the fact that the dissidents were willing to risk their lives. But such behavior is rare and indicates an intensity of opposition that would not be easy for any regime to cope with.**

* on 11 May the NID did mention that "Before this year, the bazaars had not been closed in over a decade," but this indicator was not mentioned again.

** This is not to say that warning shots never succeeded in dispersing crowds. Sometimes they did, as the Embassy reported in Tehran 10338, 23 October 1978.

IRAN'S DOMESTIC ECONOMIC SITUATION 1977–1978

1. Because the Shah's full-steam-ahead development program and its consequences of inflation, corruption, unequal income distribution, social dislocation and the like clearly affected the domestic political climate we think that some treatment of intelligence production on Iranian domestic economic matters is called for. We survey that production in this section, discuss how it was related to political intelligence, and also treat the matter of joint political-economic analysis.* One should note here that ‹12 lines redacted›

2. The volume of finished intelligence on Iran's domestic economic situation was not large. 1977 had three items. The first, responding to a request from State/INR, analyzed the impact of Iran's projected defense spending. The memorandum 7 January 1977, judged that while Iran could afford to spend the $10 billion it planned to on military equipment, defense spending at that level would have an adverse effect on the economy, because it would siphon off skilled and semi-skilled manpower, and that military spending was already helping to boost inflation.

> "Although Iran can financially afford the military program, the economy is by no means ready for it. Most of its current economic problems would be far less severe without a mammoth military effort. Military demands for construction—estimated at $2.2 billion in 1976—aggravate material and manpower shortages elsewhere in the economy. Military imports, which share top priority with foodstuffs in port off-loading, have added considerably to port and road congestion. And, the boom in military spending certainly has been a major factor in the current 20% rate of inflation."

The paper concluded that "the economic impact of the defense program is not likely to pose serious political problems for the Shah."

3. *Iran in the 1980s* contains two sections on the economy. The one on agriculture judged that agricultural performance was the key element in Iran's future development and that "the country must be able to feed its population with minimum reliance on expensive imports or that other elements of the Shah's development program . . . [would be] meaningless." Describing both the success and the extensive deficiencies of the land reform program, the section ends with the following judgment:

> "In sum, the planned agricultural development, which has been under the same sort of forced draft as the more spectacular industrial development, is lagging. The problems are likely to continue for a long period of time and become more urgent as Iran finds it necessary to import more and increasingly expensive food. The pressure for agricultural production will rise, and tension between the bureaucracy and the farmers is likely to mount."

* We have not attempted to assess the quality of all NFAC's economic analysis on Iran; we judge that to be outside the terms of our charter. It gave extensive attention to Iranian oil matters and to Iran's external economic relations.

A second section on the economy in general describes planned development in reasonably optimistic terms. It notes some problems but does not highlight them as extensive and judges that Iran "will probably come close to the Shah's goal of a per capita GNP equal to that of Western Europe by the 1980s" although there will be a serious maldistribution of income. In sum, this economic section is descriptive rather than analytical and what little analysis there is is not particularly incisive. (This paper was an early effort to carry out integrated political-economic analysis; it was not a success in that regard, a fact for which one of the authors of this report (JD) bears some responsibility.)

4. In September 1977, replying to a request from the Chairman of the Council of Economic Advisers, OER assessed Iran's economic development policy. (28 September 1977) The paper noted a series of pronouncements accompanying the appointment of a new cabinet under Prime Minister Amuzegar that the Shah was being forced to abandon his "go for broke" development policy, that the regime was adopting a policy of growth which the economy can digest, that project schedules would be stretched out and that efforts would be made to control inflation. The paper estimated that two billion dollars in private capital had fled Iran in the 16 months up to the end of 1976. It noted that by the end of the Five-Year Plan in March 1978 operating expenditures and defense spending would be far over planned levels and development spending would be well under that projected in the Five-Year Plan. The paper judged that implementation of the new program would give the Iranian economy the pause that it needed, and that a stretched out development program would be "more in step with an expected slow growth in oil production and the difficulties in increasing the pool of skilled labor."

5. From then until early summer of 1978 economic coverage on Iran focused on the international economic aspects and on petroleum and related matters. The latter were frequently mentioned in the periodical *International Energy Bi-weekly Review* and a brief assessment of Iran's oil future is contained in "The Oil Market Through 1985." August 1978.

6. On 23 June the economic contribution to NIE 34-l-78 described the Iranian economic situation, noting the problems deriving from a foreign exchange outflow which was estimated to be running at two to three billion dollars a year in 1975–77. It also described the problems of inflation, transportation bottlenecks, and the like brought on by trying to do too much too soon and the great slowdown in growth in 1977. It took special note that Iran, which has been self-sufficient in food in the late 1960s, was now only 75 percent self-sufficient and that this could drop as low as 50 percent by 1985 if observed trends continued. In later drafts of the estimates this was raised to 60 percent.

7. The contribution noted that "most Iranians have gained little from the oil and construction booms," that the Iranian emphasis on military spending and on large industrial and nuclear energy projects would leave little in the way of "funding for

programs directly beneficial to the Iranian consumer in the next several years" and that the government's efforts would "likely be confined to necessary food imports and to price subsidies, . . . [which were] costing an estimated $1 billion annually." All valid points, but not further explored in the prospective NIE.

8. The NID of 30 August assessed the economic program announced by the newly appointed Sharif-Emami. It judged that the cabinet change was not likely to convince either the Iran consumer or investor that the economy was going to improve. It judged that "solutions to Iran's deep-seated economic problems, . . . will require more than a new management team."

9. As the dimensions of the Iranian crisis began to become apparent, economic intelligence production grew in volume. September brought three publications bearing on Iran's economic situation. ‹Publication redacted› (5 September 1978) was a respectable wrap-up of Iranian agriculture. It judged that the land reform has accomplished most of the regime's political goals: "the majority of peasants now own the land they farm and the once-powerful absentee land owners have lost their political base." "The effects of the land reform on economic and social development were positive, though not spectacular." It went on to note that agriculture had been "the stepchild of the government's development efforts." Despite lip-service of food self-sufficiency, food imports were four times what they had been in 1973 and were costing about two billion dollars annually.

10. "Iran: New Government Maintains Low Economic Profile" (14 September) is a good description of Iran's economic problems especially as they faced the new government. It noted that unhappiness with the "Shah's development priorities has added to political and religious unrest" and judged that the need to placate certain elements of society might lead to shifts in government policy away from industrial and nuclear development and toward the agricultural sector. The main message of this paper was repeated in the NID of 18 September.

11. Iran's problems in feeding itself already flagged in the contribution to the NIE and in the unclassified memorandum of 5 September were discussed at some length in "Iran: Massive Rise in Food Import Needs." (21 September 1978) It noted that food imports running at $2 billion a year and expected to rise at a 15 to 17 percent rate annually, could easily triple by 1985 to more than $6 billion at today's exchange rates. It concluded:

> "Given a food import bill of this magnitude in the early-to-mid 1980s, the Shah may be forced into some difficult decisions concerning import priorities. Unless oil prices rise substantially, declining oil export volume will produce a sizeable current account deficit by 1981. At that time, the Shah may be required to moderate either politically sensitive food imports or imports of capital/military goods to avoid a quick rundown in foreign assets, which now total about $18 billion."

The main messages of this item were repeated in the NID 14 October.

12. Coverage in current intelligence publications during the fall dealt primarily with cuts in oil production and strikes in the oil fields. The industry began to be hit in late September but had little immediate impact because supervisory personnel could keep facilities operating. (NID, 29 September 1978) The government responded to strikes in many sectors by granting most strikers' demands; it saw "the hand of the Shah's religious and political opposition acting behind the scenes to manipulate workers' economic grievances into mass political protest." (NID, 7 October 1978) A few days later a political-economic article (NID, 14 October 1978) reported that "the Iranian Government is being forced to reorder its economic priorities in light of continuing political unrest. It put a finger on the limited effects of this priority shift:

> "Although a high-level decision apparently has been made to free military and nuclear program funds for rural development, infrastructure, and social welfare projects, most of the cutbacks will not impact on the current or next year's budget. The government will have to find other means to cover increased payments to public sector workers.
>
> "Government capitulation to substantial wage and benefit demands is settling widespread strikes in government and industry. The effect on the economy cannot be determined, but renewed inflation seems almost certain."

13. A series of items reported the growing difficulties in the oil fields, with production dropping to a fourth of normal by the end of October. (NID, 31 October 1978) The NID on the day following the Shah's appointment of a military government noted that "a major test of the new government's effectiveness will be its ability to convince strikers to return to work. In the vital oil industry, the strike has widened to include support workers." (NID, 7 November 1978)

14. EIWR 045 of 9 November wrapped up the Iranian economic situation as being in upheaval, the effects of which would be felt for years. It noted that capital flight, although not subject to accurate measurement, had been generally estimated at three to five billion since the beginning of 1978 and that once a measure of political stability was established government would find it a very complex and pressing problem to get the economy back on the tracks.

Conclusions and Evaluation

15. *The record indicates that Iran's domestic economic situation received relatively little attention in finished intelligence until mid-1978. It is clear that political protest grew in some part out of societal dislocation caused by a development program, and we think it not unfair to suggest that managers and analysts should have been alert to the interaction between the two. While some of the publications mentioned do refer to the political implications of economic problems, there does not seem to have been much effort put into integrating political and economic analysis. For example, no attention was paid to the political consequences of the policy of the Amuzegar government to cool off the economy, thus increasing unemployment. We recognize that there is a lack of political economy in this organization. It is not unlike university campuses*

where different disciplines are carried out by different departments. We are aware that management now recognizes this as a problem and that solutions to it are being pursued. They are not easy to come by, but in our view the lack of some systematic method of relating politics to economics (both terms used in the broadest sense) helped to prevent NFAC from appreciating the political consequences of socio-economic problems in Iran. As we noted above, maldistribution of wealth, inflation, and accompanying strains were among the elements which caused ordinary Iranians to demonstrate and riot against the Shah.

CONTACTS

1. Contacts between official Americans and oppositionists were few; those that existed were with the "modernized" political opposition. The obvious problem was noted in the FOCUS review, although its conclusion was not exactly helpful: "While it is a politically difficult and sensitive matter for Embassy officials to meet with identified opponents of the Shah, the Mission should have the widest possible range of contacts." (4 November 1976, p. 4)

Utility of Contacts with the Opposition

2. Information on the thinking and planning of the various opposition groups would not of itself have been sufficient to understand the temper of the opposition to the Shah, but it would have been of substantial benefit in four ways. First, the analysts would have been able to compare the size and strength of various demonstrations that occur with the expectations that were held by the opposition leaders. On the occasions when demonstrations were small or non-existent it would have been of some benefit to have known whether none had been planned or whether an attempt to stage one had failed. For example, the interpretation of the frequent lulls would vary depending on whether the opposition was trying to get people into the streets or not.

3. Second, benefit would have been gained if NFAC had known more about the kind and degree of organization that characterized the opposition, since this was one element in the opposition's strength. Contacts with the opposition—either overt or by penetration—might have given information about how disciplined it was, what communication networks existed, how the leaders were able to keep in touch with the views of their followers, what kinds of resources they had at their disposal, and what kinds of constraints they felt. Analysts would have had a better sense of the strengths and weaknesses of the opposition, of their depth of commitment, and of their ability to wage a sustained campaign which involved risks and sacrifices of money and lives. But this information of course would have not been unambiguous and as long as the beliefs discussed on pp. 131–133 were held it is hard to tell whether it would have led to a very different estimate of the Shah's staying power.

4. Third, greater contacts with the opposition—again through either open conversations or penetration—would have shed some light (it is hard to tell how much) on the

important question of the relations among the diverse opposition groups. We have elsewhere discussed what was known about this and the inferences the analysts drew. Greater contact might have revealed something about the discussions that presumably occurred among the top leaders of the group, and it might have given NFAC a sense of how the cooperation was working out, the kinds of frictions that were arising, and the degree of the commitment on all sides to continue a functioning alliance. Furthermore, analysts might have learned more about the distribution of power between moderates and extremists and derived a better sense of whether the former could afford to strike a bargain that the latter opposed.

5. Fourth, and perhaps most important, greater contacts might have produced information conducive to a fuller and better understanding of the beliefs and motives of the religious-based opposition. On pp. 105–107 we have discussed what we see as the problems in this regard. More first-hand reports of what the religious leaders—and their followers—were saying, the grievances they felt, and their attitudes toward modernization, might have modified the characterization of the groups, which the analysts knew was based on limited data.

Utility of Contacts in the Wider Society

6. These benefits would have been significant, but they still would not have gone to the heart of the matter, which was how much support the opposition would have outside its own circle. As in most other protests, this is a point on which the leaders of the opposition themselves could only guess. Indeed the National Front was reported "as surprised as everyone else about violence in Tabriz and at a loss to explain [it] except in terms of repressed peoples taking up cudgels of freedom and similar boilerplate." (Tehran 1879, 23 February 1978) In retrospect it seems that the boilerplate had a large element of truth and that large numbers of people hated the Shah and viewed the religious movement opposition as the symbol of and carrier for opposition to the regime. More contacts with the opposition presumably would have revealed that it was attracting large numbers of adherents, adherents who furthermore had diverse views on many issues. But more important would have been contacts with a wide variety of people who were not in the elite of either the government or the opposition. Knowledge about the views of something like a cross-section of the general population would have been extremely valuable, although it would not have yielded a clear prediction. In the absence of such evidence, the analysts were forced to make assumptions about how groups and classes would respond, and these seem to have been largely based on the belief that most people appreciated the benefits the Shah's modernization program was bringing.*

* The draft NIE argues that "Most Iranians have gained little in terms of standards of living from the oil and construction booms," and concludes that "The Shah's development program seems likely to lead to growing discontent among the urban poor." (6 September 1978, pp. II 15, II 17) But this perspective was not fully developed and does not appear to have strongly influenced most of the political analysis.

7. In this regard, it is interesting to note that the reports from the consulates in Iran were generally more pessimistic than those from the Embassy. Indeed the Embassy noted this at one point and explained that it did not share the alarming views of the Consul in Tabriz. (Tehran 1879, 23 February 1978) One possible explanation for this is that the consular officials, unlike those in the Embassy, had direct contact with people from a wide range of Iranian society. Their day to day activities involved dealing with many people outside the elite. (There are other possible explanations for their greater pessimism e.g., pre-existing views, their being stationed in cities that were more revolutionary than Tehran, and the decreased influence of policy considerations.)

8. The concentration on the elite in the reporting and in NFAC production seems to have been partly a matter of choice and partly a matter of necessity. Choice because it was believed that interactions among the elite would strongly influence the future of the country, especially when the Shah died or relinquished power. Concentrating on the elite was also a necessity since there was little information available about other segments of society. (This is not to imply that reliable and useful information about the elites was easy to come by.) Given the reporting of the Embassy, station, and the information from open sources, little was known about groups like the bazaaris, and oil workers which we now realize were so important. Even less information was available about less organized segments of society. Even now we do not know the make-up of the anti-Shah demonstrations. Thus the analysts could not say much about the groups beyond the elite. The most they could have done was to have pointed out that vital information was lacking and to have asked for a change in the priorities of information collection in the field. To determine such priorities would have involved a more thorough treatment of general Iranian politics to try to determine how much intra-elite maneuverings would set Iran's course and the extent to which other segments had to be considered as active participants. This sort of analysis is difficult and there are no general guidelines on this point. But no attempts to deal with the problem were made, perhaps because of resource limitations or because of the belief that, even if information about non-elite groups were useful, it could not have been obtained.

POLICY BIASES

1. It is often claimed that analysts distort what should be objective judgments to support official policy, but unambiguous evidence on this point is usually hard to come by. The case of Iran fits this pattern. Intelligence generally was consistent with US policy but this does not mean that the latter was influencing the former. If such an influence were present, the analysts were not aware of it.

2. In some cases, one finds that commitment to a policy—on the part of analysts as well as policy-makers—increases as more information indicating that the policy would fail becomes available. This was not the case here. In some cases the political climate was such that analysts who warned that the policy was failing had good reason to fear that they would be punished. Again, that does not seem to be true here.

3. If it were the case that the policy had a strong and direct impact on analysis, one would expect that the State Department's Bureau of Intelligence and Research, being more closely tied to US policy, would be more affected than NFAC. The former, however, in fact displayed more doubt about the Shah's ability to maintain his power than did the latter. The opposite side of this coin is that if policy were strongly influencing evaluations, one would expect news reporters, who had no stakes in the Shah's survival, to have been much more pessimistic than official accounts. But this also was not the case.

4. But it is at least possible that the belief that there was no alternative to existing policy—either because the realities in Iran would not permit an alternative or because the US Government was committed to supporting the Shah and his policy of liberalization—inhibited analysts from recognizing how precarious the situation was. If one believes that issuing a warning is useless, then one is less likely to believe that a warning is needed. We cannot be sure that this influence was at work. When it operates it does so on a subconscious level. It is possible, however, that there was some tempering of NFAC's analysis of the negative effects of the administration's human rights policy in response to signals that intelligence had already fully covered this topic.

5. The problem of determining whether analysis was influenced by policy is especially difficult because the analysts generally agreed with the policy. Looking over the range of beliefs held by people in and out of government it is clear that, as a generalization, those people who thought that the Shah's regime was on balance good for the citizens of Iran and thought that supporting him was in the American interest also thought that his government was quite strong. Those who thought he was evil also believed that it was bad for the United States to aid him and saw his regime as relatively vulnerable. Presumably the judgments about whether the Shah was good or bad for Iran influenced interpretations of the potency of dissent. Those journalists and academic analysts who opposed the Shah were more pessimistic about his chances of survival than were those in and out of government who had a more benign view of the regime. To a degree this was logical. Support for the Shah only made sense if one believed that he could survive. And if one believed that the Shah was generally acting in the interests of most of his countrymen then one would be likely to think that he had a lot of domestic support.

6. Even if analysis was not directly influenced by policy, these three inter-locking beliefs supported each other and made the analysts especially slow to give full credit to information indicating that the Shah was in very serious trouble. It is probably impossible to say which of the three beliefs came first either in time or in importance. As the Shah survived over perilous years, people became more convinced both that the United States should support him and that he was helping lots of Iranians and earning their support (or else he would not have survived). And as they came to believe that he was a good ruler they increasingly expected him to be able to survive.* ‹footnote redacted› Furthermore, the fact that those outside the government who thought in

the early autumn that the Shah might fall were people who opposed his rule gave the analysts an easy way to downgrade these warnings, for they could seem to be—and perhaps were—the product of wishful thinking.

7. A related problem was that the observers' apparent lack of sympathy with the protestors was reflected in their choice of words. They talked of "mobs" which "rampaged through the streets," 10 February 1978, "vandalism" (Tehran 5131, 30 May 1978), mullahs "agitating" (Tehran 8353, 31 August 1978), and "irresponsible" opposition. (NID, 10 August 1978) Field reporting used more highly colored terms than did finished intelligence, but we think it is fair to say that a reader of the latter could also tell what outcomes the writers wanted and which they feared. It is possible that this indicated or created a subtle bias.

8. The unprecedented nature of the revolution and the Shah's record of survival made it hard enough to see that past might not be a good guide to the future. To believe that the unrest would succeed was to expect the kind of sudden and dramatic change in affairs that strains our imaginations. The analytic task would have been extremely difficult if the United States had been neutral or even anti-Shah. But we cannot completely rule out the possibility that the subtle influence of US policy may have made it a bit harder for the analysts to realize that the Shah's position was becoming precarious.‹11 lines redacted›

In Conclusion

It will be clear to readers who have stayed with us this far that there is no one reason for NFAC's failure to assess the deterioration of the Shah's position during 1978. Life is never that simple. We have cited a number of reasons—inadequate information, pre-existing beliefs, mind sets, a small and isolated community of Iranian analysts, and a production system that emphasizes reporting events rather than underlying causes. We conclude with a dual appeal: analysts, re-examine your assumptions and beliefs; managers, create an environment conducive to analyzing foreign affairs, not just reporting them.

CIA Comments on the Report

1. Knorr to Bowie, 17 July 1979
Subject: Post-mortem

Critique of the Post-mortem

1. The post-mortem is done with great care and conspicuous analytical acumen.

2. The overall judgments are close to the mark. Obviously, NFAC failed to anticipate the course of events in Iran that took place late in 1978. It is also correct to say that NFAC did receive some evidence that pointed to the Shah's vulnerability. On the critical question of whether or not NFAC's estimates were unreasonable in the light of all information, and thus on whether there was a culpable intelligence failure, the post-mortem does not give a flat answer. The refusal to give a flat answer is clearly laudable. A flat answer, one way or another, is not supportable. The realistic question had to center on the degree (and, of course, kind) of estimative weakness. Here the balance of judgment elaborated in the post-mortem points to a higher degree of unreasonable failure than can be defended conclusively. Even though the authors know and acknowledge the difficulty of evaluating estimates made before the advent of hindsight, they do not seem to have overcome this difficulty completely. Indeed, there is considerable evidence for the thesis that the constraints of hindsight knowledge cannot be entirely neutralized in the process of post-mortem judgment.

3. It is also important to clarify the precise object of estimative failure. The Iranian revolution was clearly an unusual, virtually unprecedented, event which nobody, not even the Iranian revolutionaries themselves, were able to foresee in detail. The authors of the post-mortem, therefore, were right in limiting the object of intelligence failure to the Shah's ability to stay on top and to the strength of his opposition. Any attempt to do more, that is, to estimate not the probability of revolution but its precise evolution would have come up against an intractable order of difficulty.

4. While the post-mortem is a bit too harsh in estimating the degree of intelligence failure, it is in any case the identification and discussion of the reasons to which this failure (whatever its true degree) is to be attributed that constitutes the principal value of the post-mortem.

5. This contribution of the post-mortem deserves serious study. There is nothing new in the analytical framework which the authors bring to bear. The underlying model is taken from existing intelligence theory, especially the theory of threat perception (to which, however, Robert Jervis has made an important contribution in his previous writings).

Factors Contributing to "Intelligence Failure" (according to post-mortem) ‹9 paragraphs of summary omitted›

15. Finally—and this is an intriguing point—while analysts prefer, for understandable reasons, a short time frame for estimative purposes, the time frame set for the NIE on Iran turned out to be too extensive. The crucial problem of instability turned out to be short-term. Asking questions about longer-term stability reinforced the assumption that there was no short-term problem.

16. There is perhaps one angle—an extremely sensitive one—which the post-mortem may be said to have neglected. The post-mortem argues that there was enough information to call in question the underlying assumption on the solidity of the Shah's power and the weakness of his domestic opposition. Yet if a serious re-examination of this preconception had taken place, it would have been hard to avoid the impact of US policy toward Iran. Not only may US policy on human rights and political liberation have pushed the Shah farther than it was safe to go, there is also the question of whether he felt that his option of restoring order by using the military was weakened by US policy,

17. The post-mortem does not explicitly distribute weight to all the factors that are said to have detracted from a better estimative performance. They seem to suggest, however, that the ones listed under 6, 7, and 10 were the primary ones. This judgment, too, has merit although informational shortfalls also deserve to be ranked highly.

18. Three questions remain to be answered: (a) Which parts of the post-mortem are accepted? (b) Should the NFAC weaknesses it expressed be remedied, at least in part? (c) If so, how should this be done?

---

2. Knorr to Bowie, 18 July 1979
Subject: Earlier Estimates on Iran

Estimates on Iran: 1960–1975, The Record

‹3 pages of summary omitted›

Comment

1. Estimates were more frequent during the 1960s (especially early 1960s) than in the 1970s. Why?

2. The main focus of the first five estimates was on Iran's internal affairs. In 1966 the emphasis shifts to its foreign role. The last estimate (1975) dealt with both sides.

3. Relatively speaking, the analytical and estimative quality of estimates was better during the first part of the 1960s than afterwards. The earlier estimates reflected an understanding that rapid economic development was bound to be destabilizing in this autocracy and that a violent upheaval, though not imminent, was almost certain to occur in the longer run. (In retrospect, these estimates were very good.)

4. The NIE of March 1966 breaks with the estimative thrust of the preceding papers. The new tone is strongly established in the Special Memorandum of May 1968. The Shah's position is now seen as solid and the opposition, even though present and perhaps growing, is perceived to be weak and divided. It appears that this new estimative thrust prevailed through 1978 and the approach (seen in retrospect) of a revolutionary crisis.

5. The intriguing question is: Why did this change in basic assumptions occur in 1966 and 1967? I do not know and can only list some possibilities.

a. Was it induced by a "cry wolf" phenomenon? (This is not very plausible because the earlier estimates placed the probability of a serious upheaval in the far future.)

b. Was it induced by Iran's rapidly expanding armed forces and by their perception as an effective means of suppressing any active opposition?

c. Was it induced by a deterioration in the flow of information? And if so, why did this happen? Was it largely that information on Iran's domestic politics was given a reduced priority because of the new prevailing assumption that the Shah's hold on power was firm?

d. Was it induced by a change in US policy toward Iran? And if so, in what manner?

e. Was it induced by a change in the quality of the analysts?

f. Was it a consequence of INR's contraction?

---

3. Blee, 19 July 1979

1. The principal thrust of the Post-Mortem (P-M) is the concept that NFAC (as the rest of the analytic community) performed inadequately with respect to Iran in 1978 primarily because the analysts held a firm pre-crisis view of Iran which caused them to give inadequate weight to pieces of evidence tending to contradict this view. Two misconceptions are cited in the P-M as fundamental:

- that the Shah would use force effectively to suppress the opposition should he believe he was in serious risk of losing control of events, and

- that the opposition would split rather than follow the extreme position insisted upon by Khomeini.

2. Essentially I agree with the above position, although I believe the P-M overstates and oversimplifies it. At times the P-M even misrepresents the facts when they seem to contradict its thesis. For example, in Paragraph 48 it states that the drafting of the NIE on Iran "started early in 1978 because it had been several years since the last NIE was completed; it was not a response to specific events." This is simply not accurate.

The standard of passage of time since the last NIE would have put other countries ahead of Iran. I alone was responsible for recommending the scheduling of the Iran NIE to NFAC management and there were two principal reasons for my making this recommendation:

- the rather violent Community reaction to the suggestions in Admiral Turner's 1977 AWACS letter that the Shah's government might be subject to political and/or security weaknesses indicated to me that there were differences within the Intelligence Community regarding the stability of a nation important to our foreign policy, and

- DDO information about collaboration between the underground leftists and the underground religious rightists, compounded by the apparent inability of SAVAK to make progress in suppressing these under-grounds caused me concern that the Community was giving too little weight to these indications of potentially effective opposition to the Shah.

3. The motivation for my recommending the NIE, therefore, does not in fact support the theory that we went wrong because of our strongly held views—nor does my title, "Iran: How Reliable an Ally?"

4. The P-M makes the valid point that NFAC predictions were hampered by the fact that in many ways the Iranian revolution was unprecedented ("a major discontinuity" the P-M—unfortunately—calls it) in that an entrenched regime with the support of a well equipped military force was overthrown by an unarmed mob. Also, the P-M notes, the past success of the Shah in overcoming organized large scale opposition as well as the demonstrated willingness of the armed forces to carry out his orders in dealing with the populace reinforced pre-existing beliefs that the regime could—and would—prevail. Further, there was conventional wisdom that pro-Western dictatorships are overthrown by the left, not the right.

5. The P-M observation that we are hampered by our tendency to try to give secular explanations for religiously motivated behavior is also valid and was particularly obvious to me during my service in NFAC (DDO officers, at least those with long Asian experience, have learned better). As an NIO I noticed this to be a problem particularly with analysts of Israel who never thought I was serious when I urged them to read Genesis—if necessary in the English translation. Earlier this week in the N1D I read a long article on the Arabs of Khuzistan and found myself interested in the question of whether they are Shia (as are most Iraqi Arabs) or Sunni—only to end in frustration as the subject was never touched on. So the problem remains.

6. Unfortunately I cannot wholly agree with the P-M conclusion that there was no effort to influence analysis to support policy. As I recall, the DIA representatives were under orders to oppose my title, "Iran: How Reliable an Ally?" because it seemed to cast doubt on the wisdom of our military aid program.

7. The above notes are written off the top of my head without the benefit of any files or research, so there may well be an odd error of detail. Also, it should be remembered that I left NFAC at the end of July 1978, so I have minimal official knowledge of Iranian related events thereafter.

---

4. Bowie, 20 July 1979
Subject: Iran Post-Mortem

These comments are my first reaction upon completing the report on the NFAC performance on Iran in 1978.

1. The report seems to me to be much affected by hindsight despite the express recognition of this danger. The premise that the events which took place were bound to happen underlies much of the discussion. There does not seem to be any element of contingency where events might have taken a different turn had conditions been different or had the Shah or others followed a different course. My perception of the way in which events unfolded was certainly different at the time. That, of course, could be a mistake. But even in retrospect, I cannot convince myself that the actual course of events was inevitable until rather later than is implied in much of the discussion of the report.

2. The report stresses the fact that two assumptions which underlay much of the analysis proved to be wrong:

a. that the Shah would actually use force to supress the opposition if he thought there was a serious chance of his losing control, and

b. that the opposition had split.

The first of these premises certainly did affect much of the analysis. In view of the past it would not seem reasonable to expect substantial evidence to have reached the contrary view, especially since the Shah was clearly in full control of the army and SAVAK.

3. My memory of the second premise is somewhat different. It was not assumed that the opposition had split but rather that it would not coalesce under Khomeini. No effort was devoted to trying to analyze the sources of discontent of the different groups. This indicated the extreme disparity among them and the divergence in what they objected to in the Shah's rule. We also supported the view that a number of these groups actually preferred that the monarchy should continue though essentially as a constitutional monarchy with greatly reduced powers. Since this was diametrically opposite to Khomeini's commitment to get rid of the Shah, it did not seem probable that the various groups would be united with the sole aim of getting rid of the Shah. Events in the last six months have certainly shown how widely the various groups did differ and still do about what they really wanted to achieve.

4. The report recognizes that on many points our problem was the evidence available to the analysts. Yet it does not seem to me to give adequate weight of the effect of this on their conclusions. At various points the report refers to the estimates in the fifties and sixties which stressed the weakness of the Shah and the likelihood that he would not be able to maintain his throne (usually the Fall that is placed just beyond the period of the estimate as I recall it). The experience of nearly twenty years during which the estimates had cried wolf must have induced some self-doubt on the part of the analysts. The fact that the estimates had been repeatedly proven wrong and that the Shah had indeed endured should have led any analyst to await persuasive evidence before finding that the Shah was doomed when the evidence was so fragmentary and obviously so limited regarding the strength and extent of the opposition. This certainly contributed to the hesitation of analysts to reach a final judgment that the Shah would not be able to surmount the turmoil of the 1978 period. ‹1 paragraph redacted›

6. I want to also reread my testimony before the Senate Foreign Relations Committee in September. My recollection is that I indicated pretty clearly that I found that (a) the opposition was substantial and extensive though highly divergent in its aims, (b) that the threat to the Shah was real and substantial but that (c) on balance he still would have a good chance to surmount the troubles. My assumption, as I recall it, was that he would show the skill to reach out and tap the moderate forces which seemed to want continuance of a constitutional monarchy and that he would be prepared to make the changes in actual power which were required for that result. The second assumption was that he had the means to repress the more extreme opposition and would be prepared to use them. Both of these premises turned out to be wrong but even as late as September and October they did not seem to me to be unreasonable on the basis of past experience and the evidence up to that time.

---

5. Palmer to Bowie, 23 July 1979
Subject: Comments re "Analysis of NFAC's Performance on Iran's Domestic Crisis, Mid-1977 to 7 November 1978" dated 15 June 1979

1. In examining the subject postmortem analysis, it should first be noted that it was a limited effort. It was basically limited to the information available to NFAC analysts without the benefit of State, Defense, and CIA electronic messages and telephone conversations that were closely held. Moreover, the analysis did not delve very deeply into US policy aspects which had enormous influence over both the analytical and operational/collection sides of the Intelligence Community. Thus, a broader examination of the matter would no doubt lead to some much different conclusions. In my own view, our "failure" in Iran was considerably more one of a policy nature, to include the lack of adequate policy-intelligence linkage, than an intelligence breakdown.

2. Within the relatively narrow bounds of this effort, I feel that the authors of the analysis did a good job; their analysis is detailed, comprehensive, coherent and

reasonably free of bias. They have tried to identify those aspects of this inquiry where hindsight has influenced their views, but by their own admission, it is not possible to eliminate hindsight entirely.

3. Again, given the limitations of the study, I agree with the thrust of the author's main conclusions; namely that:

a. There were major deficiencies in the information received from the field.

b. There was a partial failure to challenge underlying beliefs and assumptions, and focus on the most important questions. Faith in the strength of the regime; the Shah's willingness to use force which in fact would save the situation (a dual assumption); a conviction that the opposition was weak and divided, and could not unite effectively—these were among the most important beliefs and assumptions. (Not realizing that the preservation of the Iranian Armed Forces was essential and central to the survival of a moderate government, with or without the monarchy—this is an example of a failure to link policy and intelligence.)

c. Current events drove the intelligence effort with respect to Iran.

d. The managerial chain of responsibility did not adequately review intelligence production in a substantive sense.

e. The Intelligence Community lacks an estimative mechanism which can focus on the issues important to policymakers and produce analytical papers in a timely manner. ‹2 pages redacted›

---

6. Knorr to Bowie, 23 July 1979
Subject: Postmortem

1. You asked for further reflection following your discussion with the SRP.

2. I still think that the postmortem is a fine report despite serious questions that can be raised about it.

3. To clarify one point I made in my review of the postmortem. If one believes in some failure of intelligence in the Iranian case, the failure was *not* that of having failed to raise as a serious possibility the precise nature and timing of the Iranian Revolution and of its development (so far). The estimating failure rather was one of attributing too much solidity to the position and capabilities of the Shah and of underestimating the strength of the opposition and of its capacity to coalesce under propitious circumstances. There was nothing inevitable about the actual developments and outcome of the events that are now known as the Iranian Revolution. Several possible intervening factors could have modified or postponed the revolutionary events or led to a different denouement.

4. There is one part of the problem which the authors of the postmortem did little to penetrate, perhaps because they felt unable to do so. US policy toward the Shah

may well have had a major impact on Iranian developments. In ways as yet unclear and speculative, the intelligence failure may have resulted in part from this policy, (a) in terms of structuring attention to Iranian realities and the procurement of information; (b) in terms of discouraging intelligence analysts from pursuing questions that might have been, or were felt to be, uncomfortable to policymakers (because they were assumed to cross the boundary between intelligence and policymaking) and (c)—and perhaps most of all—because US policy helped to bring about the actual course of events in Iran.

5. To the extent that the relative failure of intelligence resulted from the interlinkage of policy and intelligence mentioned under (4) the remedies suggested by the postmortem are *incomplete,* perhaps seriously so. But they are not, in my opinion, misplaced. Indeed, nearly all the suggestions are in line with deficiencies previously noted by the SRP and others in other estimates.

6. I find it difficult to give any advice on what should be done with the postmortem. Three possibilities occurred to me: (a) to circulate a summary and/or excerpted version; (b) not to circulate the postmortem beyond its present range; and (c) to circulate the original postmortem with a brief critical commentary. I do not like any of them because (a) and (b) might stimulate thoughts that unwelcome truths are being suppressed, and (c) might lead to a defensive reaction in NFAC and be exploited unfairly by critics elsewhere. Unless knowledge of the postmortem can be closely limited, (c) might be least undesirable course of action. I do think, however, that (a) and (b) are also legitimate choices because the purpose of a postmortem is to identify deficiencies in order to mitigate them. And that is the responsibility of NFAC management.

---

7. Leonhart to Bowie, 26 July 1979
Subject: Notes on the Iran Postmortem

I. Report as a Whole

1. The <name redacted>-Jervis examination of finished intelligence on Iran over an eighteen months period contains a number of useful insights and constitutes an interesting and informative case study of certain aspects of the analytical problem.

2. But the study has severe limitations and serious weaknesses. Some of these are inherent in the design of the study. Others, probably more important, lie in the report's failure to develop a concept of the role of intelligence analysis in policymaking—to situate NFAC in that process—and to consider the relationship between intelligence and policy. These inadequacies in scope make the study less an overall performance appraisal than a fairly sterile documentary analysis, which may too easily be read as a search for scapegoats among a handful of Iranian analysts and the management chain in NFAC for what it chooses to term "an obvious intelligence failure".

3. In so doing, the report may obscure, rather than highlight, the more important lessons to be learned from the Iranian case.

II. Limitations in the Design of the Study

4. A very short time frame is used: summer of 1977 to November 1978.

5. The study is an examination of "only the information that was available to NFAC at the time . . . not . . . the quality of that information or . . . what might have been done to improve it. (Introductory Note)

6. The authors note "several deficiencies in the information available", but they state that "the subject of collection is beyond the scope of our investigation" (12). Collection and analysis are two of the elements involved. There is a third—and more important—dimension of the problem: The relation between policy and analysis. The report has little to say about the preponderant weight of US policy and attitudes in the swiftly moving Iranian situation the analysts were called upon to examine—or about the effect those policies might have in altering at the most critical junctures the ratio of forces in a rapidly disintegrating environment.

7. At one point the authors note that "feedback from policymakers would have helped in choosing alternative interpretations to be treated" (iv). At another, they observe that, "*in the succeeding year after*" the US Government made its decision to push the Shah to liberalize, NFAC's discussions of the problems involved were never "more than a few sentences long" (5b). It does not seem to have occurred to the authors that a closer relationship between policymakers and the Intelligence Community might have had advantages in assessing the implications or consequences of policy options *before* decisions were taken on the directions and use of US influence.

III. Results

8. Limitations in design often result in limitations in product. What the study presents, in sum, is an exegesis of texts, an analysis of manuscripts—in which the postmorticians grade a mixed score card of published materials. The product is less a single critique than three separate studies woven together:

- the postmortem itself
- an essay on management and organization
- an independent analysis of Iranian events

Each of these bears a brief look.

9. *Retrospective Analysis* What the authors think they would have concluded—or examined differently—or qualified in lesser or greater degree—is of course closer to the mark. It is also possibly the least interesting part of the study. They have much of interest to say about such matters as the nature of Khomeini's appeals, the strength of the religious opposition, the Shah's moods, the political effects of economic slow-down,

and the attitudes of non-elite groups—much of which has analytic value. But their analysis of the key elements in the Iranian revolution (as contained in the sections of the report following p. 61) has surprising omissions as an illustration of what the authors maintain "a sustained and thorough evaluation of the most important questions" (43) would have involved. It is a bit surprising to find so little by way of a critque of analysis, or estimative judgments, or available information on such matters as:

- the early and progressive organization of the opposition (money, agents, initial weapons, communications, linkages)
- the effects of corruption, at many levels of Iranian officialdom
- reactions to repression and SAVAK operations
- differential impacts of inflation, living standards and social mobilities on Iranian expectations
- demographic changes in age groups, organization, unemployment
- land reform (decreasing small-holder incomes, transfer of mosque estates to the Pahlevis, operations of the Shah's village agents)
- special role of the trade unions (particularly in the oil fields)
- student organization and agitation, at home and abroad
- bases of an apparently widespread anti-Americanism below elite levels

Retro-respective views of Iranian events might have been expected to deal with many, if not most, of these matters.

10. *Management/Organization Essay* The authors seem to have in mind an organizational model which differs from NFAC, and much of their analysis reflects their preferences for:

- *a more directed research effort.* They write: "management must take the burden of re-ordering priorities and ordering that selected in-depth studies be undertaken. Working level analysts cannot be expected to take the initiative in shifting from the normal mode of analysis to one that is more appropriate to the situation" (20).
- *an office of estimates.* The authors observe that the present lack of a separate NFAC mechanism with estimative capacities "may have contributed to the difficulties" (41). They note that "the mechanism that once existed where a current office and an estimative office looked at issues from their different perspectives was not a cure-all, but it did offer on a regular basis opportunity for different approaches to surface" (vi). "The exchange involved sharpened argument and caused people to examine assumptions... Its demise is a considerable loss" (33). Absent such a mechanism, they appear to suggest the problem is

insoluable: Analysts today have been "conditioned over years to keep an eye as close as possible to the facts and reports rather than draw out the implications... The system... has stronger incentives for writing for the NID" (23). They conclude that "when people are not used to writing analytical papers, one cannot expect them to be able to do so when the need arises" (26).

11. These reflections seem part of those "general beliefs", about which the authors dilate elsewhere, that they feel largely pre-determined the subsequent analysis of the Iranian problem. Their view of analysts, particularly those at senior level, seems curiously constricted. But those who hold similar organizational preferences will no doubt be more responsive to the line of criticism which the authors make of NFAC performance during the period reviewed—criticisms which in turn generally reinforce their predilections on desirable organizational mold. The point is not so much that the authors' arguments are right or wrong, but that their implicit assumption appears to color much of their own analysis. The case for a revised or a revived estimates office should be argued on its own merits. (The old Board mechanism is not generally remembered for its immaculate record of Iranian prediction.)

12. *Postmortem* Two initial points should perhaps be made:

- No other intelligence service, whatever its organizational form, appears to have done much better.

- The report's specific findings on NFAC performance in the 1977–78 have an unusually tentative and qualified nature.

13. The postmortem itself involves at least several separate matters: (a) underlying conceptions, (b) analytical judgments, (c) process and performance.

- (a) *Underlying Conceptions* The authors' most basic judgments appear to be that: "The problem lay less in incorrect interpretation of specific bits of information than in a misleading analysis of the situation which pre-dated the crisis" (5)—that variations in analyst performance were attributable to "general beliefs about Iran which long pre-dated" the protests (4)—that those beliefs were in turn related to whether the analyst was a "liberal or conservative" person (5)—and that the authors could not analyze "how and why this belief formed" (6).

This underlying concept—in which epistemology replaces analytics—presents a number of problems. If accepted, it would undercut much of the report's subsequent critique. It would provide a somewhat uncertain criterion for the future selection and training of NFAC staff. And in a period in which crises were still unresolved, it would not provide much help to policymakers weighing their current options. The "general beliefs" argument may account for a fundamental ambiguity in the study which the drafters never openly confront or clearly resolve: whether there was an inevitability to the course of events in Iran which a "non-misleading analysis", long pre-dating the crisis, should have foreseen from the beginning—or whether the Iranian outcome lacked pre-determination, turned on options and decisions which were not fore-ordained, and remained in question until a very late stage. Was there inevitability in the overthrow of the Pahlevi dynasty? If not, how long was the outcome in doubt? If so, how much earlier than November, 1978 should it have been foreseen? Despite their meticulous inquiry, the authors never offer explicit findings on these questions which would seem to be basic to the formulation of an opinion on NFAC's Performance.

- (b) *Analytic Performance* Apart from suggestions of how the authors believe they would have handled certain aspects of the problem differently, their judgments on the specific conclusions reached by the analysts *at the time* events were unfolding, are exceedingly diffident and tempered. As examples:

    - "...even in retrospect it is hard to say why he (the Shah) did not crack down" (74)

    - "No definitive answers were possible, but a more thorough weighing of the evidence and a more penetrating analysis of the problem were" (85)

    - (White Revolution) The problem of liberalizing a repressive regime "was great enough to have called for much more attention and analysis" (67). Analysis which was made was "plausible", "made sense", "made eminent sense", but was also "a typically American view" (sic). The authors note that they differ on the extent to which such ethnocentrism may have affected intelligence production" (68)

    - (Shah's willingness to use force) Various signs should have been noted, "but it would have been impossible to say exactly how significant they were" (71)

    - (Splits in the opposition) "This is not to say that the evidence was so overwhelming that the analysts should have automatically accepted it. But there should have been a probing of the reports..." (84) "No definitive answers were possible, but a more thorough weighing of the evidence and a more penetrating analysis of the problems were." (85)

    - (Religious Opposition) "Unless one used that (a pro-Khomeini, anti-Shah) perspective, the evidence would not stand out as especially significant" (92)

    - (Contacts) "The most they (the analysts) could have done was to have pointed out that vital information was lacking and to have asked for a change in the priorities of information collection in the field" (106)

    - (Policy Biases) Policy did not have a strong and direct impact on analysis. "But we cannot completely rule out the possibility that the subtle influence of US policy may have made it a bit harder for the analysts to realize that the Shah's position was becoming precarious" (108)

• The foregoing quotations—largely from the italicized "Conclusions and Evaluation" sections of individual chapters—have an elusive quality. No explicit judgments are given on what "more probing", "more thorough weighing", etc. would have produced. They stand in some contrast with the values the study elsewhere attaches to "sharp and explicit predictions" by analysts. And, as the authors note elsewhere "it is much harder to tell whether there was an intelligence failure in (the sense that)... given the information available, did NFAC ignore or misinterpret events in ways and to an extent that consumers can legitimately expect should not and will not occur." (35)

• (c) *Process and Performance* Similarly, in dealing with the particulars of the people involved and their interactions, the study seems reluctant to come to grips with specifics:

(i) *Analysts* A total of ‹number redacted› analysts on Iran are noted. There are a few generally favorable references to the senior analyst; little on the others. The study obviously considers their products, in greater or lesser degree, inadequate, but avoids the more central question of the competence of the analysts for their tasks, in such matters as selection, background, training, and previous evaluation. Were there variations in their individual performance or output? Were the published assessments mainly individual or joint products? If both, which was more effective? Were there differences in their coordination practices, abilities to integrate Community materials, access to or skill in the use of Embassy or Station materials and reports? Did observable differences in products or practices correspond with length of experience, tenure on Iran, language capability, field trips, advanced training, if any? The study does not treat such matters. Its undifferentiated use of the term "the analysts" is not of much help to managers seeking to improve performance.

(ii) *Management* Similarly the study uses "management" and "managers" scores of time without discrimination or definition. What was the approval chain above "the analysts", and how numerous and layered? What is the evidence for "an absence of substantive review", as asserted in the author's statement that: "In the case of Iran, there was also a failure of what can be called intellectual or analytical management in the absence of substantive review of what the analysts were writing." (47) Were there no exceptions? Where in the management chain, should critical, substantive reviews have been made? How many times? At what levels? Where did the breakdown in systematic evaluation occur? How was coordination carried out among the analysts and between NFAC's several offices concerned with Iran? With what results? Was this, in practice, an analyst or a management responsibility? What should it have been? Were there no challenges to NFAC's analysis on Iran by other agencies prior to meetings on a prospective NIE in the fall of

1978? What was the nature of NFAC-DDO relationships during the period? Were there differences in NFAC and Station assessment? If not, this bears on NFAC performance. If so, whose management responsibility was it to probe for discrepant bases? The study does not tell us much about how the system worked in practice. ‹half page redacted›

14. These matters seem far from peripheral to an exercise styled an "Analysis of NFAC's Performance on Iran's Domestic Crisis". Textual criticism alone is flat and one-dimensional, and, whatever its merits for documentary analysis, should not of itself constitute a performance appraisal.

IV. Summary

15. The issues touched upon in the study are broader than those analyzed by a report which is essentially a documentary critique. They include the basic question of how the United States Government organized itself to report on Iranian developments as an integral part of the policymaking process—the place of NFAC in that process and in that integration of effort—and the specific operations of NFAC which resulted in its finished production. The Devlin-Jervis study is interesting and informative, and obviously done with painstaking care. For reasons noted above, it should not be regarded as a definitive appraisal of NFAC performance on the Iranian crisis.

---

8. Bruce C. Clarke, Jr., Director, National Foreign Assessment Center, 19 December 1979

Introductory note:

I am disseminating this report, completed under the auspices of my predecessor as D/NFAC, because I believe it will be helpful both to analysts and to managers in improving our substantive product. Although it is directed to one issue at one moment in history, it is a careful examination of some of the pitfalls that are endemic to intelligence analysis. I urge each of you to read it carefully and thoughtfully. I particularly urge those of you who are line analysts and first-line supervisors to draw from it useful ideas for further improving our analytical work.

Bear in mind that this report was initiated and executed as a limited endeavor. It was intended to look only at NFAC itself within a short, specific time frame and in the light of the circumstances that actually prevailed. It is not:

- a retrospective analysis of the Iranian situation
- a study of collection as well as analysis
- an inquiry into the impact of policy on intelligence
- an examination of the role of intelligence in policymaking
- an attempt to assess the role or competence of any individual

Read it, therefore, for what it is.

[3]

The Iraq WMD Intelligence Failure

What Everyone Knows Is Wrong

> [The tool of preemptive war] has to be used carefully. One would want to have very good intelligence.
>
> —National Security Adviser Condoleezza Rice

Perhaps the most studied intelligence failure since Pearl Harbor is the misjudgment of Iraq's programs for WMD, which was especially striking because it dealt with capabilities rather than intentions, and these are supposed to be less difficult to discern. It was followed by endless journalistic accounts, official British, Australian, and American postmortems, and CIA self-studies.[1] As we will see, these yielded something like a consensus. It is an incorrect one, however, almost as flawed as the original estimates and partly for the same reason: the postmortems neglected social science methods, settled for more intuitive but less adequate ways of thinking, and jumped to plausible but misleading conclusions.[2]

The American concern with Iraq's WMD sharply accelerated with Iraq's invasion of Kuwait in August 1990, the subsequent American-led war, the discovery that Iraq's programs had been highly advanced, the regime's refusal to abandon its efforts, and the continued hostility between Iraq and the West. The terrorist attacks of September 11, 2001, brought the issues even greater attention, especially because the Bush administration believed that Saddam Hussein might share with terrorists any WMD that he developed. Few questions then had higher priority for the United States, and the fact that American intelligence was so wrong was particularly striking.

Less well understood is that just as most of what intelligence "knew" about Iraq's WMD programs in 2002–3 was wrong, so much of the prevailing explanation for the failure is also wrong. The studies provide a wealth

Rice made her remark in Online NewsHour, "Rice on Iraq, War and Politics," September 25, 2002, available at www.pbs.org/newshour/bb/international/july-dec02/rice_9-25.html.

of raw material, but the failure that occasioned them provides a context that we need to take account of. The very fact that the failure was seen as so important meant that many of the commentaries were strongly influenced by individual, organizational, and partisan politics, if not being driven toward predetermined conclusions. It is worth remembering that there were four official investigations in the years following Pearl Harbor, and while they made public much valuable information, they could not explain what had happened or settle the political debate.[3]

The general consensus is that judgments about Iraq's WMD were characterized by egregious errors.[4] My summary view is that while there were not only errors but correctable ones and that analysis could and should have been better, the result would have been to make the intelligence assessments less certain rather than to reach a fundamentally different conclusion. As I noted in chapter 1, this judgment is psychologically disturbing and politically unacceptable. We like to think that bad outcomes are explained by bad processes and that fixing the intelligence machinery will solve the problems, but this needs to be demonstrated rather than assumed. If Secretary of State Powell had not spent several days closely querying intelligence officials about the information that would go into his crucial February 2003 UN speech that sought to rally support for the invasion, I am sure his critics would have said that many of the mistakes would have been caught if the secretary had exercised this kind of due diligence.

To analyze the performance of the intelligence community (IC) we need to avoid hindsight and the automatic association of being wrong with having made avoidable and blameworthy errors. The report of the Senate Select Committee on Intelligence (SSCI) fell most deeply into this trap, as shown by the fact that it almost always equated reasonable, well-grounded inferences with those that proved to be correct. We can see the problem by asking the counterfactual: would the same reports have been written if the estimates about WMD had turned out to be correct? This is implausible, yet it is what most accounts imply. After all, they argue not that the conclusions were wrong—we knew that already—but that the analytical processes were badly flawed. Often this was indeed the case. But as I noted in chapter 1, the conflation of incorrect answers with deficient if not incompetent ways of thinking makes more sense politically than intellectually. We need to come to grips with the unfortunate fact that the most warranted inference may be incorrect.

Did Intelligence Matter?

Most discussions of intelligence failures assume that they mattered in the sense that national behavior would have been different if intelligence had rendered a different verdict, and it was this presupposition more than intellectual curiosity that justified the plethora of investigations into the Iraq WMD case.[5] Reinforcing this impression, politicians who favored the war but grew uneasy after WMD were not found conveniently blamed intelligence, although there were partisan differences here. Putting the onus on intelligence allowed Democrats to shield themselves from the unfortunate consequences of supporting the war, but doing so also protected the Bush administration by treating it as the innocent victim of intelligence incompetence. This stance also forced Democrats to face the uncomfortable question that several of their candidates for president in 2004 and 2008 alternately dodged and mishandled: "Would you have supported the war if you had known that Saddam did not have active WMD programs?" For Democrats, then, the best way out was to argue that while they had followed faulty intelligence, the errors stemmed from politicization in that intelligence had yielded to administration pressure. They had been misled; the administration was responsible for the misleading.

For Republicans in general and the Bush administration in particular, the first line of defense was that intelligence had not been badly in error, that WMD would be found or had been spirited across the border to Syria. Once this became untenable, the claim of politicization had to be refuted in the face of common sense. The Republicans also had to deflect attention from the ways in which the administration had distorted intelligence to make its case to the public, and they resisted allowing the official investigations to look at this question.[6]

The Republicans still could be asked whether they would have favored the war if they had known the truth about Saddam's programs. President Bush was forthright in his affirmation that he would have proceeded anyway, arguing that Saddam wanted WMD, especially nuclear weapons, and that sanctions and inspections could at best have slowed him down.[7] Furthermore, Saddam was a tyrant and so there was a great danger that once he had WMD he would dominate the region or hand them over to terrorists, a risk that was no longer acceptable after 9/11.[8] This argument, also made by Prime Minister Tony Blair in the United Kingdom, is not without its logic, but it implies a much reduced role for intelligence. If the fundamental danger is the existence of a tyrannical regime with a history of aggressiveness, neither spies nor satellites are needed.[9] In this view the intelligence errors, although unfortunate, were irrelevant. Although we should not take these self-justifications at face value, they do hint at the possibility that what intelligence was saying cannot explain the policy.

But the fact that Bush and Blair said that they would have favored going to war even if they had known of Saddam's reduced capabilities does not mean that they would have done so and that the intelligence did not matter.[10] In fact, these two points are somewhat different. Intelligence might have strongly contributed to the policy despite the preferences of Blair and

Bush because the reluctance of many members of the Labor Party, Democrats, and Secretary of State Powell was overcome only by the belief that the Iraqi dictator had growing WMD capabilities. Had they been better informed, it is doubtful whether they would have supported the war, and it would have been harder for Bush to launch it.[11]

Would he have wanted to? His numerous statements in the affirmative are not definitive. For him to say that he would have followed a different policy had he known the truth would have shifted the blame to intelligence but would also have made him seem credulous and implied that the war was unnecessary. In fact, it is unlikely that Bush knew what he would have done had he understood the status of Saddam's programs. People are not aware of many of the reasons that move them; even an introspective person with incentives to accurately estimate how he or she would have behaved with different information cannot do this.[12] Nevertheless, I think that what Bush said is essentially correct in that once he moved toward war in the winter of 2001–2, he would not have been deflected by new information.[13] At best, intelligence could have said that there was no firm evidence that Saddam had stockpiles of chemical and biological weapons or was actively pursuing nuclear bombs. It could not have said that he had ceased his efforts. Even the much-praised verdict of the State Department's Bureau of Intelligence and Research on Saddam's nuclear program was that the evidence was insufficient to establish that he was reconstituting it, not that he was not doing so.[14] Furthermore, intelligence could not have said that Saddam would not resume pursuit of WMD at some point in the future. The only way intelligence could have mattered for Bush would have been if before September 11, and probably before he assumed office, it had been more accurate. In this case Bush and others might not have brought with them an image of Saddam's regime as strong and threatening. There would have been a greater burden on those calling for war, and the entire tone of the discussions might have been different. This possibility aside, the intelligence failure was not responsible for the invasion. But it is worth exploring in its own right.

Description of the Intelligence Failure

Before turning to the standard explanations for the Iraq failure and why they are flawed, I want to mention three points on which conventional wisdom is indeed correct.

Too Much Certainty

Many of the IC's judgments were stated with excessive certainty, and while the preponderance of evidence indicated that Iraq probably had

WMD, it was not sufficient to prove their existence. The public versions of the assessments were especially culpable in this regard, but even the classified ones gave an unjustified impression of certainty.[15] In effect, the IC should have said that the evidence was good enough to convict Saddam in a civil suit but not, as it implied, in a criminal prosecution.[16]

Part of the reason for this error is that the October 2002 National Intelligence Estimate was produced in great haste. The items in the President's Daily Brief were even more stark, in part because they reflected first impressions derived from recent information and had to be brief.[17] Other reasons for the excess certainty were that analysts overestimated the number of independent sources reporting to them, and they failed to consider the significance of negative reports and the absence of evidence, as we will discuss below. Analysts may also have been influenced by the desire to please policymakers, not so much by telling them what they wanted to hear but by being able to reach a firm conclusion rather than writing in the typical and disliked style of "on the one hand, on the other hand."[18] Furthermore, when the NIE was being drafted, the National Intelligence Officers and top decision makers received reports from a high-level source (apparently Naji Sabri, Iraq's foreign minister) that were so sensitive that they were withheld from the working-level analysts. Although the extent of Sabri's access remains unclear and accounts disagree on exactly what he said, the NIOs perceived it as powerful confirmation, and in February 2004 Tenet declared, "Now did this information make any difference in my thinking? You bet it did."[19] Those at the top then became more confident, an attitude the analysts probably sensed.

A related problem was that finished intelligence did not do a good job of conveying levels of certainty to consumers, in part because there were no accepted standards for how to do this. The Butler report on the British performance notes that while consumers thought that terms such as "likely" and "probable" were conveying subtle differences of meaning, intelligence actually used the terms interchangeably.[20] It is doubtful, however, that consumers were looking for subtle degrees of certainty in this case. In other cases they may be, and the problem of conveying degrees of confidence is a continuing one. Although NIEs now carry an explicit discussion of the meaning of terms such as "likely," the British and American ICs have grappled with this problem for years, and the fact that several alternatives have been tried and abandoned indicates the depth of the difficulties.

No Alternatives Considered

A second facet of the failure was that alternative explanations were not considered. This is not to say there were no disagreements. To the contrary, there were sharp splits over whether the aluminum tubes that Iraq was surreptitiously importing indicated that Iraq was reconstituting its nuclear program and whether a threat to the American homeland was implied by the Iraq procurement of software for its unmanned aerial vehicles (UAVs) that included maps of the United States. But no general alternative explanations for Saddam's behavior were offered. There were no "red teams" to attack the prevailing views, no analyses from devil's advocates, no papers that provided competing possibilities.[21]

Most strikingly, no one proposed a view close to the one we now believe to be true. Indeed, as the president's WMD Commission put it in its postmortem, "Failing to conclude that Saddam had ended his banned weapons programs is one thing—not even considering it as a possibility is another."[22] This was a serious failure but one that needs to be placed in context. No observers, including opponents of the war, proposed serious alternatives, and no one, including analysts in the Arab world, provided a description of Saddam's motives and behavior that was close to what we now think is correct. Furthermore, there is no reason to think that any alternative would have been seen as credible had it been proposed, and as we will see, it is hard to argue that even the story we now believe to be true fit the available evidence better than the prevailing one. So while alternatives should have been considered, doing so probably would not have changed the estimates.

Insufficient Imagination

Related to the fact that alternatives were not considered is the argument that the IC should have been more imaginative. This claim is familiar, being the standard view of intelligence before 9/11, where intelligence failed to "connect the dots." This phrase betrays a fundamental misunderstanding of the problem, however. There are countless dots, and they can be connected in a great many ways. To take the 9/11 case, I am sure that if we look back at all the information rather than only at the bits that we now know could have led us to the plot, we will find many alarms that looked as troubling as the danger that turned out to be the real. In retrospect the presence of a handful of Arabs in flying schools without obvious employment prospects called for immediate investigation, but if the attacks had been delivered by chemical trucks, we would now be bemoaning the failure to see the significance of the scattered warnings—which I am sure we could find—about Arabs who were enrolled in truck-driving schools.

The fact remains, however, that the IC *was* unimaginative.[23] Just as intelligence thought it was clear that the Shah would live up to his reputation for ruthlessness and crack down if the disturbances grew serious in 1977–78, few in the IC felt the need to go beyond the obvious proposition that Saddam was developing active WMD programs. This pattern makes sense.

Intelligence analysts are selected and trained to stay close to the information and to eschew speculation. Although the result is that they will miss the truth on some occasions, there are few limits on what can be imagined, and those who urge more imagination say little about how it should be disciplined. Furthermore, in one sense the IC was too imaginative about Iraq in putting together scattered and ambiguous information and so ended up speculating without realizing it was doing so. While one can legitimately reply that this kind of outrunning the evidence was not imaginative because the picture that resulted was a familiar one, the analysts were seeing a world beyond the incoming reports.

On at least one major question—Saddam's actions leading up to the war—the British and American ICs not only declined to speculate but apparently were not aware that there was anything important to speculate about. Although Saddam's refusal to cooperate with the inspectors did seem to imply that he was conducting forbidden activities, his behavior in the eighteen months preceding the war was hard to understand even if he had things to hide. His actions made it almost certain that the United States would overthrow him, and his behavior therefore was figuratively and indeed literally suicidal. Since national leaders seek to avoid this fate, this was a puzzle whether or not Saddam had WMD. It would not have been reasonable to expect the IC to unravel it, but noting that Saddam's behavior was inexplicable might have sparked doubts and productive thought. The analysts displayed an unfortunate lack of curiosity here, in part because they were trained to work from the reports from the field rather than to be sensitive to generalizations that were apparently being violated.

Common but Misleading Explanations for the Failure

To proceed further, I will first outline and criticize the explanations that are commonly given for the intelligence failure, then turn to smaller but quite significant factors that were in fact at work, and finally focus on the most important reasons why the IC reached its conclusions.

Groupthink

One of SSCI's main conclusions is that the IC fell victim to groupthink.[24] Taken literally, this is simply incorrect. Groupthink is, as its name implies, a small-group phenomenon, with the driving motor being the posited tendency for tightly knit groups to seek the comfort and confidence that come from mutual agreement and approval.[25] Such an atmosphere leads people to refrain from disturbing the group consensus and even to shy away from disturbing thoughts. Intelligence on Iraq was not developed by small groups, however. A great deal of work was done by individuals working in relative isolation, and many of the groups were large and of a shifting composition.

Excessive Consensus

In fairness to SSCI, it is using the term "groupthink" in a colloquial rather than a technical sense. What is claimed to be at work are general pressures of conformity and mutual reinforcement. Once the belief that Iraq was developing WMD was established, there were few incentives to challenge it, and each person who held this view drew greater confidence from the fact that it was universally shared.

There is much to this, but it needs more careful scrutiny. The general consensus did not prevent vigorous disagreements on specific issues, especially over UAVs and the aluminum tubes, and individuals and agencies did not meekly go along with what others thought. More centrally, we need to probe the notions of conformity and consensus. In many cases, everyone believes the same thing because there are good reasons to do so, which is one reason why I suspect that cases of success are as likely to be characterized by high levels of agreement and mutual reinforcement as are cases of failure. Furthermore, the fact that several conscientious and intelligent people believe something is a valid reason for others to be ready to believe it. What needs to be avoided is unthinking conformity in which everyone quickly accepts conventional wisdom, thereby reinforcing and perpetuating it without further examination. In practice, however, it is not easy to separate justified from unjustified conformity, and while the latter may have been the case in Iraq, this has yet to be demonstrated.[26]

Failure to Challenge Assumptions

Parallel to the diagnosis of excessive conformity is the argument that assumptions were insufficiently examined. Thus according to SSCI, the NIE "suffers from a 'layering' effect whereby assessments were based on previous judgments without carrying forward the uncertainties."[27] This was especially true for the belief that Saddam's policy was consistent, coherent, and unchanging. He had used poison gas in the war with Iran, sought other WMD before the 1991 Persian Gulf War that followed his invasion of Kuwait, and afterward he had tried to continue them in the face of sanctions. The elements of his behavior, although distressing, fit together and embodied a comprehensible plan, and since Saddam was a dictator, there was every reason to expect the regime to be a unitary actor. In fact it now appears that Saddam did not have a coherent plan, his control was less than complete, and the regime was less than fully competent.[28] More important, almost everyone assumed that Saddam's behavior and plans remained relatively stable, whereas it now appears that in the 1990s he realized that he would not be able to develop robust WMD programs in the face of sanctions and inspections. As David Kay, first head of the postwar Iraq Survey Group, says, "One of the hardest things to do in the world of intelligence is to discern change.... When people's behavior has been consistent, you tend to predict the future based upon the past."[29] It appears that the IC never asked whether Saddam's approach had changed.

Although the impact of assumptions and beliefs is central to the explanation I will give later, the processes involved need to be understood rather than merely criticized. There is no such thing as "letting the facts speak for themselves" or drawing inferences without using beliefs about the world, and it is inevitable that the perception and interpretation of new information will be influenced by established ideas.[30] Indeed, many correct inferences about Iraq were based on strong assumptions, and it is impractical to reexamine all assumptions all the time. One wants to concentrate on assumptions that are not subject to dispute in the ordinary course of analysis, are central to the conclusions (what some in the IC call "linchpins"), and are amenable to sensible analysis. It now appears that intelligence needed to question whether the regime's refusal to cooperate with inspectors could have been explained by anything other than forbidden programs and whether its past use of chemicals and history of WMD programs explained what it was doing in 2002. While it is not quite correct to say that these assumptions were so deep that the analysts were not aware of them, they were never explicitly defended because they seemed obviously true and were widely shared. (It is worth noting that outside observers also failed to question these beliefs, which did not rest on classified information.)

It is difficult to specify ahead of time which assumptions should be reexamined, however. It would be challenging but worthwhile to try to specify these for current estimates, or for beliefs held by the academic community on any subject.

Politicization

The most prominent explanation for the WMD failure is that the IC bowed to pressures to tell the policymakers what they wanted to hear.[31] Although this view has been rejected by the official reports, most observers have endorsed it, partly because the reports themselves were written with an eye to political objectives. Indeed, this narrative so conforms to common sense that it has been a barrier to more careful thought. But, contrary to my initial impressions, I think the official reports are largely correct. Director of Central Intelligence (DCI) Tenet may have gotten too close to policymakers,[32] and everyone in the IC knew that the unfolding Iraq policy was premised on Iraq's having WMD, but it does not follow that analysis would have been markedly different had the political environment been different.

This is not to say that there was no politicization in the form of leaders giving inaccurate accounts about intelligence in order to garner political support. Most famously, the president said that the British reported that Saddam had sought uranium from Africa (true, but the implication that American intelligence agreed was not), the vice president and the secretary of defense said that there was solid evidence for connections between Iraq and al Qaeda, and many policymakers insisted that the WMD threat was "imminent." The intelligence community disagreed, and Tenet testified that he had privately rebuked the vice president for claims like these.[33] But this kind of twisting of evidence by policymakers is a substitute for politicization in that it was necessary only because the IC did not provide decision makers with the messages they wanted the public to believe.[34]

Officials also engaged in "cherry-picking" and "stovepiping." The former is highlighting reports that support the policy to the exclusion of contradictory ones that are more numerous and better established; the latter in this context refers to the delivery of selected bits of raw intelligence to policymakers, bypassing intelligence analysts who could critically evaluate them. These practices can be defended as within the prerogatives and even the duties of top officials to reach their own conclusions, but when used to justify policies to the public they incorrectly imply the backing of the intelligence community.

In some cases, the line between distortion and legitimate if questionable emphasis is hard to draw, as I will discuss further in chapter 4. The most striking case is Tony Blair's use of intelligence that Saddam could employ chemical weapons within forty-five minutes of deciding to do so.[35] He not only implied that the information was solid (blame on this point must be shared with British intelligence) but left the impression that these weapons could reach the entire region and so showed that Saddam was a great menace with evil intent. Blair omitted the crucial point that these were short-range battlefield weapons, which actually pointed to Saddam's *defensive* orientation because such readiness would have had value only as a safeguard against a swift attack on him.

Most central here, however, is the claim for politicization in the form of pressure on the IC to provide analysis that supports decisions. The head of Britain's MI6, Richard Dearlove, came back from a trip to Washington in July 2002 convinced that "Bush wanted to remove Saddam, through military action, justified by the conjunction of terrorism and WMD. But the intelligence and the facts were being fixed around the policy."[36] This often-repeated quotation at first seems to provide good evidence for politicization but on closer examination does not: it refers to intelligence on the links to al Qaeda, not to WMD programs. On the former topic, while some decision makers saw or claimed a link, the American IC did not, and on WMD British and American intelligence were in almost complete agreement. Dearlove could hardly have claimed that political pressures were being put on U.S. intelligence to reach a conclusion that the British felt was justified.

A second bit of testimony is the exchange between a member of SSCI's staff and Richard Kerr, who headed one of CIA's internal reviews:

> *Mr. Kerr:* "There's always people who are going to feel pressure in these situations and feel they were pushed upon."
> *Committee Interviewer:* "That's what we've heard. We can't find any of them, though."
> *Mr. Kerr:* "Maybe they are wiser than to come talk to you."[37]

A great line, but Kerr's own report does not stress this factor, and it appears that almost everyone involved in the estimates was interviewed by the investigating committees.[38] Another possibility, even harder to detect, is that dissenters and potential dissenters were taken off the Iraq case. Those who remained were not pressured or politicized, but the entire process was. The WMD Commission, although downplaying politicization as a central explanation, asserts that this happened, but its account is lacking in detail.[39]

I cannot dismiss these two claims, but while my confidential interviews with IC officials at several levels of the hierarchy did yield hints that some people were transferred, I did not find anyone attributing his or her errors to political pressure. Of course they might have felt that admitting to having given in was worse than having been honestly mistaken, and as I noted earlier, people are often unable to understand how they reached their judgments. As an analyst put it at the Senate hearings to confirm Robert Gates as DCI, "[P]oliticization is like fog. Though you cannot hold it in your hands, or nail it to a wall, it does exist, it is real, and it does affect people."[40] Indeed, what one person interprets as probing questions another will feel as pressure.

The crudest form of politicization is easy to dismiss: superiors did not change the papers coming up to make them conform to policy. Less direct forms are harder to judge, especially the subtle form of politicization in which the desire to avoid the painful value trade-off between pleasing policymakers and following professional standards created what psychologists call "motivated bias" in favor of producing estimates that would support, or at least not undermine, policy. Analysts come to believe what they say, but the ultimate cause is the political environment. This is not unusual. In Britain during the 1930s, even without explicit pressure, estimates of the balance of power with Germany shifted in the wake of policy shifts.[41] But on Iraq many of the incorrect beliefs formed before the issue became politically salient, and evidence that analysts and policymakers really believed that

Saddam had active and advanced programs is provided by the measures taken to protect the soldiers from WMD attacks and, even more, by the uniform surprise—indeed disbelief—in the IC over the results of the postwar search and the slow and grudging acceptance of the truth.[42]

Evidence from Comparisons

Better evidence may be provided by relevant comparisons. It appears that the belief that Iraq had active WMD programs was held by *all* intelligence services, even those of countries that opposed the war.[43] While this does not mean that the U.S. and U.K. ICs were not affected by the political atmosphere, it does show that they did not need political pressure to reach their conclusions. The failure of the commentaries to discuss this fact is an instance of how the neglect of standard social science methodology lowered the quality of the public understanding of the intelligence failure, just as it weakened contemporary intelligence.

Other comparisons are also important and neglected, most obviously the fact that on two key aspects of Iraq the American IC resisted strong administration pressures. Although not asked for its assessment, it warned that the aftermath of the invasion was not likely to be easy and that invading might increase support for terrorists, thereby contradicting the rosy picture painted by the administration and implicitly weakening the case for war.[44] Even more strikingly, although the IC did say there were "senior level contacts between Iraq and al-Qa'ida," it consistently denied that there was credible evidence of Saddam's role in 9/11, of a collaborative relation with bin Laden, or of a significant chance that Saddam would turn over WMD to al Qaeda. It held to this position in the face of administration statements to the contrary, repeated inquiries and challenges that can only be interpreted as pressure, and the formation of a unit in the Defense Department dedicated to finding such connections.[45] The administration's pressure was illegitimate, but the lack of success not only speaks to the integrity of the intelligence officials but also undermines the claim that the WMD analysis was biased by the desire to please. It is also interesting that intelligence judgments were more accurate when they cut against administration policy than when they were supportive, although this may be only a coincidence.

Comparing positions taken by different parts of the American IC also casts doubt on the politicization thesis. The State Department's INR was the most skeptical member of the community about nuclear weapons, and Air Force intelligence dissented on the UAVs, yet State and Defense were the two most policy-oriented agencies. The Department of Energy (DOE) dissented on the aluminum tubes, and there is no evidence that political pressure was exerted in response. In reply it can be argued that Secretary

Powell's standing permitted him to shield his intelligence officers (even as he rejected their arguments), and the fact that for much of the country intelligence is equated with CIA may have meant that the latter, perhaps because it was ostensibly removed from politics, in fact bore the brunt of the pressure.

A final comparison is with the Clinton-era estimates. There were differences, especially in the claim that Saddam had reconstituted his nuclear program, was increasing his stockpiles of chemical weapons, and definitely had mobile biological laboratories. But the latter possibility emerged in 2000 as detailed (but erroneous) reports started coming in, and indeed, it was in this period that CIA accepted the claim that Saddam had developed the ability to prepare and spread dried, and thus highly potent, biological agents.[46] The changes in the nuclear and chemical assessments also corresponded to new information, and the alarming and flawed analysis of the aluminum tubes, discussed in more detail below, began in the spring of 2001—i.e., before there was significant pressure on intelligence. Thus much of the gap between the Bush and Clinton estimates can be explained in terms of reports from the field, and the gap between the two sets of estimates is less than that which separated their conclusions from what we now believe to have been true.

This does not mean that political pressure had no role. At the very least, it created an atmosphere that was not conducive to critical analysis, encouraged excessive certainty, and eroded subtleties and nuances.[47] Analysts and intelligence managers knew that any suggestion that Saddam's capabilities were limited would immediately draw fire from their superiors. In this climate it would have been hard for anyone to reexamine the conventional wisdom. The vehemence and certainty with which the policymakers, especially Vice President Cheney, expressed themselves may also have had an impact. Thomas Ricks quotes a senior military intelligence official as saying, "When the vice-president stood up and said 'We are sure'—well, who are we to argue? With all the compartmentalization, there's a good chance that a guy that senior has seen stuff you haven't" (which actually was the case, although much of this information was incorrect).[48] It may well be that this kind of stance at the top would not inhibit analysts when they were sure of their judgments but would have an effect when they were less certain. At bottom, however, political pressures cannot explain the intelligence failure.

Politicization Late in the Day

Perhaps the best evidence of politicization has received little attention, probably because it was something that did not happen: the ICs did not make any reassessments once UN inspections (UNMOVIC, United Nations

Monitoring, Verification, and Inspection Commission) resumed and found no traces of WMD. One reason may be that analysts believed that UNMOVIC had not visited the right sites. The Butler report says that the inspectors had time to follow up only half the leads provided by the British government, and the United States may not have given them all the information it had, which meant that UNMOVIC's reports could not be definitive.[49] Nevertheless I think the Butler Commission was right to note that the lack of interest in what UNMOVIC found—or rather did not find—was "odd," and it is interesting that Tenet says little about this period in his memoirs.[50] Especially striking is the lack of reaction when UNMOVIC found nothing at what was supposed to be a key biological weapons facility and saw the aluminum tubes being used as parts of artillery rockets, although it is not clear how much detail the inspectors gave to CIA.[51]

I suspect that the explanation is that once people came to see that the United States and United Kingdom were committed to overthrowing Saddam, they understood that reevaluations would be unacceptable and stopped examining the evidence with much care.[52] This may be another reason for the insufficient scrutiny of Powell's UN speech, discussed more below. When an agent questioned the use of information in the speech from a key source named Curveball, his boss replied: "[L]et's keep in mind that this war's going to happen regardless of what Curveball said or didn't say, and that the Powers That Be probably aren't very interested in whether Curveball knows what he's talking about."[53] I think that different people and parts of the IC shut down at different times, depending largely on their assessments of the administration's commitment to war. When critics level the charge of politicization, they usually point to evidence in the winter of 2002–3 but imply that it characterized intelligence throughout.[54] The entire period should not be homogenized.

Specific Puzzles and Analytical Errors

If administration pressure and intelligence's desire to please do not explain the intelligence failure, then what does? The answer lies in a series of specific problems and errors and in a general factor that raises one of the fundamental dilemmas of intelligence.

Minor Problems and Missed Opportunities

Let me start with a few minor problems and puzzles. One is that each bit of evidence the IC used was ambiguous or impeachable, and yet together they formed the basis for far-reaching conclusions as each questionable account lent credence to the others. The IC is criticized for this, but the procedure may not be unwarranted. If Saddam was producing one kind of WMD, it was likely that he was producing others as well. Although some might have argued that different types of WMD could substitute for one another, it seemed more plausible that if he had programs, he would move ahead with all of them. Of course, evidence of nuclear activities did not prove that Curveball was correct about biological weapons, for example, but it did paint a picture in which his reports made a great deal of sense. If each report were worthless, the sum total of even a large number of them would still be zero, although listing them together would give them an air of credibility. But if each one of them had some probability of being correct, the fact that there were several did make the positive finding more reasonable (and it is not clear that all relevant pieces of information have been declassified).[55] Multiple pieces of information, each ambiguous in itself, can together provide quite convincing evidence. Thus it appears that Curveball's reporting led the analysts of the chemical program to increase and harden their estimates.[56] In retrospect this was a mistake, but as a study of how scientists came to accept the argument for global warming explains, "each story [about an aspect of the phenomenon], bizarre in itself, was made plausible by the others."[57] How we are to determine whether this procedure is justified in any particular case is a difficult question, but the IC erred in not being explicit, and perhaps not even aware, about the inference processes involved.[58]

One specific puzzle was overlooked at the time and later as well. This is that Hussein Kamel, Saddam's son-in-law who defected from Iraq in 1995 and provided a great deal of valuable information about Iraq's forbidden programs, told interviewers that the old chemical and biological material had been destroyed and that the programs were moribund. The version that reached the public, however, was that he had said that the programs were continuing. Indeed, for many outside observers this was a major reason for believing that Saddam was still vigorously pursuing WMD. There are two mysteries here. First, who spread the false reports and why were they not corrected? Bush's administration had an interest in maintaining the myth, but it is hard to see how Clinton's did. Second, why did the IC not pay more attention to Kamel's testimony? In retrospect his reports were very revealing and might have led intelligence to at least consider the possibility that Saddam no longer had active programs. In failing to raise this question, the postmortems fell victim to one of the analytical problems committed by the intelligence, that of ignoring nonevents. Kamel did not loom large in the assessments, and later critiques did not think the absence needed to be explained.[59] It does, but unfortunately I can only raise the question without being able to answer it.

Secretary Powell's speech to the Security Council was a missed opportunity to reexamine the evidence for Saddam's programs. It seemed quite persuasive to most observers at the time, in part because in keeping with Iraq's inept diplomacy, his arguments went unrebutted. But the speech was almost entirely fallacious.[60] As we have seen, some of the doubts did not reach the secretary and may not have reached the DCI and his top assistants, which raises questions of how the optimal flow of information can be established. The whole point of organizations is to compress and filter information, but crucial issues, uncertainties, and disagreements are supposed to reach the top. Here it appears that the disagreement about Curveball between analysts and some members of CIA's Directorate of Operations (DO) was slow to receive attention,[61] that until very late in the process no one understood that Curveball's information would be so central to the presentation, and even more strikingly that Tenet was not aware of the dispute about the uses to which the aluminum tubes could be put. Part of the reason for the clogged flows lay in the circumstances of the speech, which was designed not to provide a well-rounded summary of the evidence, let alone to reevaluate established conclusions, but rather to make the case for the prosecution. I suspect that another aspect of the context helps explain why Powell did not go over some of the IC's claims more carefully. Cheney's office supplied him with a draft that was filled with wild accusations that Powell had to spend significant time analyzing and rejecting. This exercise made the remaining claims look more reasonable and lowered the resistance to scrutinizing arguments that had garnered IC approval.

The writing of the NIE on Iraq's programs was an earlier opportunity for reassessment, but it was done in a great rush. In fact, neither the consumers in the executive branch nor the IC thought the document was needed because there had been such a steady and apparently clear stream of information, and it was only because Congress insisted that the NIE was produced. But as Tenet acknowledges, he should have called for this much earlier,[62] and had he done so it might have provided the occasion for stepping back from current reporting and asking critical questions. Given the political atmosphere and dominant beliefs, however, I doubt that the conclusions would have been much different.

Overlearning

In the Iraq case as in many others, the inferences people drew are explained in part by the lessons learned—and overlearned—from the past.[63] Recent and important events leave a deep imprint on people, especially when they have been proved wrong. They will be sure not to make the same mistake again but are likely to commit the opposite one. After the 1991 Gulf War the IC found to its dismay that it had greatly underestimated Saddam's WMD activities, partly because Iraq had deployed an extensive deception program. It was therefore especially vigilant, which meant it was unlikely to miss activities that were taking place but was primed to make more out of the information than it should have.[64]

Denial and Deception

Analysts knew that they were seeing less than a full WMD program. But this was easy to explain—and explain away—by Iraq's denial and deception campaign. The lessons of 1991 were reinforced by the experiences with the UN inspectors, which were clear and vivid. Iraqi officials would own up to activities only when confronted by direct evidence, and they did what they could to thwart the inspectors, including moving materials and records out the back door when the inspectors arrived at the front. Machinery would be hidden, even buried, and information was hard to come by. Analysts knew that the Iraqis had been trained by the Soviet Union, which had developed elaborate schemes and succeeded in concealing its biological warfare program from the West. So it made sense for intelligence to conclude that it was seeing only a fraction of the Iraqi program.

The problem was that the British and American ICs treated deception and denial as a given rather than as a hypothesis to be tested, and they never asked what information might indicate that activities were absent rather than being hidden. The ambiguous intercepted commands to military bases telling them to remove traces of WMD that Powell quoted in his UN speech were interpreted as evidence of continuing deception rather than as attempts to show that the programs had been abandoned, and overhead photography that appeared to contradict one of Curveball's crucial claims was "set aside" in the belief that it represented Iraqi deception.[65] Analysts then fell into a trap by not realizing that the proposition that much was being concealed, which was central to their conclusions, was only a proposition, not a fact, and one that did not rest on direct evidence such as a series of recent deceptions that had been unmasked. Neither did they appear to realize that their belief was essentially impossible to disconfirm.[66]

The very failure to detect concealment testified to its success, and nothing could make salient the possibility that there was little to be seen. Thus one CIA memo reported that "we have raised our collection posture in a bid to locate these [biological weapons] production units, but years of fruitless searches by UNSCOM [United Nations Special Commission] indicate they are well hidden," and when Saddam accepted renewed inspections in the fall of 2002, the IC assessed that he did so in part because he was confident in his ability to conceal his forbidden programs.[67]

Because deception is indeed common, there are no easy solutions. But what the ICs should have done was to flag the central and hard-to-confirm role of beliefs about Iraqi denial and deception, increase their efforts to penetrate it, and stress to policymakers that the projected activities could not be directly observed. The ICs could also have asked themselves what should be concluded if what they were seeing was not the tip of the iceberg but the bulk of it. Goethe famously said, "We are never deceived, we deceive ourselves." The irony here is that the United States and the United Kingdom deceived themselves into believing that Iraq was engaging in widespread deception. The final embarrassment was that when Secretary Powell came to this subject in his speech to the UN, he called his "colleagues' attention to the fine paper that the United Kingdom distributed yesterday which describes in exquisite detail Iraqi deception activities": it soon became clear that this paper had been plagiarized.[68]

HUMINT

Shortfalls of human sources of intelligence (HUMINT) contributed to the overestimate of deception and the WMD programs.[69] Most obviously, the amount of HUMINT was slight. It is not clear how many sources the Americans relied on; the British had five, none of whom claimed firsthand knowledge of the programs.[70] Compounding the problem, the IC did not realize how much depended on so few individuals, especially where biological weapons were concerned. Earlier the ICs had relied heavily on information from the UN inspectors, and when they were forced out in 1998, adequate sources were not developed to fill the gaps. It seems clear that insufficient attention was given to the problem throughout the 1990s, but as I noted in chapter 1, it is hard to say what reasonable expectations in this area should have been. The full-court press for HUMINT instituted to support the invasion produced a great deal of information, but much of it appears to have been wrong.[71]

A second problem was that even before then most of the HUMINT was misleading. These two points call to mind Woody Allen's famous line, "Such bad food, and small portions too." The best-known and perhaps most important source was Curveball, whose fabricated testimony convinced analysts that Iraq was using mobile laboratories to produce biological agents.[72] It turns out that although some of the other sources may have been accurate in relaying what they heard from others, little if any of the information was true. The most obvious explanation was that the sources had come through the Iraqi National Congress (INC), an organization that had an interest in leading people to believe that Saddam was vigorously pursuing WMD. But it now appears that the INC sources were discounted by the ICs, though not by the vice president's office, the civilians in the Defense Department, and the media. The reasons for the extent of the misinformation remain a mystery and probably vary from one source to another.[73] Without knowing other cases we cannot say whether the problems with HUMINT were unusually great here, but it is also worth noting that apparently no national service did much better than the others in cultivating human sources or separating truth from fiction.

The third difficulty, which contributed to the second, was that the analysts did not know enough about the sources they were relying on. The chain of transmission resembles the game of telephone, with room for distortion at each of many stages. Sources are loath to disclose all the details about the subsources who report to them; officers in the field rarely give a complete picture of their sources; Reports Officers in DO at CIA headquarters remove significant identifiers before passing the material to the analysts, as well as deciding what material is valuable enough to send on at all. The result is that analysts are given only a generic description of the source, and indeed one that can vary from one report to another, which in the Iraq case led the analysts to overestimate the number of different sources who were reporting.[74] This may explain why officials who vetted Secretary Powell's UN speech did not know that the important claim that the Iraqis were able to produce biological weapons in dried form (which were easy to disperse and highly lethal) was based on a single source. Even worse, in some cases analysts did not realize that the source being relied on was known to be a fabricator.[75] In other cases, the descriptions omitted important details about the source's specific expertise and access. Clearly it was not helpful for DO to describe Ambassador Joseph Wilson's reporting on the possibility that Saddam was seeking uranium from Niger as coming from "a contact with excellent access who does not have an established reporting record."[76] (This is not a new problem: in 1920 an official in the British Foreign Office said that "the value of a report is always increased by fifty per cent if we know exactly how the information was obtained.")[77]

There is even less transparency when the source is under the control of a foreign service, as was the case with Curveball. German intelligence kept him to themselves, arguing incorrectly that he did not speak English and was anti-American, and the only direct contact was a single meeting with an American who came away skeptical about Curveball's reliability.[78] Unfortunately, the fact that the Americans found his information of such interest may have increased the stake that Curveball's German handlers had in him and reduced their incentives to examine him critically.[79] Furthermore, his information flowed through the Defense Intelligence Agency (DIA), which was unwilling or unable to push the Germans for information about him or to conduct an independent evaluation. There were language problems as well since Curveball spoke little German, and the American analysts received not transcripts but only DIA's summaries of the summaries that the German service provided.

There were major problems with DO's role as well. Only in late 2002 did DO begin to vet Curveball by looking at his behavior, credentials, and consistency, and only at the last minute did the skeptics confront the analysts.[80]

It remains unclear why DO did not become involved earlier, and this was an important source of error because this was the section of the organization with the most expertise in spotting fabricators. Part of the reason seems to have been that because Curveball was a German asset and his reports came through DIA, DO felt that it had little responsibility for him, and some DO Reports Officers apparently believed that the analysts were in the best position to validate the source by determining whether the information fit with other evidence at their disposal. Not only did many analysts fail to understand this, but the danger of circularity was heightened by this approach, as the fact that information fits with prevailing views will validate the source, and the reliability of the source will lend credence to the information. This kind of thinking may explain why insufficient attention was paid to the possibility that Curveball's information fit so well with what was known because he had searched the Internet for it.[81]

It is clear that the paucity of HUMINT was a major cause of the Iraq debacle. But the quality of information is more important than its quantity. When dealing with WMD capabilities, let alone with the country's intentions, the number of potential informants may be small. Furthermore, even if vetting is done much better, it will remain more an art than a science and will produce both false positives and false negatives. Indeed, for this reason HUMINT is generally suspect, and it seems to have been given unusual credence in this case only because little else was available. HUMINT then contributed greatly to the failure, and it is ironic, although not necessarily foolish, that the common prescription was to gain more of it.

The Puzzle of the Aluminum Tubes and Uranium from Africa

The bitter and prolonged battle over whether Iraq's purchase of aluminum tubes showed that it was reconstituting its nuclear program revealed several IC errors.[82] The issue was the focus of intense concern because if the tubes could be used only for uranium enrichment, their acquisition would unambiguously point to a nuclear program. But partly because the discussion was not well structured, people sometimes talked past one another, blurring the claim that the tubes could have been used for uranium enrichment and the much stronger argument that Iraq had procured them for this purpose.[83] The evidence for the former was stronger (although still weak), but what made the most impact was the even less substantiated inference that the tubes were uniquely suited for enrichment.

Five factors contributed to the incorrect analysis. First, one of the grounds on which the 1998 Rumsfeld Commission had faulted the IC's estimates of adversaries' missile programs was that it had assumed that those countries could not alter products that were ostensibly purchased for other uses. For both intellectual and political reasons, the IC took this lesson to heart.[84] Second, the Army's National Ground Intelligence Center (NGIC) argued that "the tubes were, technically speaking, poor choices for rocket bodies," which we now know was their true use.[85] For reasons that are still unclear, NGIC, which presumably had great expertise in this area, missed the Italian rockets that served as the model for the Iraqis.[86] This error was highly consequential because it meant that those who doubted that the tubes were intended for enrichment could not mount a credible alternative account. Third, there was a history of strong disagreement between CIA and DOE about centrifuges dating back a decade or more, something that was both a cause and a product of bad feelings among the individuals involved. Because of this background, the interagency group designed to rule on such matters never did so. Although the debate was fierce, it was not conducted in a forum that might have produced, if not agreement, then at least a shared understanding of where the differences lay. The IC's leadership failed to either revive the interagency group or develop a substitute for it.

Fourth, although DOE dissented from the judgment that the tubes were designed for enrichment, it agreed that Iraq was reconstituting its nuclear program. DOE's analysts must have believed that Iraq was developing weapons through some other, unspecified, route, but their reasoning was not queried when the NIE was being written because for the task at hand all that was crucial was the conclusion that Iraq was reconstituting. This was what was of most concern to the policymakers, and there seemed to be no point in exploring why DOE disagreed on the tubes but agreed with the conclusion. In fact, it would have been worth learning whether the rest of the IC felt that DOE's analysis of how Iraq could develop weapons without the tubes had merit because, if it did not, there would have been more reason to question the conclusion. Although how DOE reached its judgment remains unclear, my discussions indicate that its analysts may have believed that Saddam was seeking uranium from Africa, a conclusion that was tenable because a technical failure led to their not receiving the cable from CIA that discredited these claims. Furthermore, the communication channels within DOE were clogged, in part because segments of it were scattered around the country, and the views of their experts were not always well represented at high-level meetings.[87]

The fifth problem, although in some sense accidentally, is related to a recurring one. Immediately after gaining access to the tubes, the lead CIA analyst concluded that they were designed for a centrifuge. Since he had a background in the enrichment industry, his opinion carried great weight. His superiors were then quick not only to endorse his conclusions but to convey them to policymakers, and even put them into the PDB, before other agencies had a chance to analyze the material and reach a different verdict. Although the NIE acknowledged the disagreement and uncertainties, CIA could not easily give up its established position.[88] The effect of this error was magnified by the fact that the DCI was the head of the CIA as well as the IC. In the latter capacity he was supposed to arbitrate differences among the intelligence agencies, but as director of CIA, Tenet was closer to CIA analysts than to those from other parts of the IC. The dissents from INR and DOE therefore received less of a hearing than they might have in a similar situation today, when there is a Director of National Intelligence. Indeed, it appears that Tenet did not even know that there was a dispute until the NIE was being written, a stunning failure that presumably is to be explained not only by the press of other business but also by the fact that he was physically, politically, and psychologically at some distance from analysts outside CIA.

The intelligence system then operated to push the organization as a whole as well as the individual CIA analyst into the common trap of premature cognitive closure. When General Tommy Franks was designing a force for the war in Iraq that would be quick and agile, he said that "speed kills"; unfortunately speed can also kill good judgment. In retrospect, it would have been better to have waited, to have kept the information about the tubes from policymakers until a full IC evaluation. But it is rarely possible to do this on a pressing issue. Policymakers want to be informed immediately, and the incentives are for every individual and agency to move as quickly as possible. If one group holds back, the result is less likely to be a fruitful period of deliberation than another group's taking its message forward, and few things are worse for a subordinate than having the boss ask why he or she had to hear the news from another policymaker. So while the error here was a significant one, it is unlikely that the proper process can be followed in most cases.[89]

This may be the appropriate place to note that the issue of whether Saddam was seeking uranium from Africa was less important in the intelligence at the time than it became after the president's mention of it in his 2003 State of the Union Address, Ambassador Joseph Wilson's op-ed piece claiming the White House had ignored his negative report, the associated leaks about the role of his spouse in sending him on the mission, and the conviction of Vice President Cheney's chief of staff, Lewis "Scooter" Libby, for perjury and obstruction of justice in denying the White House's role in trying to discredit Wilson.[90] Except for the unfortunate case of DOE just discussed, the IC placed little faith in reports that Saddam was seeking uranium (he had quite a bit stockpiled) and even less in the forged letter acquired in Italy saying that he was. (British intelligence did believe that Saddam was making such efforts and still holds to this conclusion. It has not made public the underlying evidence or even shared it with the United States.) While Ambassador Wilson's reporting reinforced IC doubts, it had little impact because there was a great deal of skepticism to begin with.

This may be why CIA failed to tell the vice president what Wilson had concluded or even that he had made the trip despite the fact that Cheney had flagged an earlier report on the subject. Indeed, Wilson's trip was not even deemed important enough to tell Tenet about.[91] In a further irony, this means that when Wilson's op-ed appeared with its implication that the White House had ignored evidence that disagreed with its position, all the White House had to do was to tell the truth and explain that it did not know that Wilson had been sent and did not receive a copy of his report and that if there was any blame, it was with CIA's failure to pass the information on. At the start it took this tack, but it soon reverted to its standard procedure of seeking to discredit critics instead of meeting their arguments.

Empathy and Context

In parallel with many other cases, the failure to understand Iraq has been attributed to a lack of area knowledge and empathy. It is true that few members of the IC spoke Arabic, had lived in Iraq, or were familiar with the country's culture. But we need some cautionary notes here, starting with the fact that the countries in the region had reached the same basic conclusions that the West did. Furthermore, even though knowledge was limited in the United States and United Kingdom, their ICs were not without empathy. They did try to see the world through Saddam's eyes and so believed that he had great incentives to get WMD (which was correct) and that he viewed the United States as the main enemy (which was not). The attempt to empathize may have made it more difficult to understand how little information reached Saddam, how isolated he was from even his inner circle, and how corrupt his regime had become. Nevertheless, three aspects of the limits on empathy are relevant, including an especially troubling one that brings us to the heart of the failure.

First, intelligence failed to sufficiently integrate technical and political analysis. Most estimates of Iraq's WMD programs were supervised by the NIOs for the relevant weapons and drew most heavily on the Weapons Intelligence, Nonproliferation, and Arms Control (WINPAC) division of CIA. Regional analysts were involved but were not central, which meant that questions of Iraqi WMD capabilities were not treated in the context of Saddam's political system, fears, and intentions.[92] I doubt that this was an exceptional case. The division of labor and caution that characterizes large organizations like CIA is more conducive to studying trees than forests, and combining political and technical considerations is difficult in any context and is rarely done well anywhere. Furthermore, to return to one of my dismal themes, it is unlikely that greater integration would have produced the correct answer. Indeed, in some ways the analysts not only implicitly took account of the political context but overweighted it. It was less the specific signs of WMD activity that led them to conclude that Saddam had active programs than their implicit sense of his political objectives and outlook.

Second, here as elsewhere, analysis assumed that foreign actors were rational as Americans understand rationality. Empathizing with confusion, improvisation, and corruption is rare and difficult. As Douglas Ford explains, during World War II the United Kingdom never was able to understand Japanese "long-term plans and the [strength of the military] opposition to be encountered [in Burma] owing to the Japanese high command's failure to devise a coherent strategy."[93] The strategy that Saddam's Iraq followed was similarly incoherent, and it is not surprising the ICs had great trouble discerning it.

Third, and central to the Iraq case, empathy is difficult when the other's beliefs and behavior are strange and self-defeating. As I will discuss further in the next chapter, many intelligence failures are then bilateral in that one state is taken by surprise because it is unable to anticipate the other's intelligence failure, as the quote from Sherman Kent at the head of chapter 1 indicates. This was true in Iraq. It is particularly difficult for analysts to get it right when the truth is implausible, and the role of plausibility is central to this and many other cases.

The Importance of Plausibility

The fundamental reason for the WMD intelligence failure in Iraq was that the inferences were very plausible, much more so than the alternatives. Saddam had vigorously pursued WMD in the past, had used chemical weapons to good effect, had powerful incentives to rebuild his programs, had funds, skilled technicians, and a good procurement network at his disposal, and had no other apparent reason to deceive and hinder the inspectors. The UNSCOM inspectors, who provided so much information to U.S. and British intelligence, had left a vivid impression of Saddam's commitment to his WMD programs. Important also were beliefs that extended beyond Iraq. According to INR's biological weapons specialist, one reason why the IC was quick to accept the evidence that Iraq was developing mobile labs was that "the U.S. BW [biological warfare] analysts generally think that BW programs historically have shifted [away] from large-scale fixed facilities."[94]

There are other indications that plausibility played a central role in the inferences, starting with the fact that other countries, who had different bits of specific information than did the United States and the United Kingdom, reached the same general conclusion, although perhaps with less confidence. Differences in inferences within the U.S. IC are also better explained by different views of what was likely rather than by different information. Thus while INR is to be praised for rejecting the reports that Iraq was making a serious effort to buy uranium from Niger, the explanation is not that their analysts read the evidence more carefully but that they found the whole idea implausible because Iraq would not "risk such a transaction when they were 'bound to be caught.'" In the same way, those in Air Force intelligence who dissented from the judgment that the procurement of mapping software covering the United States meant that Iraq might be planning to use UAVs against the American homeland did so "because they did not believe that the UAVs were intended for CBW [chemical and biological weapons] delivery use and, therefore, Iraq would have no need to use the UAVs in the U.S."[95] For the majority, the inference that the UAVs were being configured to deliver chemical and biological agents was made compelling by the fact that this had been Iraq's intent in the past, although these analysts probably failed to understand that the history weighed on them so heavily.[96] In this light it is not surprising that CIA analysts (rightly) inferred that there was no close and collaborative relationship between al Qaeda and Iraq since such ties did not fit with how they believed the regime saw its self-interest. While information pointing to a connection was unreliable, there were enough scattered reports that someone who had a different reading of the regime could have placed more faith in them, as the vice president and many civilians in the Defense Department did.[97] In fact, because of differences in background beliefs, terrorism analysts in the IC were more prone to see links than were those with regional expertise.[98]

For all groups, it did not make sense that Saddam had nothing to hide. If before the war someone had produced studies of Iraq like the postwar Duelfer Report or the parallel analysis by Woods and his colleagues, they would no doubt have been praised as imaginative but would not have come close to persuading. Who would have believed that the reason why Saddam's scientists would not account for much of the missing anthrax was that they feared his anger if he learned that they had dumped it near one of his palaces? Did it make any sense that "by late 2002 Saddam had persuaded himself... that the United States would not attack Iraq because it already had achieved its objectives of establishing a military presence in the region," that private meetings between the inspectors and scientists were resisted because "any such meeting with foreigners was seen as a threat to the security of the Regime," and that "Iraq did not want to declare anything that documented use of chemical weapons [in the war with Iran] for fear the documentation could be used against Iraq in lawsuits"?[99] A bit more understandably, Saddam feared that unlimited inspections would allow the United States to pinpoint his location and assassinate him, and we can now see that the combination of fear, incompetence, and corruption explains many of the suspicious ways in which equipment was purchased.[100] Thus one reason why the aluminum tubes had such precise specifications was that the Iraqi engineers needed to compensate for problems that could not be addressed more directly because that would have involved quarreling with one of Saddam's cronies who was in charge of the rocket program.[101]

More generally, Duelfer and Woods tell us that Saddam sought to maintain the appearance of WMD in order to keep power at home and deter Iran. The United States was a secondary concern. Indeed, Saddam told a postwar interrogator that while he opposed American policies, he did not consider the United States an enemy![102] It appears that he hoped first to end sanctions and inspections and then to reconstitute his programs, all the while keeping his real and perceived adversaries at bay. "This led to a difficult balancing act between the need to disarm to achieve sanctions relief while at the same time retaining a strategic deterrent. The Regime never resolved the contradiction inherent in this approach."[103] This is putting it mildly. The sanctions regime might decay over time but (especially after 9/11) would be lifted only if he showed that he had abandoned his WMD programs. Even in retrospect, it is hard to understand the priority he placed on maintaining his WMD bluff: the fear of such weapons could not prevent an American attack, and Iran was hardly spoiling for a fight and in any event could not have assumed that the West would stand aside while it greatly increased its influence by moving against Iraq. Furthermore, even if nuclear weapons would deter Iran, it is hard to see how a nuclear *program* could do so. Saddam's policy, then, was foolish and self-defeating, and this goes a long way to explaining the intelligence failure. When the situation is this bizarre, it is not likely to be understood.

In many previous cases behavior that was puzzling comes into focus when one understands the other's situation and strategy. Thus the United States and Israel were surprised by Egypt's attack in 1973 because they failed to appreciate that Egyptian president Anwar Sadat thought that what was needed was not a massive military victory but enough of an effort to convince Israel that the status quo was untenable and to bring in the United States as a broker. Here empathy would have been difficult but not out of the question.[104] In other cases the adversary's plans and perspectives are hard to grasp because they are a product of motivated bias—i.e., the adversary has come to believe quite improbable things because doing so meets pressing political and psychological needs. Although this layer is hard to penetrate, in many cases this can be done. But Saddam's behavior was even harder to understand, even with the information now at our disposal. While it is true that rampant corruption and fear of coups and of a neighbor with whom he had fought an eight-year war should not have seemed so unlikely, the way Saddam's regime functioned and how he saw the world were outside the normal range and particularly hard to understand.

The claim that the contemporary inferences made a great deal of sense is contrary to most discussions of the failure, although it is hinted at by the WMD Commission and the Butler Report. Such a conclusion is politically unacceptable to most people, who want to believe that such a gross misjudgment must stem from flagrant and correctable errors. As I will discuss further in chapter 4, few members of the elite have incentives to understand either the utility or the limits of intelligence, and it is frustrating to believe that incorrect conclusions may be warranted. In this case, even if there had been no errors in tradecraft, I believe that the analysts would *and should* have judged that Saddam seemed to be actively pursuing all kinds of WMD and probably had some on hand.[105] The assessment should have been expressed with much less certainty, the limitations on direct evidence should have been stressed, and the grounds for reaching the conclusion should have been explicated. But while it would be comforting to believe that better analysis would have led to a fundamentally different conclusion, I do not think this is the case.

This does not mean that the analysis was as good as it should have been. The central analytical error was not that inferences were driven by their plausibility as established by previous Iraqi behavior and the sense they made of what Saddam appeared to be doing but that the analysts did not make this clear, in part because they did not understand their own thinking. The ICs should have tried to separate the role of plausibility from the impact of the specific reports, and they should have done more to understand and communicate how they reached their final judgments.[106] This also helps explain what SSCI means when it says that many IC conclusions were "not supported by the intelligence" and instead were the products of "analytical judgments."[107] This is correct but is misguided in implying that the latter are somehow illegitimate—in fact, they are the bread and butter of intelligence analysis. Direct reports that are valid and unambiguous are rare. To tell the IC to shy away from analytical judgments would be to condemn it to silence, just as a similar prescription for science would stymie any comprehension of our world. Deductions and indirect inference are central to the enterprise of understanding. The real problem was that the ICs and policymakers were unaware of the extent to which the conclusions rested on these kinds of judgments.

To say that inferences are drawn because they are plausible may seem circular, but it is not. The point is that the interpretation of individual bits of information depended less on their content than on more general ideas and images that were off the paper. Analyses of the aluminum tubes and the mobile biological weapons laboratories rarely mentioned Saddam's previous behavior or his refusal to cooperate with inspectors. These were well known and could also be seen as irrelevant to the narrower task at hand, but in fact they were crucial in predisposing people to seeing the new evidence as pointing to active WMD programs. Thus if the reports about removing all traces of WMD that Secretary Powell quoted in his UN speech had been received about Canada, very different inferences would have been drawn, and with good reason.[108] Intelligence strives to follow the scientific method, and every day scientists see results that contradict basic scientific laws, which they react to not by rushing to publish but by throwing out the data because they know that it cannot be right.[109]

Of course, in science as in intelligence, being strongly influenced by plausibility can be criticized as being closed-minded or assumption-driven. But this is a powerful and legitimate habit of the mind, necessary for making sense of a complex and contradictory world, and although it was responsible for the WMD failure, most of the inferences it produces are right. Richard Betts makes the important point that while the implicit theories of the world that we bring to cases usually are correct and most of the time we are better off being guided by them rather than adopting exotic alternatives, we will be misled and surprised when the other's behavior is extraordinary.[110] If we are more imaginative in the latter cases, we may get them right; but if we are generally more imaginative, we will be wrong in many standard cases. Of course, what we want is a way of determining when the normal patterns will hold and when they will not, and perhaps this is the main task of intelligence. But without some magic key, we must live with the conundrum that many of the same ways of thinking that produce an accurate picture of normal behavior will fail when the country or situation is odd.

For the IC to have explained more carefully why judgments were reached would have had multiple benefits, however. It would have alerted consumers to trains of reasoning that they could question; it would have told consumers and analysts what evidence, direct and indirect, was being relied on; it would have sensitized analysts to instances in which they not only see evidence as consistent with established views because of the latter's plausibility but take this evidence as an independent reason to accept these views. This bootstrapping is a form of circular thinking that leads to excessive confidence, as I will discuss further in the next chapter. For example, the only reason why the analysts were impressed by the admission of Iraq officials that they had considered (but rejected) the idea of producing BW in trucks was that they expected this kind of activity.[111]

Confirmation Bias, Negative Evidence, and the Comparative Method

Related to the analysts' failure to understand the role of plausibility was their falling victim to the propensity for people to seek information that confirms their beliefs and to fail to see the significance of evidence whose absence is diagnostic.[112] In early 2002, CIA agents around the world were told to seek information about Iraq's WMD programs. This made sense but inadvertently was dangerous because asking people to be on the lookout for something increases the chance that they will find it whether it is there or not. During World War II, British intelligence understood this trap, and when it received preliminary reports about a new German weapon, it was careful to phrase inquiries to other agents in neutral terms that did not disclose what it believed the Germans might be developing. It appears that CIA did not take this precaution.[113]

Even more strikingly, intelligence failed to see the significance of the lack of confirming information where there was reason to expect it to be present. "Absence of evidence is not evidence of absence," Secretary of Defense Rumsfeld tells us.[114] Like many mantras, there is quite a bit to this, but it disguises quite a bit as well. There are indeed numerous cases in which an adversary's action or capabilities were not preceded by any detectable signs, and it is chastening to note that for years the West was unaware that the USSR—and then Russia—continued BW programs despite having signed a treaty banning them and that Albania's chemical weapons program went undetected.[115] But presumably even Rumsfeld would acknowledge that absence of evidence can be significant. If it were not, one would have to argue that lacking positive evidence that a country is not pursuing WMD (and it is not clear what this could be), we should assume that it is.[116]

It was rare for negative information to be solicited, reported, or noticed, however. CIA officers were not likely to press their sources on what they did *not* see or for the field to report that various sources did *not* have any information that Saddam was actively pursuing WMD even if these people were well placed. Had such messages come in, I doubt that they would have been passed on to the analysts, and it appears that any negative reports that made their way to the analysts stopped there instead of being reflected in finished intelligence. The fact, glaringly significant in retrospect, that the increased collection efforts yielded little was not considered noteworthy.[117] Similarly, in the debate over whether Saddam had meaningful links to al Qaeda, no one seems to have noticed that he never opened an embassy in Kabul after the Taliban took power.[118] By its nature, positive evidence is much more striking than its absence, and vivid information has an impact out of proportion to its diagnostic content because it stands out. Negative evidence and things that do not happen tend to be overlooked. Often they should not be, and it is disturbing but not surprising that the IC found it hard to comply with SSCI's request that it turn over this kind of evidence because there is no simple way to retrieve it from memory or files.[119]

What the IC failed to appreciate was that instances in which specified behavior does not occur or evidence is absent are highly significant *if* this contradicts an important proposition or argument. Political scientists refer to this kind of evidence as "dogs that do not bark," borrowing a concept from Sherlock Holmes, who realized that the dogs' failure to bark on the night of the crime showed that the perpetrator was an acquaintance. It is not that negative evidence and events that do not occur are automatically or uniformly important; their significance arises when the claim under consideration implies that they *should* be present. A heightened awareness of this logic and the attendant research design of focusing on negative cases have greatly improved social science over the past decade. But intelligence (and the postmortems as well) did not see this, just as Watson, Holmes's assistant, did not, even though he was very smart. What is required in such a case is thinking in a counterintuitive way that comes from an explicit consideration of the hypothetico-deductive method. We move naturally from evidence to inference, but it takes greater self-consciousness to see that testing our propositions requires us to ask what events should occur and what evidence should be observable if a particular argument or explanation is correct.[120]

In the Iraq case, doing so would have helped in four ways. First, an explicit focus on the importance of negative information could have restrained the confirmation bias in collection. Headquarters in both the United States and the United Kingdom could have instructed their agents to look for and report not only what sources were claiming they knew about WMD activities but also cases in which people who might have known about them if they were occurring in fact saw nothing. Second and relatedly, sensitivity to absence could have corrected for the propensity to note only corroborating facts. Thus although intelligence pointed to the use of code words as evidence that some activities were likely to be related to BW, it appears to have missed the fact that code words were *not* used to "conceal acquisition of BW-related equipment, and impair Western measures to monitor Iraqi technology acquisition."[121] Third, if the IC had asked, "If Iraq has reconstituted its nuclear and biological programs, what would it have to do?" inquiry might have been pointed to areas that should have been probed more deeply, such as the lack of evidence that Iraq was seeking centrifuge components other than tubes and the absence of safety measures that would have been expected to accompany mobile facilities that were manufacturing biological weapons.[122] Fourth, the ICs would have had to think harder about the meaning of the negative results from the major effort to probe relevant Iraqi scientists around the world (and even in Iraq itself). Of course these people could have been lying or the WMD programs could have been run by a network that was unknown to the ICs, but proper methodology would have meant that these claims would have been made explicitly and that the negative evidence would have been discussed in the NIE.

Analysts similarly did not utilize the standard social science comparative method to probe either the significance of specific bits of information or the relative validity of alternative explanations. They failed to realize that some evidence that was consistent with their interpretation was consistent with other views as well. Indeed, analysts often seemed to incorrectly assume that anything that fit with their views contradicted the alternatives, which meant that they were engaging in bootstrapping. For example, Iraq's use of fronts and other surreptitious means of obtaining dual-use material was taken as evidence that it was pursuing forbidden programs. While this inference was consistent with the behavior, it neglected "the fact that Iraq typically used front companies and evaded UN sanctions for imports of purely legitimate goods." More specifically, the majority of the IC believed that the fact that Iraq used intermediaries to procure the aluminum tubes meant that they were intended for uranium enrichment. But, as DOE noted at the time, Security Council resolutions prohibited Iraq from importing such material for conventional military uses, which meant that the behavior did not discriminate between the two main hypotheses.[123] More generally, because it was believed that Saddam had active programs, multiple bits of evidence were seen within this frame without much consideration of alternatives that could have been the explanation—and in retrospect were. Thus many analysts saw the presence of special tanker trucks at suspicious sites as indicating chemical weapons without considering that they were likely to be deployed around conventional munitions, which also pose safety risks, or even to be deployed for routine activities.[124] While the analysts were correct to infer from the fact that these trucks had been associated with chemical weapons during the Gulf War that they would likely accompany the movement of chemicals thereafter, they failed to consider that the trucks might be put to other uses as well. Indeed, if the Iraqis were not producing chemical weapons, they would need to find some other ways to employ them.

An Alternative—Individuals, Not the System

Intelligence on Iraq is rightly criticized for not considering alternatives, and so I would like to note one, which is that the failure contained a significant element of randomness or accident. The most dramatic and I think significant elements of the Iraqi assessment concerned the nuclear program and, to a slightly lesser extent, biological weapons. As I noted earlier, each positive finding reinforced the others, and we now know that they all rested on slight and insecure foundations. But what is particularly interesting is that the nuclear and BW conclusions were strongly influenced by particular individuals. This is most obvious in the case of BW, for which Curveball was crucial. Had he not appeared on the scene, the IC almost certainly would have assessed that while the regime was pursuing the ability to make BW, little could be said about the scope of the program or the existence of stockpiles. The resulting judgment, while not being entirely accurate or completely reassuring, would have been closer to the truth and less alarming.

In the case of the nuclear program, the individual involved was not an Iraqi source but a CIA analyst. As I noted, the assessments of the CIA and the wider IC were strongly driven by the view of one person who quickly concluded that the tubes were designed for uranium enrichment. Had others within CIA been technically qualified to challenge him or had a different individual been in this position, CIA probably would have taken a less definitive and extreme position on the tubes, and the final assessment of the nuclear program would have been much less certain and less worrisome, probably along the lines of the one that INR made in the actual case—i.e., that while the evidence did not rule out the possibility that Iraq was reconstituting its nuclear program, neither could it support the conclusion that it was.

In this hypothetical world, decision makers would still have been able to exaggerate the intelligence to justify the war, and so perhaps the policy outcome would have been the same. But the intelligence failure itself would have been of a much lesser magnitude. Viewed in this light, the reason for the dramatic nature of the failure, lay not in fundamental flaws in the IC but in an unfortunate appearance of two individuals at key times and places.

There is quite a bit to this, and these individuals did have great impact. But intelligence should be able to cope with such problems, and the case still illustrates serious flaws in the system and does not, I believe, disturb my arguments that the prevailing methodologies were deficient and that the assessment was driven by plausibility, something neither the analysts nor the consumers realized.

Conclusion

It would be comforting to believe that feasible reforms could avoid false conclusions like the finding that Iraq had active WMD programs. This is indeed the implication of many of the critics of the IC's performance, especially the Senate Select Committee on Intelligence.[125] Even the more discerning reports leave the impression that some (unspecified) alternative fit the evidence better than the IC's assessments. To have admitted that although errors were made and the process could be improved, appropriate procedures would not have led to the correct judgment not only would have been met with incredulity but would have defeated the political purposes and undercut the recommendations. The main explanation provided by most journalistic accounts is political pressure, a view rejected by the official reports. I think the reports are correct in this regard, but they share a fundamental weakness with the intelligence analysis in neglecting social science procedures. Thus both intelligence on Iraq and the postmortems fail to use the comparative method, ignore the power of asking what evidence should be seen if alternative accounts of the reality being described are correct, neglect the importance of negative evidence, and do not probe the psychology that lay behind many of the inferences, both correct and incorrect.

In retrospect, the most reasonable assessment would have been that Iraq probably (but not certainly) had active and broadly based WMD programs and a small stockpile of chemical and perhaps biological weapons. A responsible judgment could not have been that the programs had ceased. It would have noted the wide band of uncertainty and indicated that much of the support for the conclusion came from the plausibility generated by Iraq's previous behavior rather than from specific bits of evidence about the current programs. This would not have made policymakers' lives or decisions easier and would not have been happily received, but it would have been truer to the evidence.

The official reports and other commentaries are right to find fault, and better analysis would have highlighted the central role of assumptions, preexisting beliefs, and implicit views of Saddam's goals and outlook. By doing so, it would have facilitated their reexamination, although it probably would not have changed them. Carl Sagan reminds us that "extraordinary claims require extraordinary evidence," and by the mid-1990s the claim that Saddam was actively pursuing WMD was ordinary and therefore did not require extensive evidence to be confirmed. Indeed, by this point, it would have required extraordinary evidence to call this claim into question. This makes sense of the exchange in which Bush reacted to CIA's presentation of what could be declassified to convince the public that Saddam was developing WMD by asking if "this is the best we've got" and receiving Tenet's infamous reply, "Why, it's a slam-dunk!"[126] Bush was focusing on the specific evidence he had just heard; Tenet was moved by the plausibility of the entire picture.

If the ICs had done a better job, they would have been more sensitive to the paucity of direct evidence and would have been less certain in their conclusions. They would have been closer to the truth, which of course is to be applauded. But policymakers would not have applauded. Even had they not wanted to believe that Saddam had active programs in order to bolster their desire to overthrow him, they would not have been likely to welcome uncertainty. Although decision makers call for better intelligence, under many circumstances they do not want it, a topic to which I will turn in the next chapter.

[4]

The Politics and Psychology of Intelligence and Intelligence Reform

Estimating is what you do when you do not know.

—Sherman Kent, chair of CIA's Board of National Estimates

In judging the performance of any intelligence organization we need first to come to a realistic understanding of the limits to intelligence.

—Sir Percy Cradock,
chairman of the UK Joint Intelligence Committee

There is nothing a Government hates more than to be well-informed; for it makes the process of arriving at decisions much more complicated and difficult.

—John Maynard Keynes

Let me tell you about these intelligence guys. When I was growing up in Texas, we had a cow named Bessie. I'd go out early and milk her. I'd get her in the stanchion, seat myself and squeeze out a pail of fresh milk. One day I'd worked hard and gotten a full pail of milk, but I wasn't paying attention, and old Bessie swung her shit-smeared tail through the bucket of milk. Now, you know that's what these intelligence guys do. You work hard and get a good program or policy going, and they swing a shit-smeared tail through it.

—Lyndon Johnson

Kent's statement is in his "Estimates and Influences," *Studies in Intelligence*, Summer 1968, reprinted in *Sherman Kent and the Board of National Estimates: Collected Essays*, ed. Donald Steury (Washington, DC: CIA Center for the Study of Intelligence, 1994), p. 35; Cradock's statement is from Percy Cradock, *Know Your Enemy: How the Joint Intelligence Committee Saw the World* (London: John Murray, 2002), p. 290; Keynes is quoted in Robert Skidelsky, *John Maynard Keynes: The Economist as Saviour 1920–37* (London: Macmillan, 1992), p. 630; Johnson is quoted in Robert Gates, "An Opportunity Unfulfilled: The Use and Perceptions of Intelligence at the White House," *Washington Quarterly*, vol. 12, Winter 1989, p. 42.

INTELLIGENCE AND POLICYMAKERS

These four quotations summarize the insoluble dilemmas of intelligence and policymaking. Many of the sources of intelligence errors have been outlined in the previous chapters, but a fuller picture requires more explicit treatment of why intelligence is so hard and what improvements and reforms are possible. We should start by considering the pressures on decision makers who consume intelligence and drive much of the process, and the conflicts with intelligence that result.

Policymakers say they need and want good intelligence. They do need it, but often they do not like it. They are also prone to believe that when intelligence is not out to get them, it is incompetent. Richard Nixon was only the most vocal of presidents in wondering how "those clowns out at Langley" could misunderstand so much of the world and cause his administration so much trouble.[1] Unfortunately, not only will even the best intelligence services often be wrong, but even (or especially) when they are right, they are likely to bring disturbing news, and this incurs a cost. As a former high-ranking CIA officer put it, intelligence is like a guest at a dinner party in that although it is valued, if it spills the wine and insults the host, it will not be invited back.[2] But by its mandate, intelligence is prone to be unruly, and if it is excessively tame it will lose its value.

Intelligence, then, will not win any popularity contests. As Director of Central Intelligence Richard Helms said shortly after he was let go in 1973, he was "the easiest man in Washington to fire. I have no political, military or industrial base."[3] Although DCI James Woolsey's view was colored by his bad relations with President Clinton, he was not far off the mark in saying that the best job description for his position was "not to be liked."[4] Intelligence is even less liked than it might be because policymakers understandably live by the saying "There is no such thing as a policy failure, only intelligence failures," thereby exaggerating the role of the latter, as was the case with the war in Iraq.

For the general public, intelligence is not popular for the additional reasons that its two prime characteristics of secrecy and covert action clash, if not with American traditions, then with the American self-image, and even those who applaud the results are likely to be uncomfortable with the means. As I noted in the introduction, it is telling that discussions of interventions in others' internal politics, and especially attempts to overthrow their regimes, are couched in terms of *CIA's* interventions despite the fact that CIA acts under instructions from the president. Critics, even those on the left, shy away from the correct label, which is that it is a *U.S. government* intervention. Political leaders see little reason to encourage a better understanding.

A New York clothing store has as its slogan "An educated consumer is our best customer." Intelligence can say this as well, but its wish for an educated consumer is not likely to be granted. Many presidents and cabinet officers come to the job with little knowledge or experience with intelligence and with less time to learn once they are in power. Even presidents like Nixon who were more informed and who doubted CIA's abilities often held unreasonable expectations about what it could produce. Henry Kissinger sometimes knew better, as revealed by what he told his staff about the congressional complaints that the United States had failed to anticipate the coup in Portugal:

> Why? Now goddam it, I absolutely resent—anytime there's a coup you start with the assumption that the home government missed it.... Why the hell should we know better than the government that's being overthrown.... I mean what request is it to make of our intelligence agencies to discover coups all over the world?[5]

Although Kissinger was right, even he sometimes expected more information and better analysis than was likely to be forthcoming and displayed the familiar schizophrenic pattern of both scorning intelligence and being disappointed by it.

The knowledge that intelligence can be wrong is useful for shifting blame onto the assessments and convenient in rationalizing the rejection of them when they clash with desired policies. But decision makers as well as scholars need to realize that not all the problems can be fixed (and certainly will not be by the latest "reforms"), and that even an optimally designed system will produce many errors. Just as intelligence analysts should always ask themselves what evidence could lead them to conclude that their views were incorrect, so policymakers should think about the extent to which their policies depend on accurate intelligence and try to reduce their vulnerabilities.[6] These efforts would leave decision makers with greater uncertainty and increase their psychological and political burdens, however. Thus parallel to the limits on how much policymakers can expect from intelligence are the limits on how educated intelligence can expect the customers to be. But a lack of education is not the only source of friction between policymakers and intelligence; the tasks of the two put them in conflict. If there is any doubt about this, we need only remember that it would be hard to find two more educated consumers than Donald Rumsfeld and Richard Cheney.

Decision Makers' Needs and How Intelligence Conflicts with Them

The different needs and perspectives of decision makers and intelligence officials guarantee conflict between them. For both political and psychological reasons, political leaders have to oversell their policies, especially in domestic systems in which power is decentralized,[7] and this will produce pressures on and distortions of intelligence. It is, then, not surprising that intelligence officials, especially those at the working level, tend to see political leaders as unscrupulous and careless, if not intellectually deficient, and that leaders see their intelligence services as timid, unreliable, and often out to get them.

Although it may be presumptuous for CIA to have chiseled in its lobby "And ye shall know the truth and the truth will make you free," it can at least claim this as its objective. No decision maker could do so, as the more honest of them realize. When Secretary of State Dean Acheson said that the goal of a major National Security Council document was to be "clearer than truth," he understood this very well.[8] Some of the resulting tensions came out when Porter Goss became DCI and told the members of the CIA that they should support policymakers.[9] On the other hand, the job of intelligence is to inform policymakers and in this way to support better policy. But support can also mean providing analysis that reinforces policies and rallies others to the cause. The first kind of support fits with intelligence's preferred mission, the one that decision makers pay lip service to. But given the political and psychological world in which they live, it is often the latter kind of support that decision makers seek. In light of the charges that CIA had previously undercut President Bush's policies, it is not surprising that many people thought Goss was using the term in the latter sense. Decision makers need confidence and political support, and honest intelligence unfortunately often diminishes rather than increases these goods by pointing to ambiguities, uncertainties, and the costs and risks of policies. In many cases, there is a conflict between what intelligence at its best can produce and what decision makers seek and need.

Because it is axiomatic that a good policy must rest on an accurate assessment of the world, in a democracy policies must be—or at least be seen as being—grounded in intelligence. Ironically, this is true only because intelligence is seen as proficient, a perception that developed in the wake of the technologies in the 1960s, and the pressures on intelligence follow from its supposed strengths.[10] When Secretary of State Powell insisted that DCI Tenet sit right behind him when he laid out the case against Iraq before the UN Security Council, he was following this imperative in a way that was particularly dramatic but not different in kind from the norm. It is the very need to claim that intelligence and policy are in close harmony that produces conflict between them.[11]

In principle, it could be different. Bush could have said something like this: "I think Saddam is a terrible menace. This is a political judgment, and I have been elected to make difficult calls. While I have listened to our intelligence services and other experts, this is my decision, not theirs." In other cases the president could announce, "The evidence is ambiguous, but on balance I believe that we must act on the likelihood that the more alarming possibilities are true." At times in the run-up to the war in Iraq and other cases, policymakers indicated that they were expressing their own convictions, not an intelligence assessment. But the line often is a thin one,[12] and speeches that clearly separate themselves from intelligence will seem weak and be politically unpersuasive. Indeed, in the years since the Iraq debacle, while Britain has renounced its experiment with issuing public intelligence papers, the United States has moved in the opposite direction, releasing the key judgments of several estimates, especially on Iran and Iraq. It can be argued that this is appropriate for a democracy—and in today's climate the information would be leaked in any event—but the results are to increase the pressures on intelligence.

Conflicting Pressures

For reasons of both psychology and politics, decision makers want not only to minimize actual value trade-offs but to minimize their own perception of them. Leaders talk about how they make hard decisions all the time, but like the rest of us, they prefer easy ones and will try to convince themselves and others that a particular decision is in fact not so hard. Maximizing political support for a policy means arguing that it meets many goals, is supported by many considerations, and has few costs. Decision makers, then, want to portray the world as one in which their policy is superior to the alternatives on many independent dimensions. For example, when a nuclear test ban was being debated during the cold war, proponents argued not only that atmospheric testing was a major public health hazard but also that a test ban was good for American national security and could be verified. It would have undercut the case for the ban if its supporters had said, "We must stop atmospheric testing in order to save innocent lives even though there will be a significant cost in terms of national security."

Psychological as well as political dynamics are at work. To continue with the test-ban example, proponents who were deeply concerned with public health did not like to think that they were advocating policies that would harm national security. Conversely, those who felt that inhibiting nuclear developments would disadvantage the United States came to also believe that the testing was not a health hazard. They would have been discomforted by the idea that their preferred policy purchased American security at the cost of hundreds of thousands of innocent lives. Decision makers have to sleep at night, after all.[13]

The run-up to the war in Iraq is an unfortunately apt illustration of these processes. In its most general form, the Bush administration's case for the war was that Saddam was a great menace and that overthrowing him also was a great opportunity for changing the Middle East. Furthermore, each of these two elements had several supporting components. Saddam was a threat because he was very hard to deter, had robust WMD programs, and had ties to terrorists, whom he might provide with WMD. The opportunity was multifaceted as well: the war would be waged at low cost, the postwar reconstruction would be easy, and establishing a benign regime in Iraq would have salutary effects on the region by pushing other regimes along the road to democracy and facilitating the resolution of the Arab-Israeli dispute. Portraying the world in this way maximized support for the war. To those who accepted all components, the war seemed obviously the best course of action, which would justify supporting it with great enthusiasm; and people could accept the policy even if they endorsed only a few of the multiple reasons. Seeing the world in this way also eased the psychological burdens on decision makers, which were surely great in ordering soldiers into combat and embarking on a bold venture. What is crucial in this context is not the validity of any of these beliefs but the convenience in holding them all simultaneously when there was no reason to expect the world to be arranged so neatly. This effect was so strong that Vice President Cheney, who in previous years had recognized that removing Saddam could throw Iraq into chaos, was able to convince himself that it would not. There was no logical reason why the situation could not have presented a threat but not an opportunity (or vice versa), or for there to have been threat of one kind—i.e., that Saddam was on the verge of getting significant WMD capability—but not of another—e.g., that he had no connections to al Qaeda. Logically, Cheney's heightened urgency about overthrowing Saddam should not have changed his view on what would follow. But it did.

As we saw in the previous chapter, most members of the American intelligence community did believe that Saddam had robust WMD programs. As far as we can tell, intelligence said little about how difficult Saddam was to deter, which was unfortunate because this was a central part of the justification for the war (which is probably why intelligence did not analyze it).[14] But because the IC did not feel the psychological need to bolster the case for war, it did not have to pull other perceptions into line and so gave little support to the administration on points where the evidence was to the contrary. And this is where the friction arose. Intelligence denied any collaboration between Saddam and al Qaeda, and it was very skeptical about the possibility that Saddam would turn over WMD to terrorists. So it is not surprising that here the administration put great pressure on intelligence to come to a different view and that policymakers frequently made statements that were at variance with the assessments. It is also not surprising, although obviously it was not foreordained, that the intelligence here was quite accurate.[15]

Intelligence also painted a gloomy picture of the prospects for postwar Iraq, noting the possibilities for continued resistance and, most of all, the difficulties in inducing the diverse and conflicting groups in the country to cooperate with one another.[16] Because this skepticism did not receive public attention, these estimates were subject to less political pressure, although the fact that the administration not only ignored them but frequently affirmed the opposite must have been frustrating to the analysts. Fortunately for them, however, on these points the administration was content to assert its views without claiming that they were supported by intelligence, probably because the judgments were of a broad political nature and did not rely on secret information. Later, when the postwar situation deteriorated and intelligence officials revealed that they had in fact provided warnings, the conflict heightened as the administration felt that intelligence was being disloyal and furthering its own political agenda.

It is tempting to see the browbeating and ignoring of intelligence as a particular characteristic of the George W. Bush administration, but it was not. Although available evidence does not allow anything like a full inventory, it does reveal examples from other administrations. Because Bill Clinton and his colleagues were committed to returning Haiti's Jean-Bertrand Aristide to power after he had been ousted in a coup, they resented and resisted intelligence analysis that argued that he was unstable and his governing would not be effective or democratic.[17] Neither the Eisenhower nor the Kennedy administration, both of which favored a test-ban agreement, was happy with analyses that indicated that verification would be difficult. Although on many issues liberals are more accepting of value trade-offs than are conservatives,[18] and many liberals like to think of themselves as particularly willing to confront complexity, once they are in power, they, too, need to muster political support and live at peace with themselves.

Intelligence does not feel the same pressures. It does not carry the burden of decision but "merely" has to figure out what the world is like. If the resulting choices are difficult, so be it. It also is not the duty of intelligence to build political support for a policy, and so even intelligence officials who do not oppose the policy will—or should—feel no compulsions to portray the world in a helpful way. In many cases, good intelligence will then point to the costs and dangers implicit in a policy. It will make it harder for policymakers to present the policy as clearly the best one and will nurture second thoughts, doubts, and unease. It is not that intelligence usually points to policies other than those the leaders prefer, but only that it is likely to give decision makers a more complex and contradictory view than fits with their political and psychological needs. Ironically, it can do this even as it brings good news. One might think that Lyndon Johnson would have welcomed CIA's telling him that other countries would not fall to Communism even if Vietnam did, but since his policy was justified (to others and probably to himself) on the premise that the domino theory was correct, he did not.[19]

We like to think that more information and better analysis will yield a clearer picture. But this is often not the case. To the extent that good intelligence will remain open to alternative interpretations and sensitive to discrepant information, it will be problematic for political leaders. As we saw in the previous chapter, in the Iraq WMD case better intelligence would have produced judgments that were *less*, not more, certain, and some of the subsequent reforms were designed to ensure that the excess certainty would not be repeated. These reforms are valid and useful but decision makers are likely to be happy with this change only when intelligence contradicts their preferred policy, in which case the greater modesty of the assessments will reduce their impact.

Resistance to Fallback Positions and Signs of Failure

The same factors that lead decision makers to underestimate trade-offs make them reluctant to develop fallback plans and to resist information that their policy is failing. The latter more than the former causes conflicts with intelligence, although the two are closely linked. There are several reasons why leaders are reluctant to develop fallback plans. It is hard enough to develop one policy, and the burden of thinking through a second is often simply too great. Probably more important, if others learn of the existence of Plan B, they may give less support to Plan A. Even if they do not prefer the former, its existence will be taken as betraying the leaders' lack of faith in their policy. It may also be psychologically difficult for leaders to contemplate failure.

Examples abound. Clinton did not have a Plan B when he started bombing to induce Serbia's Slobodan Milosevic to withdraw his troops from Kosovo. Administration officials thought such a plan was not needed because it was obvious that Milosevic would give in right away. In part they believed this because they thought it was the brief and minor bombing over Bosnia that had brought Milosevic to the table at Dayton, an inference that even if it had been correct would not have readily supported the conclusion that he would give up Kosovo without a fight. The result was that the administration had to scramble both militarily and politically and was fortunate to end the confrontation as well as it did. The most obvious and consequential recent case of a lack of Plan B is Iraq. Despite intelligence to the contrary, top administration officials believed that the political and economic reconstruction of Iraq would be easy and that they needed neither short-term plans to maintain order nor long-term preparations to put down an insurgency and create a stable polity.[20] Thinking about a difficult postwar situation would have been psychologically and politically costly, which is why it was not done.

Having a Plan B means little unless decision makers are willing to shift to it if they must, which implies a need to know whether the policy is working. This, even more than the development of the plan, involves intelligence, and so here the clashes will be greater. Leaders tend to stay with their first choice for as long as possible. Lord Salisbury, the famous British statesman of the end of the nineteenth century, noted that "the commonest error in politics is sticking to the carcasses of dead policies."[21] Leaders are heavily invested in their policies. To change their basic objectives will be to incur very high costs, including, in some cases, losing their offices if not their lives. Indeed the resistance to seeing that a policy is failing is roughly proportional to the costs that are expected if it does. Iraq again provides a clear example. In early 2007 Senator John McCain explained, "It's just so hard for me to contemplate failure that I can't make the next step," and President Bush declared that American policy in Iraq will succeed "because it has to."[22] This perseverance in what appears to be a losing cause may be rational for the leaders, if not for the country, if there is any chance of success and if the costs of having to adopt a new policy are almost as great as those for continuing to the bitter end.[23] An obvious example is Bush's decision to increase the number of American troops in Iraq in early 2007. The previous policy was not working and would have resulted in a major loss for the United States and for Bush, and even a failed "surge" would have cost him little more than admitting defeat and withdrawing without this renewed effort. Predictions of success or failure were not central to the decision. In most cases, however, predictions are involved, and it is hard for decision makers to make them without bias.

Intelligence officials do not have such a stake in the established policies, and thus it is easier for them to detect signs that the policies are failing. The fact that the leaders of the Bush administration saw much more progress in Iraq than did the IC is not unusual.[24] President Johnson's sentiments quoted at the start of this chapter rest on accurate observations. He probably was thinking about Vietnam, and appropriately so. The civilian intelligence agencies were quick to doubt that bombing North Vietnam would either cut the supply lines or induce the leadership to give in; they issued pessimistic reports on the pacification campaign and gave higher estimates of the size of the adversary's forces than the military or Johnson wanted to hear.[25]

Leaders are not necessarily being foolish. The world is ambiguous, and indicators of success are likely to be elusive. If it were easy to tell who would win a political or military struggle, it would soon come to an end (or would not start at all), and Vietnam is not unique in permitting a postwar debate on the virtues of alternative policies. Although it was a pernicious myth that Germany lost World War I because of a "stab in the back," it could have gained better peace terms if the top military leaders had not lost their nerve in the late summer of 1918. Furthermore, leaders can be correct even if their reasoning is not. The classic case is that of Winston Churchill in the spring of 1940. He prevailed over strong sentiment in his cabinet for a peace agreement with Germany in the wake of the fall of France by arguing that Britain could win because the German economy was badly overstretched and could be broken by a combination of bombing and guerrilla warfare. This was a complete fantasy; his foreign secretary had reason to write in his diary that "Winston talked the most frightful rot. It drives one to despair when he works himself up into a passion of emotion when he ought to make his brain think and reason."[26] Fortunately, Churchill's emotion and force of character carried the day, but intelligence can get no credit. But regardless of who is right, we should expect conflict between leaders and intelligence over whether Plan B is necessary.

Confidence and Perseverance

We should perhaps not underestimate the virtues of perseverance, as stubborn—if not pigheaded—as it may appear to opponents and to later observers when it fails. Not a few apparently hopeless cases end well. Thus despite widespread opinion to the contrary, the mujahedeen in Afghanistan were able to force the Soviets out of the country. Similarly, two scientists spent over twenty years working on what almost everyone else believed was a misguided quest to understand the workings of the hypothalamus, producing no results until they independently made the breakthroughs that earned them Nobel Prizes.[27] Albert Hirschman points to the "hiding hand" in many human affairs. If we saw the obstacles in our path, we would not begin many difficult but ultimately successful endeavors.[28] For example, how many scholars would have started a dissertation had they known how long and arduous it would be?

So while the desire to see the world in a certain way can lead to errors, strong motivation may also be necessary to make the effort and to seek the information necessary to establish a position that is in fact correct. In many cases, the first and obvious interpretation is wrong, and only those who find this conclusion troubling have the motive to look hard for an alternative. This was true of the reaction of Matthew Meselson and his colleagues to the Reagan administration's claim that "yellow rain" and illness in Cambodia were caused by illegal toxins used by the Vietnamese and their Soviet sponsors. It was their deep skepticism that the Soviets would do this and their strong opposition to the policies that would follow from such an interpretation that motivated them to mount the arduous and painstaking expeditions to Southeast Asia that showed yellow rain to be a natural phenomenon unconnected with the reported illnesses.[29] That Meselson and his colleagues wanted to reach this conclusion does not mean that they were wrong (in retrospect, they almost surely were correct), and without such strong preferences it is unlikely that they would have made the great efforts that were needed to challenge the administration's interpretation.

Confidence is necessary for perseverance and for embarking on any difficult venture. While it can be costly, it also is functional in many situations, which helps explain why people are systematically overconfident.[30] Although it might seem that we would be better off if our confidence better matched our knowledge, it turns out that the most mentally healthy people are slightly overoptimistic, overestimating their skills and ability to control their lives.[31] This is probably even more true for decision makers, who carry heavy burdens. As Henry Kissinger says, "Historians rarely do justice to the psychological stress on a policy-maker."[32] A national leader who had no more confidence than an objective reading of the evidence would permit probably would do little or would be worn down by mental anguish after each decision. Former secretary of state Dean Acheson understood this when he told the presidential scholar Richard Neustadt, "I know your theory [that presidents need to hear conflicting views]. You think Presidents should be warned. You're wrong. Presidents should be given confidence."[33]

There is little reason to think that President Bush was being less than honest when he told Bob Woodward, "I know it is hard for you to believe, but I have not doubted what we're doing [in Iraq]." He was aware that a degree of self-manipulation if not self-deception was involved: "[A] president has got to be the calcium in the backbone. If I weaken, the whole team weakens.... If my confidence level in our ability declines, it will send ripples throughout the whole organization. I mean, it's essential that we be confident and determined and united."[34] During the air campaign phase of the Gulf War, when CIA estimated that the damage being inflicted was well below what the air force reported and what plans said was needed to launch the ground attack, the general in charge, Norman Schwarzkopf, demanded that CIA get out of this business. His reasoning was not that CIA was wrong but that these estimates reduced the confidence of the men and women in uniform on which success depended.[35]

Of course there are occasions in which intelligence can supply confidence. The breaking of German codes in World War II not only gave allied military and civilian leaders an enormous amount of information that enabled them to carry out successful military operations but provided a general confidence that they could prevail. At the height of the Cuban missile crisis in 1962, Kennedy was given confidence by the report from his leading Soviet expert that Khrushchev would be willing to remove the missiles the Soviets had installed in Cuba without an American promise for a parallel withdrawal from Turkey.[36] In most cases, however, intelligence is likely to provide a complicated, nuanced, and ambiguous picture.

When they are not prepared to change, leaders are then prone not only to reject the information but to scorn the messenger, claiming that intelligence is unhelpful (which in a real sense it is), superficial (which is sometimes the case), and disloyal (which is rare). Intelligence may lose its access or, if the case is important, much of its role. Thus in the 1930s when a unit in Japanese military intelligence showed that the China campaign, far from leading to control over needed raw materials, was draining the Japanese economy, the army reorganized and marginalized it.[37] Something similar was attempted in Vietnam by the U.S. military, which responded to the pessimistic reporting from the Department of State's Bureau of Intelligence and Research by having Secretary of Defense Robert McNamara argue that INR should not be permitted to analyze what was happening on the battlefield.[38]

It might be comforting to believe that only rigid individuals or organizations act in this way, but what is at work is less the characteristics of the organization and the personalities of the leaders than the desire to continue the policy, the need for continuing political support, and the psychological pain of confronting failure. When the research arm of the U.S. Forest Service turned up solid evidence that the best way to manage forests was to permit if not facilitate controlled fires, the unit was abolished because the founding mission and indeed identity of the service was to prevent forest fires.[39]

Too Early or Too Late

For intelligence to be welcomed and to have an impact, it must arrive at the right time, which is after the leaders have become seized with the problem but before they have made up their minds. This is a narrow window. One might think that early warning would be especially useful because there is time to influence events. But in many cases decision makers will have an established policy, one that will be costly to change, and early warnings can rarely be definitive.

Intelligence about most of the world is irrelevant to leaders because they are too busy to pay attention to any but the most pressing concerns. Intelligence on matters that are not in this category may be useful for building the knowledge of the government and informing lower-level officials but will not receive a hearing at the top. This was the case with intelligence on Iran before the fall of 1978. As I discussed in chapter 2, intelligence was badly flawed here, rarely going beyond the inadequate reports from the field or assessing the situation in any depth. But even better analysis would not have gained much attention because the president and his top assistants were preoccupied by other problems and projects, most obviously the attempt to bring peace to the Middle East that culminated in President Carter's meeting with President Sadat and Prime Minister Begin at Camp David. As one

CIA official said to me, "We could not give away intelligence on Iran before the crisis." Almost as soon as the crisis hit, however, it was too late. Top officials quickly established their own preferences and views of the situation. This is not unusual. On issues that are central, decision makers and their assistants are prone to become their own intelligence analysts.[40]

Perhaps intelligence can have most influence if it operates on questions that are important but not immediately pressing. In the previous chapter I argued that there was nothing that intelligence could have reasonably told President Bush that would have affected the basic decisions on Iraq. But things might have been different if intelligence in the mid-1990s had been able to see that Saddam had postponed if not abandoned his ambitions for WMD. Had this been the standard view when Bush came to power, he and his colleagues might have accepted it because they were not then far down the road to war.

As a policy develops momentum, information and analyses that would have mattered if received earlier now will be ignored. This can be seen quite clearly in military operations because it is relatively easy to mark the stages of the deliberation. At the start the focus is on whether the operation can succeed, which means paying careful attention to the status of the adversary's forces and the possibilities of gaining surprise. But as things move ahead, new information is likely to be used for tactical purposes rather than for calling the operation into question. The greater the effort required to mount it and the greater the difficulty in securing agreement to proceed, the greater the resistance will be to new information that indicates it is not likely to succeed.

A clear example is Operation Market Garden in the fall of 1944. After the leading British general, Bernard Montgomery, was rebuffed by Eisenhower in his arguments for concentrating all Allied forces behind his thrust toward Berlin, political as well as military reasons lead Eisenhower to agree to a bold but more limited attack deep into German-held territory culminating at Arnhem. The need for allied unity and conciliating Montgomery, combined with the fact that Eisenhower had been urging him to be more aggressive, meant that "once he was committed, retreat for Ike was all but impossible."[41] Shortly before the attack was to be launched, code breaking revealed that the Germans had more and better-trained forces in the area than the allies had anticipated. Had they known this earlier, the operation would not have been approved. But once the basic decision was made, the political and psychological costs of reversing it were so high that the intelligence was disregarded, to the great cost of the soldiers parachuted into the final bridge. The refusal or inability of a leading British general to heed the intelligence indicating that the British move into Greece in 1941 would almost surely fail can be similarly explained, as can the fact that pessimistic CIA assessments about the planned American invasion of Cambodia in

1971 were not forwarded to the president when DCI Helms realized that Nixon and Kissinger had made up their minds and would only be infuriated by the reports, which turned out to be accurate.[42]

Importance of Cognitive Predispositions

Of course it is not only decision makers who become committed, and even if intelligence does not advocate policy positions, it does—and must—develop views about the world and other states in it. It is perhaps the most confirmed proposition in cognitive psychology that once a belief or image is established, new material will become assimilated to it, with discrepant and ambiguous information being ignored or fitting into the established views. Change is difficult and slow; the tendency for premature cognitive closure is powerful and, like many other psychological processes, often is useful because it conserves cognitive resources and facilitates decision making.[43] In a perfect world, intelligence could consciously strive to keep an open mind for as long as possible and to encourage alternative perspectives. But the minds of individuals race ahead, and they and their organizations have powerful incentives to bring new information and their views of it to the attention of the leaders as quickly as possible. Intelligence also has incentives to counteract the stereotype that it is never willing to reach a firm conclusion, and as we saw in the previous chapter, CIA quickly adopted one interpretation of Saddam's aluminum tubes that it was unwilling to modify despite mounting evidence to the contrary.

Intelligence, then, often has its own strongly held beliefs, which can operate at multiple levels of abstraction, from general theories of politics and human nature to images of adversaries to ideas about specific situations.[44] These need not be uniform, and the IC, like the policymaking community, often is divided and usually along the same lines. During the cold war some factions were much more worried about the USSR than were others, and the China analysts were deeply divided in their views about the role of Mao and how internal Chinese politics functioned. In these cases, analysts, like policymakers, were slow to change their views and saw most new information as confirming what they expected to see. This is true on the level of tactical intelligence as well. A striking case was the accidental shooting down of an Iranian airliner by the *USS Vincennes* toward the end of the Iran-Iraq War. One of the key errors was that the radar operator misread his screen as indicating that the airplane was descending toward the ship. What is relevant here is that the *Vincennes'* captain had trained his crew very aggressively, leading them to expect an attack and giving them a mind-set that was conducive to reading—and misreading—evidence as indicating that one was under way. A destroyer that was in the vicinity had not been drilled in this way, and its operator read the radar track correctly.[45]

The previous paragraphs provide another reason why decision makers so often reject intelligence. The answers to many of their most important questions are linked to their beliefs about world politics, the images of those they are dealing with, and their general ideas if not ideologies. Bush's view of Saddam rested in large measure on his beliefs about how tyrants behave, for example. If intelligence had explained that Saddam was not a major threat, being unlikely to aid terrorists or to try to dominate the region, this probably would not have been persuasive to him, and not only because he was particularly closed-minded. This kind of intelligence would have been derived not only from detailed analysis of how Saddam had behaved but from broad understandings of politics and even of human nature. Here it is not only to be expected but legitimate for decision makers to act on their views rather than those propounded by intelligence. It is often rightly said that "policy-makers are entitled to their own policies, but not to their own facts."[46] Facts do not speak for themselves, however, and crucial political judgments grow out of a stratum that lies between if not beneath policies and facts.

Although it was not appropriate for a member of the NSC staff to ask whether the Baghdad station chief who produced a gloomy prognosis in November 2003 was a Democrat or Republican,[47] it would not have been illegitimate to have inquired as to the person's general political outlook, his predisposition toward optimism and pessimism, his general views about how insurgencies could be put down, and his beliefs about how difficult it would be to bring stability to a conflicted society. Not only is it comforting for decision makers to listen to those who share their general values and outlook, but it makes real sense for them to do so. They are right to be skeptical of the analysis produced by those who see the world quite differently because however objective the analysts are trying to be, their interpretations will inevitably be influenced by their general beliefs and theories.

It is, then, not surprising that people are rarely convinced in arguments about central issues. The debate about the nature of Soviet intentions went on throughout the cold war, with few people being converted and fewer being swayed by intelligence or competing analysis. Without going so far as to say that everyone is born either a little hawk or a little dove, to paraphrase Gilbert and Sullivan, on the broadest issues of the nature and intentions of other countries and the existence and characteristics of broad historical trends, people's beliefs are determined more by their general worldviews, predispositions, and ideologies than they are by the sort of specific evidence that can be pieced together by intelligence.[48] The reason why DCI John McCone expected the Soviets to put missiles into Cuba and his analysts did not was not that they examined different evidence or that he was more careful than they were but that he strongly believed that the details of the nuclear balance influenced world politics and that Khrushchev would therefore be strongly motivated to improve his position. Similarly, as early as February 1933, Robert Vansittart, the United Kingdom's permanent undersecretary in the foreign office, who was to become a leading opponent of appeasement, said that the Germans were "likely to rely for their military power...on the mechanical weapons of the future, such as tanks, big guns, and above all military aircraft." Eighteen months later, when criticizing the military for being slow to appreciate the rise of Nazi power, he said, "Prophesy is largely a matter of insight. I do not think the Service Departments have enough. On the other hand they might say that I have too much. The answer is that I know the Germans better."[49] Although contemporary decision makers might not refer to intuition, they are likely to have deeply ingrained beliefs about the way the world works and what a number of countries are like, and in this sense they will be prone to be their own intelligence analysts.

The discrepancy between the broad cognitive predispositions of the IC and those of political leaders explains why conflict has tended to be higher when Republicans are in power. With some reason, they see intelligence analysts as predominantly liberals. Their suspicions that intelligence has sought to thwart and embarrass the administration are usually false, but to the extent that the worldviews of most members of the IC are different from those of the Republicans, the latter are justified in being skeptical of IC analysis on broad issues. For their part, intelligence analysts, like everyone else, underestimate the degree to which their own interpretations of specific bits of evidence are colored by their general predispositions and so consider the leaders' rejection of their views closed-minded and ideological. Although not all people are equally driven by their theories about the world,[50] there is a degree of legitimacy to the leaders' position that members of the IC often fail to grasp. President Reagan and his colleagues, including DCI Casey, probably were right to believe that the IC's assessments that the Soviet Union was not supporting terrorism and was not vulnerable to economic pressures were more a product of the IC's liberal leanings than of the evidence. They therefore felt justified in ignoring the IC when they did not put pressure on it, which in turn led to charges of politicization, a topic to which I will now turn.

Politicization

In the previous chapter I explained why I did not think that the WMD failure in Iraq could be attributed to intelligence's bowing to political pressures to tell the leaders what they wanted to hear. But this does not mean that politicization is not real. It can take many forms, from the most blatant in which intelligence is explicitly told what conclusions it should reach to the less obvious, including demoting people who produce the "wrong" answer, putting in place personnel whose views are consistent with those of the top leaders, reducing the resources going to units whose analyses are troubling, and the operation of unconscious bias by analysts who fear that their careers will be damaged by producing undesired reports. Even more elusive may be what one analyst has called "politicization by omission": issues that are not evaluated because the results might displease superiors.[51] Also subtle are the interactions between pressures and degrees of certainty in estimates. I suspect that one reason for the excess certainty in the Iraq WMD assessments was the knowledge of what the decision makers wanted. Conversely, analysts are most likely to politically conform when they are uncertain about their own judgments, as will often be the case on difficult and contentious questions.

Only rarely does one find a case like the one in which President Johnson told DCI Helms, "Dick, I need a paper on Vietnam, and I'll tell you what I want included in it."[52] Almost as blatant was Kissinger's response when CIA experts told Congress that intelligence did not believe that the new Soviet missile with multiple warheads could menace the American retaliatory force, contrary to what policymakers had said. He ordered the reports to be revised, and when they still did not conform, told Helms to remove the offending paragraph on the grounds that it was not "hard" intelligence but merely speculation on Soviet intentions, a subject on which intelligence lacked special qualifications.[53]

Even this case points to the ambiguities in the notion of politicization and the difficulties in drawing a line between what political leaders should and should not do when they disagree with estimates.[54] Intelligence said that "we consider it highly unlikely [that the Soviets] will attempt within the period of this estimate to achieve a first-strike capability."[55] This prediction was reasonable—and turned out to be correct—but it rested in part on judgments of the Soviet system and the objectives of the Soviet leaders, and these are the kinds of questions that the top political leadership is entitled to answer for itself. On the other hand, to demand that intelligence keep silent on adversary intentions would be bizarre, and indeed, when the hard-liners forced an outside estimate on the IC at the end of the Ford administration, the group of selected hawks who formed "Team B" strongly criticized the IC for concentrating on capabilities and ignoring intentions.

So it is not surprising that arguments about whether politicization occurred are rarely easy to settle.[56] In some cases the only people with firsthand knowledge will have major stakes in the dispute, and in others even a videotape of the meeting might not tell us what happened. Was the office chief bemoaning the fact that an estimate would cause him grief with policymakers, or was he suggesting that it be changed? Was the DCI or his top assistant just doing his job when he strongly criticized a draft paper, arguing that the evidence was thin, alternatives were not considered, and the conclusion went beyond the evidence, or was he exerting pressure to get a different answer? When people in the vice president's office and the office of the secretary of defense told the IC analysts to look again—and again—at the evidence for links between Saddam and al Qaeda and repeatedly pressed them on why they were discounting sources that reported such links, were they just doing due diligence?[57] Are analysts being oversensitive, or are leaders and managers being overassertive? Winks and nods, praise and blame, promotions and their absence are subject to multiple causes and multiple interpretations. In many of these cases I suspect that one's judgment will depend on which side of the substantive debate one is on, because commentators as well as the participants will bring with them their own biases and reasons to see or reject claims of pressure.

Ironically, while many of the critics of the IC's performance on Iraqi WMD highlighted the dangers of politicization, some of the proposed reforms (ones that appear after every failure) show how hard it is to distinguish a good intelligence process from one that is driven by illegitimate political concerns. It is conventional wisdom that good analysis questions its own assumptions, looks for alternative explanations, examines low-probability interpretations as well as ones that seem more likely to be correct, scrutinizes sources with great care, and avoids excessive conformity. The problem in this context is that analysts faced with the probing questions that these prescriptions imply may believe that they are being pressured into producing a different answer. The obvious reply is that consumers and managers must apply these techniques to all important cases, not just when they object to the initial answers. There is something to this, and it would make sense to look back at previous cases in which politicization has been charged and see whether only those estimates that produced the "wrong" answers were sent back for further scrutiny.

But even this test is not infallible. If I am correct that political leaders and top intelligence managers are entitled to their own broad political views, then they are right to scrutinize especially carefully what they think are incorrect judgments.[58] Thus the political leaders insisted that the IC continually reassess its conclusion that there were no significant links between Saddam and al Qaeda not only because they wanted a different answer but because their feeling for how the world worked led them to expect such a connection, and they thought that the IC's assessment to the contrary was based less on the detailed evidence than on the misguided political sensibility that was dominant in the IC.[59] It is not entirely wrong for policymakers to require a higher level of proof from intelligence when the evidence cuts against their desired policy.[60] This means that the greater probing of the grounds for judgments and the possible alternatives that are the objectives of good intelligence procedures may increase the likelihood both of politicization and of analysts' incorrectly levying such a charge.

Finally, it should be noted that some phenomena labeled politicization actually are substitutes for it. In the aftermath of the invasion of Iraq, administration leaders were often criticized for politicizing intelligence, and the proof offered was that they distorted what intelligence said and engaged in cherry-picking in the form of selectively publicizing those reports that supported their policy. But such acts, inappropriate as they are, show the lack or failure of politicization rather than exemplifying it. If intelligence had bent to the administration's will, then there would have been no need to cherry-pick or distort, since an accurate portrayal of what intelligence was saying would have served the administration's purposes. It is only when intelligence does not yield that policy-makers may have to misreport what it is saying.

Intelligence Errors

If the expectation that intelligence will be accurate leads policymakers to seek assessments that bolster their positions and give them confidence, the knowledge that intelligence is often wrong permits them to override or ignore it when the reports are inconvenient. Intelligence errors indeed are common and, although reforms can lead to improvement, there are inherent limits to what can be achieved. The problems start with the prevalence of incomplete and misleading information and the difficulties in understanding our world.[61] Even our ability to understand our physical environment is limited when we deal with difficult questions. For example, although experts agree that the world's climate is changing and doing so at least in part because of human activities, an enormous number of puzzles remain. Any ecological experiment or alteration similarly reveals many unexpected connections and consequences,[62] and anyone with an unusual illness knows the limitations of medical diagnoses.[63]

Deception

Foreign intelligence is more difficult still. The adversary is often engaged in concealment and deception, and as the many cases of surprise attack show, even the large-scale preparations that are necessary for the launching of a war often can be plausibly portrayed in other terms.[64] Furthermore, officials may try to deceive their colleagues, with the result that good information about what a person is saying in private may turn out to be misleading. One reason why the United States was deceived about Iraqi WMD was that Saddam was deceiving others in his government, and a similar problem plagued the British in the war in North Africa in 1941–42. The German general Erwin Rommel was in the habit of sending his superiors messages that exaggerated his shortages of supplies in order to bolster his case for additional shipments, and the British who decoded the radio traffic forgot the simple rule that "reading a man's correspondence is not the same thing as reading his mind."[65]

This is not to say that deception is simple or always effective, of course. But it has an illustrious past and a glorious future. If people in everyday life keep getting surprised by their unfaithful partners, why would we expect governments to do much better?[66] Indeed, the knowledge that deception is common is troublesome because it degrades much correct information, as when Stalin dismissed the reports of his atomic spies at Los Alamos on the grounds that the Americans could not have been so incompetent as to permit this most secret facility to be penetrated.

The other side of this coin is that the belief that the other side is deceiving you can account for almost all discrepant information. As I discussed in the previous chapter, the United States was led astray by the belief that Iraq was engaging in extensive denial and deception, which explained why the IC was seeing only scattered signs of the program. Similarly, in 1941 Stalin rejected the enormous amount of information pointing to an imminent German attack on the grounds that it had been produced by the British in order to provoke a war between Germany and the USSR.[67]

International Politics as Rashomon

The fundamental cause of intelligence errors is that in many if not most cases countries see the world and one another very differently, and grasping the other's worldview is difficult. Unless the other's behavior is determined by the situation it is in and this situation is readily ascertainable, the state has to understand what the other's goals are and how it sees the world. The end of the cold war spawned a number of conferences bringing together officials from several countries, and it is striking how hard it was even in retrospect for each to comprehend why the other had acted as it did. International politics is sometimes portrayed as a game of chess. This is clearly wrong because in chess everything is in the open. More sophisticated observers use the analogy of poker. But even this is misleading as the participants often are playing very different games and, furthermore, fail to realize this. International politics, then, more closely resembles Rashomon, the Japanese fable in which each participant sees the interaction and the others in very different ways.

A full treatment would require little short of analyzing all of international politics, so my discussion will be truncated. Understanding how others think is an essential job of intelligence and the fundamental reason why it is so frequently wrong. The problems occur even among allies and even when differences in cultures and political systems are not involved, as British and American officials found in the Suez crisis of 1956.[68] Enmity and distance on many dimensions make understanding even more difficult. One reason why the Soviets invaded Afghanistan was that they feared that the regime was about to seek American support. This possibility was not perceived by U.S. analysts, who then underestimated the pressures the Soviets were experiencing. In turn, because the Soviets knew that they were not threatening the Persian Gulf, the strong American response was seen not as a reaction to what they had done but as the manifestation of a preplanned offensive.[69] Similarly, both Britain and Argentina badly misread each other in the run-up to the latter's invasion of the Falklands/Malvinas islands in 1982. Ironically, the fact that the British understood the weakness of their position, especially in the form of the vulnerability of the islands to the severing of the ferry to Argentina, made the task of British intelligence more difficult. As Lawrence Freedman explains, because "the lesser forms of pressure posed difficult enough problems for Britain there seemed to be little need for Argentina to overstep the line so far by such a crude violation of basic norms of international law, and certainly not before they had made every effort to demonstrate that alternative forms of pressure had been exhausted."[70] One of the things that Britain did not understand was that Argentina believed that giving an ultimatum, openly preparing to invade, or cutting the links to the islands was too risky because Britain could respond by an alliance with Argentina's rival, Chile. This idea never occurred to the British, and it would have been dismissed out of hand because Pinochet's repressive regime was anathema.

This example helps explain why so many cases of surprise attack succeed tactically but fail strategically. Although in this case the British military victory was not foreordained, the Argentine attack was still unwise. States expect their adversaries to be crafty and ruthless but not to be foolish, let alone to commit suicide. Thus the fundamental reason why the United States was taken by surprise at Pearl Harbor and by Saddam's conquest of Kuwait was that these moves did not make sense in light of the responses they would call up. American analysts and decision makers similarly failed to anticipate the Soviet deployment of troops to Afghanistan because they knew that this would be a mistake, and analysts and Soviet experts who understood that thoroughgoing reforms would undermine the stability of the USSR could not believe that Gorbachev was serious.[71] Three days before Hitler attacked the Soviet Union, the British ambassador told a Soviet diplomat that the German military buildup was "one of Hitler's moves in the 'war of nerves'.... But a war?... An attack? I find it difficult to believe. It would be crazy!" The Soviet ambassador agreed: "An invasion [of Russia] always ends badly for the initiators."[72] One reason why the United States was taken by surprise by the Indian nuclear tests in 1998 was that intelligence believed that testing would not be in that country's best interests because of how others, including the United States, would react.[73] Intelligence failures, then, often are mutual: the United States failed to understand its adversaries because it could not comprehend their misperceptions of the United States, misperceptions that almost guaranteed that the adversaries' policies would fail. The importance of this pattern is why I introduced this book with what Sherman Kent, the head of CIA's Board of National Estimates, said about the intelligence failure that led to the Cuban missile crisis: "We missed the Soviet decision to put missiles into Cuba because we could not believe that Khrushchev could make such a mistake."[74]

The Rashomon effect operates with a vengeance here because the other side's behavior is based on an image of the actor that the actor will find disturbing and hard to grasp. The Japanese attacked Pearl Harbor in part because they thought the United States would be willing to fight and lose a limited war. This would not have been comprehensible to the American leaders, not only because they saw the confrontation with Japan as part of a broader life-and-death struggle with fascist tyranny but also because the idea of being willing to accept defeat and Japanese domination of the Pacific was insulting. Similarly, to see that Saddam might annex all of Kuwait would have been to recognize that he thought the United States would acquiesce in the violation of international law and American interests. Individuals and countries often talk about needing to understand how others see them, but this can be very painful, which sharply reduces the incentives to make the effort.

In cases like these the other side's actions and underlying perceptions are hard to understand because they are in part a product of motivated biases. As discussed earlier, these distortions stem from the actor's need to understand the world in a certain way in order to avoid painful value trade-offs.[75] The problem for the perceiving state's intelligence is that the other side's perceptions are generated by psychological pressures that cannot readily be replicated or empathized with. For intelligence to see that the adversary is in a difficult situation is not enough; it must somehow feel the other's pain. After Bill Clinton this phrase is both familiar and hard to take seriously, yet it is what is necessary and challenging. Indeed, an analyst who succeeds may find his or her assessments dismissed as far-fetched and demeaning to both the adversary and the state.

The Rashomon effect and mutual intelligence failures were clearly at work in the Iraq case. In the previous chapter I explored Saddam's fears and beliefs and stressed how hard they were for outsiders to grasp. In parallel, Saddam failed to understand the United States or predict what the Bush administration would do. This was not an aberration. The post–cold war era has seen four other instances in which the United States failed to understand and communicate with adversaries, with the result that force had to be used despite the fact that coercive threats should have succeeded because of the enormous American military advantages and its incentives to fight if need be. In the overthrow of Manuel Noriega in Panama in 1989, the Gulf War in 1991, Haiti in 1994, and Kosovo in 1999, the other side's intelligence failures were more egregious and consequential than the American ones, but the latter were not insignificant and illustrate how difficult intelligence can be. Indeed even in retrospect we lack a complete understanding of how these countries' leaders saw the United States and expected events to unfold.[76]

This is not to say that the situation is hopeless or that intelligence is always wrong. In fact, studying accuracy is difficult because of the selection bias that draws us to crises and policy failures, and these are likely to involve intelligence errors. If each side understands the other, both sides are likely to adjust their behavior in a way that minimizes costly conflict, and these cases seem unremarkable and not worth studying. As a result, we do not have the data that would enable us to estimate the "batting average" of intelligence, and indeed this endeavor would require a number of difficult judgments about what constitutes a failure and how we are to count cases. Nevertheless, I think it is fair to say that on difficult and important issues we are better off thinking about intelligence having a batting average rather than a fielding percentage. That is, we may hope to get a decent percentage of the cases correct but cannot expect to do so nearly all the time. The fact that intelligence has inherent limits may decrease the incentives to invest in increasing the IC's capacities, although, as I will argue, that is what is needed.

Reforms: What Is Wanted?

Intelligence failures inevitably are followed by proposals for reform. Obviously, these either are not implemented or are not effective, because failures continue. Although we lack a good measure, it is not at all apparent that the failure rate is decreasing, and the limits to reform underscore my central points that intelligence is inherently fallible and that possible improvements are not likely to reduce conflicts between political leaders and intelligence.[77] Here, as in the rest of this book, I will concentrate on intelligence analysis, say less about changes in structure, and ignore collection.[78]

Intelligence organizations are not unique in their inability to respond creatively to failures. The official commission to investigate the loss of the space shuttle *Challenger* and its crew in an explosion in 1986 was superficial, with the best work being the independent analysis of its maverick member, Richard Feynman. But it took a decade of research by an outside sociologist, Diane Vaughan, to understand the organizational routines that both made it possible for the National Aeronautics and Space Administration (NASA) to operate smoothly and laid the foundations for the accident.[79] Furthermore, NASA ignored this analysis, with the result that the same organizational flaws led to the disintegration of the *Columbia* in 1993. The reaction of the Catholic Church to sexual abuse followed a similar pattern: to protect the organization, wrongdoing was first ignored and then covered up, with short-run benefit to the clergy but at great cost to some parishioners and eventually to the institution itself. Universities are no better, arguing that outsiders must fund but not police them and then doing little self-examination and self-correction.

Tasks for "Better" Intelligence

At first glance, the meaning of better intelligence seems obvious: a more accurate picture of the world or, to put it slightly differently, getting more things right. But in fact there are a number of ambiguities here.[80] What are we to do with cases in which intelligence was right for the wrong reasons? Can we expect success when the other side is badly torn about what to do and when there is very little time between its decision and its action? Do we want to distinguish between easy and hard cases? Are we concerned about all cases or only (mostly?) the important ones? Some subjects are more consequential than others, and there probably is a trade-off between breadth and depth in intelligence coverage. Indeed, although the resources devoted to intelligence have increased greatly since 9/11, terrorism and "rogues" have absorbed most attention, leaving the rest of the world as unstudied as was true during the cold war when the IC focused on the USSR and the PRC. This may be appropriate, but reforms that concentrate on terrorism and WMD may lock in a focus that misses other topics that will turn out to be important.

A second question is whether we care about intelligence or *actionable* intelligence. An accurate picture of the world does no good unless policy can change and be effective on the basis of it. The other side of this coin is that while all surprises are embarrassing, only those that harm the country and could have been mitigated by actions that would have been taken had there been warning are instances in which the intelligence failure mattered. In some cases actors have a dominant strategy—i.e., their preferred behavior is insensitive to most information about the adversary. In other cases, there may be nothing that the state can do with better information because of limitations imposed by the external environment, its own capabilities, or its domestic politics. Academics and intelligence analysts value good information for its own sake; policymakers correctly do not.[81]

When intelligence serves a warning function, there is likely to be a trade-off between type 1 and type 2 errors, between being too sensitive and giving false alarms on the one hand and being less sensitive and running a greater risk of failing to detect a threat on the other. There is no such thing as a perfectly designed system in this regard, and a great deal depends on the actions the state can and will take, especially whether it can react to alarms in a way that will not be excessively costly if they should prove to be false. One could argue that the IC should simply provide its best assessment and leave it up to policymakers to decide how to respond, but this puts too much of a burden on the latter and excuses intelligence from the responsibility for giving only sensible warnings. We are not happy with the apocryphal story of a British Foreign Office official who proudly said on his retirement that throughout his entire career he had said there would be no European war and was wrong only twice, but it is difficult even in retrospect to say how a system should respond in this respect.

In parallel, there often is a trade-off between speed and accuracy. Although quick judgments based on the initial analysis of preliminary information are likely to be less accurate than what can be said after a longer period of collection and contemplation, there are reasons to deliver the news quickly. In some cases, immediate action may be necessary. In others, it is natural curiosity combined with the competition between intelligence units that leads to haste. In retrospect, CIA would have done better to have delayed telling consumers anything about the Iraqi aluminum tubes other than that they had been intercepted and were being analyzed. But in other cases withholding judgment would have been a luxury that might have been costly for the country as well as for the intelligence unit.

Much of the previous discussion has been couched in terms of right or wrong intelligence. But many assessments are phrased in terms of estimates of the likelihood of specified events. This can reflect either limits on our knowledge or the irreducible uncertainty about what others will do.[82] For example, the number of bombs that North Korea possesses is a fact, but limits on what the IC knows means that estimates must talk of ranges and probabilities. Probabilities also are involved in estimates of what North Korea will do in the future, but this reflects not only the IC's lack of sources but the fact that some of the factors on which state behavior rests are highly contingent. Dealing with uncertainties of both kinds complicates our ability to say how well intelligence is doing. Decision makers generally dislike "on the one hand, on the other hand" assessments, so would doing better mean producing fewer judgments in the range of "somewhat likely/somewhat unlikely"? This has some appeal but does not work well in situations where the evidence is limited, ambiguous, or contradictory or in the cases in which the other side's action is yet to be determined. Since different decision makers have different tastes for ambiguity, perhaps the best-designed system would vary from one administration to another. More fundamentally, the desire for greater certainty clashes with the limits on the IC's knowledge and with the argument that perhaps the most common intelligence error is to pretend to have excessive insight and foresight.

The IC often renders judgments in terms of how likely an outcome is. In retrospect, we can usually tell what did happen, but using this knowledge to see how well these estimates tracked with reality entails difficulties that are both empirical and theoretical. How do events show whether an earlier probabilistic judgment was right or wrong? The fact that the outcome did not occur does not mean that it was not likely; conversely, if the IC said that the outcome was likely but not certain and it does occur, perhaps the IC was too cautious. Can we make a sensible statement about whether the other's action was fully determined ahead of time? If the state did act but only after unusual circumstances intervened, the IC's earlier judgment that the action was 80 percent likely may have been wrong, not by being too timid but by putting such a high probability on the outcome. In fact, it is far from clear how we could establish the correct likelihood estimates even in retrospect. Historians endlessly debate whether actions would have been different under slightly different circumstances, and we can similarly debate how confident intelligence should have been on the basis of the evidence at its disposal.

For judgments about the adversary's current capabilities as opposed to what it will do in the future, the problems are a bit different. The statement that there is an 80 percent chance that another country has a nuclear weapon clearly cannot be true because the country either has the weapon or it does not. If the other country does have a weapon, we would judge the IC performance as better the higher the probability it attached to this fact, but without a large number of cases we would not be able to track changes in how well the IC was doing.

The previous paragraphs have concentrated on the answers intelligence gives. But perhaps the more important function of intelligence is to raise questions. It should tell decision makers what the fundamental issues are, what beliefs are crucial for their decisions, and what concerns, risks, and opportunities they should keep in mind. Intelligence might also inform decision makers about the role of motivated biases. This would not tell them what was right but would alert them to the fact that both they and their opposite numbers are prone to underestimate the costs of their preferred policies and to hold beliefs that appear implausible to those who do not feel the political and psychology pressures that have generated them. Perhaps more politically acceptable, intelligence can highlight the judgments on which decisions should turn and that may lie beneath the surface of the debates. In many cases the questions that receive most attention are tangential to those that do and/or should determine the policy. At its best, intelligence can probe the structure of disagreements and point policymakers to the beliefs and expectations on which they should concentrate. In a crucial meeting in which Secretary of Defense McNamara and the Joint Chiefs of Staff argued about whether the United States should deploy an antiballistic missile system, President Johnson asked, "What determined the difference in judgment?" a question that led McNamara to a fallback position that resembled the limited deployment that Johnson later decided to advocate.[83] Here a main job of intelligence would be to try to keep the arguments honest. Although this role would make intelligence even less popular than it is now and risk its becoming more deeply involved in policy disputes, there is much to be said for this, especially when it involves the entire government rather than just the top leaders.

As it is now, the IC considers the president its most important intelligence consumer. This is correct, but the president does not act alone, and perhaps some of the resources devoted to the White House might be better directed toward better informing all levels of the foreign policy apparatus. This is not as glamorous as writing items for the President's Daily Brief but in the long run may do much to improve the quality of policy. It would also mean that we would judge the quality of intelligence less by whether it was right or wrong and more by whether it helped the government come to grips with difficult questions. The reply, of course, is that in the end it is the president's decisions that matter and that we are not dealing with academic arguments that are graded by their acuity and sophistication but with policies that get tested in the real world. Nonetheless, it may be more than an academic conceit to believe that raising the level of understanding and argument within the government would have a favorable impact on policy over the long run.

These complications help explain why few reform proposals discuss what they seek to accomplish. With all the difficulties that stand in the way of significant change, this may not be a major problem. But it does make it harder to evaluate reforms.

Reform: Structure

Two major structural reforms have been put in train in the wake of the attacks of September 11, 2001: the establishment of a Director of National Intelligence (DNI) and the related push for greater sharing of information within the IC. After discussing them we will turn to actual and possible improvements in analysis.

Director of National Intelligence

The main intelligence reform in the past several decades is the establishment of a DNI. Called for in several studies, it was the central recommendation of the 9/11 Commission. A full evaluation of the commission report and of the establishment of a DNI are beyond the scope of this book, but a few points are relevant.[84] Because the 9/11 Commission was even more political than the groups that examined the Iraq WMD intelligence failures and because its members felt that consensus was necessary, it could not allocate blame for 9/11 among the political leaders. Most obviously, although the public record, journalistic accounts, and testimony before the commission all showed that Bush paid little attention to terrorism before 9/11, the report had to remain silent on this point. This meant that the recommendations had to focus on intelligence and, lacking a verdict on the responsibility for 9/11, had to come up with a proposal of some consequence. The establishment of DNI met these needs even though the links between the problems the commission described and the proposed remedy are loose at best. There are few reasons to believe that 9/11 would have been prevented had there been a DNI, but in a pattern familiar to organization theorists, a proposal that had been around for a while was seized on even though it did not match the precipitating problem.[85] To his credit, President Bush recognized this and initially opposed the new office, but an aroused public led by relatives of the 9/11 victims coupled with the coming presidential election overcame his resistance.

We should not forget that even before the DNI was established, the United States had an official who was to oversee the entire IC. Many people referred to the DCI as the director of the CIA, but his title was Director of Central Intelligence, and he was supposed to direct the entire community. Although in practice it did not work out that way, the reason was not so much a defective statute as it was the political power of other agencies, most obviously the Department of Defense. Without a new law, the president could have given the DCI most of the missing powers by telling the secretary of defense that his budget requests in the intelligence area, especially the enormous sums for spy satellites, had to be approved by the DCI before they went to the White House. Whether the DNI will be able to enforce his will is yet to be seen, but if he can, the primary reason will be a changed political climate, not the new law.[86] It is also important to realize that there is much to be said for a decentralized intelligence system, since different agencies need different intelligence for different purposes.[87] We also need to be aware that although proponents of the reform have said they do not want the DNI to become an additional layer of bureaucracy, this outcome may be hard to avoid.

There is at least one clear advantage to be gained, however. Under the old system, for reasons of both geographic proximity and organizational loyalty, the DCI almost always listened more to "his own" analysts than to those from other agencies. When it came time for crucial community judgments, it was hard for him to be impartial. This demoralized non-CIA analysts and, more important, gave CIA an edge when disagreements arose. At times, this was warranted because the other analysts tended to reflect the self-interest of their agencies, and this was especially true of the Defense Intelligence Agency. But even absent these biases, DCIs tended to give CIA views greater weight, and this reduced the quality of the judgments. As I noted in the previous chapter, this was a significant part of the reason why George Tenet adopted the more alarming interpretation of Saddam Hussein's purchase of aluminum tubes. Had the agencies' positions been reversed, with INR and the Department of Energy arguing that they were designed for centrifuges and CIA pointing out the implausibility in this claim, there would have been a much greater chance that the final community judgment would have been correct. More generally, had there been a DNI, it is more likely that the issues would have been aired before the highest authorities, and the playing field would have been more level. As far as I can tell, however, this advantage remains theoretical as no cases like this have arisen in the years since the DNI was established.

Few objected to the DNI's taking over the National Intelligence Council (NIC), which had previously been under the DCI in his community-wide responsibilities, and making the PDB an IC rather than CIA publication. While appropriate, these changes call into question the future of CIA's Directorate of Intelligence. Although the NIC was always an IC body, DI played a large role in supporting it because it was located at CIA headquarters,[88] and the DCI oversaw CIA as well as the NIC and could call on DI analysts to do much of its work. Indeed, other agencies tended to see NIC products such as National Intelligence Estimates as diversions from the more important work of serving their own agencies, and so it was hard to get them to provide the NIC with resources and their best analysts. The DI also produced the PDB, which increased in importance and prestige under George W. Bush. (At the start, the PDB was supposed to be a community-wide document, but CIA soon captured it as its own.) Although DI still plays the central role here, it has lost its special place. DI used to be uniquely attractive by being only one or two steps removed from the DCI (if that—the organization was small enough so that the DCI would meet many analysts personally), and even beginning analysts were startlingly close to top policymakers. Although DI analysts will still be heard, the reorganization has removed some of their access and cachet.

A further pressure on DI is that aside from the crucial areas of counterterrorism and counterproliferation (tasks that are largely being handled by special centers under the DNI), most of the relevant information will be from unclassified sources. The DNI has established an Open Source Center to facilitate the use of this information, although how it will be linked to or made use of by DI remains unclear. What is clear is that on a series of questions such as the likely political future of various countries, the impact of the Internet on the stability of closed societies, or the political implications of changing trade and investment flows, DI analysts are not likely to have any comparative advantage, and even less than in the past will policymakers need turn to them.

If DI is to thrive in this new environment, it will need to reinvent itself. One possibility is that the losses just described will allow it to pay less attention to current intelligence, build up its research and analytical skills, and develop a deeper knowledge base for the entire government. Alternatively, DI may become absorbed into the DNI's office. As it is now, the DNI does not have many of "his own" analysts but has to borrow them, especially from CIA. It is not only ego and empire building that will lead him to seek more analytical support. As the president's main intelligence adviser, he needs close contact with and control over the analytic talents on which he has to draw.[89] Whether this will happen is not clear, but it would fit with the old argument that analysis should be in a different organization from collection and covert action. On the other hand, this would contradict the prescription arising from the 9/11 and WMD failures that analysts should know more about their sources and that information should be more widely shared within the IC, reforms to which I will now turn.

Information Sharing and Knowledge of Sources

One of the reasons why the United States was taken by surprise on September 11, 2001, was that data was not shared between CIA and the FBI and passed to the Immigration and Naturalization Service.[90] Likewise, we saw in the previous chapter that one of the reasons for the Iraq WMD intelligence failure was that analysts did not know enough about their sources. It was almost as though CIA and FBI were not in the same government, and the proprietary attitude of the directorates within CIA are legendary. The remedy is simple in principle even if difficult to implement: there should be much more information sharing within the IC. In what seems like common sense, Pat Roberts, then chair of the Senate Select Committee on Intelligence, argued that "[k]ey terrorism analysts . . . must be given access to every single piece of relevant intelligence data concerning threats to the homeland," and the WMD Commission remarks that the terminology we use may implicitly accept undesirable boundaries within the IC: "To say that we must encourage agencies to 'share' information implies that they have some ownership stake in it."[91] But there are problems with the prescription. Not only will it meet a great deal of resistance, but sharing all information would swamp the system, which like all organizations is built on a division of labor. Furthermore, the withholding of information reflects not only the fact that the information is power but also legitimate security concerns. Spies like CIA's Aldridge Ames and FBI's Robert Hanssen would have done even greater damage had there been less compartmentalization.

While some barriers need to be pulled down, there is no perfect way to balance the competing needs involved, and I suspect that some years from now a distinguished panel will attribute a security debacle to the excessive availability of information within the intelligence community.

The freer flow of information should not be limited to human sources. One reason why analysts believed that Iraq had stepped up production of its chemical weapons was that they saw increased activity at the suspected production sites. But the WMD Commission says that what the analysts did not know was that the satellites had been reprogrammed to provide more frequent coverage, and so what they were seeing reflected a change in American surveillance, not Iraqi behavior.[92] A footnote in the report undercuts this claim, but the point remains that discussion of who needs what information should not be restricted to HUMINT. In some instances analysts need to know about the technical details of a collection system in order to think about what information could and could not have been gathered.

Other reforms deal with keeping more careful track of sources that support judgments, clarifying the degree to which the IC is confident of its assessment, and avoiding unwarranted consensus. These are not unlike the measures that were supposed to have been instituted after previous failures, and it remains to be seen how deep they will go and how long they will be sustained. A good sign is that NIEs now employ footnotes as scholars do. Instead of or in addition to their traditional function of expressing dissent, they link statements with supporting reports.[93] This should allow—indeed force—analysts to track the number of sources that they are relying on and may also prompt them to note any contradicting reports.

Reforms: Analysis

The start of this chapter presented some of the inherent limits on intelligence, explained why even (or especially) good intelligence will be unpopular, and noted that conflict between the IC and policymakers is inevitable. But improvements are possible. The IC can do a better job of learning from its failures (and from its successes), adopt appropriate social science methodologies, and invest more in its own capabilities. Since many observers have made recommendations like these, I do not expect much to come of them. They are nevertheless worth reiterating.[94]

Postmortems and Product Evaluation Staffs

Improvement is not likely without learning. But the IC has not had a robust program of postmortems, and those that have been done have generally been of cases of dramatic failure.[95] Not only do these need to be of higher quality, but the IC needs retrospective analyses of a wider range of cases, including false alarms (almost always neglected although they represent intelligence failures),[96] successes, and standard performances. Causal inferences drawn from failures select on the dependent variable and may detect procedures and ways of thinking that characterize accurate as well as inaccurate estimates. Even if we found that certain factors were present in all the cases of failure, we would not be on firm ground in providing explanations and prescriptions unless we could also establish that those factors were absent in cases of intelligence success. Oxygen is not a cause of intelligence failure despite being present in all such cases. Doing this broader evaluation is not easy and may not yield useful recommendations, and the lessons may be hard to act on. But without careful and sustained self-study, few improvements are likely.

The idea of a Product Evaluation Staff (PES) is closely linked to postmortems. It is a good sign that CIA has reinstituted a PES and that the DNI has established an office of analytic integrity and standards, but a bad sign that units like this have been established (and abolished) several times in the IC's history. This is not surprising, because a good PES is likely to be as unpopular with the IC as the IC is with policymakers, and for much the same reason. The PES cannot help but second-guess even if it avoids the trap of hindsight that has marred so many postmortems. If it functions well, it will find weaknesses, question established ways of proceeding, and generally make a pest of itself.

For a PES to significantly improve the IC, two difficult requirements must be met. First, it must be staffed by excellent people who will return to other units after their tour of duty. The easier and more common pattern is to treat it as a dumping ground for misfits or a less than arduous assignment for people who are about to retire. The obvious advantage of making this a final tour is to encourage people to write hard-hitting reports, but this advantage is purchased at too high a price. A PES should infuse the entire organization with more sophisticated knowledge, and a significant amount of the benefit is what its members carry with them to their next assignments. If serving on the PES is seen as a mark of distinction, its lessons will not be as readily dismissed. Of course line managers will not want to surrender their best analysts, and this is one of the reasons why a PES will succeed only if the top leaders of the organization are committed to it, something that is true for many of the other reforms as well.

The second requirement is that evaluation of IC products be separated from personnel judgments. As I noted in chapter 2, when conducting the Iran postmortem I was initially surprised at the nervousness of the people I interviewed. Being only a bit dense, I soon realized that they understood that their careers were on the line, which inhibited their viewing this as a learning opportunity. Of course in some cases people should be punished as well as corrected, but the price of refraining from doing this through a PES is worth paying in order to gain and spread knowledge that will reduce the chance of later errors. Other professions have managed to separate learning from punishment, although not without difficulties. Hospitals learn through morbidity and mortality conferences, which occur on a routine basis, and the National Transportation Safety Board similarly insulates its investigations from criminal and even disciplinary proceedings.[97] In this respect, the refusal of the IC to punish those involved in the 9/11 and Iraq WMD cases may have been wise, although because it was not linked to learning exercises, the reason behind it was more likely standard organizational self-protection.

Management and Peer Review

Some of what can be learned by postmortems has been set out in the two previous chapters, and so here I will just summarize. The Iranian case and, to a lesser extent, the Iraqi one reveal the need for stronger middle management and more peer review. The purpose of both is to provide appropriate critical scrutiny to the analysts' ideas. It is not that supervision is now lacking but that it is too often of the wrong kind. Papers are carefully examined before they can be published, but all too often this is done to check style and ensure that they are consistent with other IC products. These functions are legitimate, but they too rarely improve the intellectual level, raise new questions, or catch methodological shortcomings. The problem is especially great now because of the "barbell" distribution of experience within the IC. Because recruitment was cut shortly after the cold war and then expanded enormously after 9/11, something like half of the current IC analysts have less than five years' experience, while another significant percentage is close to retirement. The middle cohort is very thin, a problem compounded by the failure to give managers adequate training.[98]

Peers as well as superiors can provide the kinds of comments, questions, and criticisms that could bring to the surface implicit assumptions, raise alternatives, and catch questionable inferences. I do not think it is entirely an academic conceit to believe that the forms of peer review that characterize the scholarly world could be usefully applied in modified form to intelligence. Of course, many IC products are produced by groups, but what I and others who have made this point have in mind is something different: review by other analysts who can bring to bear their general knowledge and experience with intelligence. Having some distance from the area and its disputes may compensate for deficiencies in specific expertise, and outsiders are more likely to ask naive but important questions.

Of course, peer review uses resources that are scarce, especially when there are not enough experienced analysts to go around. No manager wants to release one of his or her stars for several days to work in a different area. But the main barrier is the lack of appropriate incentives and culture. Members of the IC are not rewarded for this kind of activity and are not socialized to see its advantages. Peer review is possible, and indeed the NIC does it regularly, but only if top management sees its virtues and works hard at nurturing it will it become widespread. As Jack Davis, an experienced intelligence officer who devoted much of his career to improving analytical standards, puts it, "CIA has everything it needs for peer review except the will to do it."[99]

Methodology

The Iran and Iraq cases revealed cognitive and methodological weaknesses in the analysis as well as sociological weaknesses in the organization. Several could be reduced if not eliminated by more self-conscious attention to methodology. This is much more difficult than it seems, however, which is why these errors recur and why it will take concerted efforts to deal with them.

Most obviously, IC products on Iran and Iraq misleadingly implied that the inferences rested on the specific facts being reported rather than on broad background factors and the plausibility of the claims. The problem is not that there is no legitimate role for beliefs about how the world works and what the actor being assessed is like. As I noted in the previous chapter, the use of general theories is an essential part of the scientific method, although in science as in intelligence this way of thinking can lead to overlooking fundamental discoveries and incorrectly affirming what is already believed. But facts do not speak for themselves, and broader beliefs are necessary for making sense of a complex and contradictory world. Thus the fact that Saddam had used chemical weapons in the war with Iran and refused to cooperate with the inspectors should not have been ignored in reaching judgments as to the status of his WMD programs. But analysts not only fooled the consumers by implying that their inferences were driven entirely by reports about current WMD activities; they fooled themselves as well. This is not unusual because like riding a bicycle, much of the mental processing that goes into reaching a judgment is inaccessible to our consciousness.[100]

The problem with the lack of awareness is threefold. First, the fundamental reasons why the inference seems plausible are taken for granted instead of being examined. In the Iraq case, analysts should have asked if there were alternative explanations for why Saddam was refusing to cooperate with the inspectors, for example. They could also have asked whether anything might have changed to render his past pursuit of WMD less relevant. In the case of Iran, they could have asked whether they were seeing the Shah of old (or rather, their image of the Shah of old). In neither case would the answer that now appears to be right have seemed obvious or entirely persuasive, but raising these questions could have revealed the implicit foundations of the analysis. Second, both the IC and the consumers overestimated the importance of the specific bits of evidence they cited. As noted in the previous chapter, President Bush may have had some understanding of this in the briefing that elicited Tenet's infamous "slam dunk" response, an exchange that could have but unfortunately did not lead the participants to see what the inferences rested on. In other cases, this lack of understanding leads to unproductive disputes as participants bitterly contest the meanings of reports and activities without realizing that the disagreement is rooted in larger issues and beliefs on which they should focus. Third, as people assimilate new information to their preexisting views, they fail to realize that this evidence seems supportive only because of what they already believe, leading them to overestimate the extent to which their conclusions are supported by independent bits of information. This is one reason why the Iraq analysts became more confident in their judgments as they received a steady stream of information that was in fact quite ambiguous. Similarly, the striking Iraqi military communications that Secretary of State Powell quoted in his speech to the Security Council seemed incriminating largely because most of his listeners fit them into a frame of Iraqi WMD and deception, and the words in turned reinforced this frame. Awareness can combat this illegitimate bootstrapping.

A related error is that analysts failed to understand the extent to which their inferences rested on propositions that were extremely difficult to disconfirm. When one state masses troops on another's borders and analysts believe invasion would be unwise, they often conclude that the move is a bluff without realizing that by the time they discover they were wrong, it will be too late. In the Iranian case, what was crucial was the unarticulated belief that the Shah would crack down if the situation became really serious. This was reasonable and fit with the common reading of the Shah's personality and the good social science generalization that dictators with well-functioning security forces will not be overthrown. The analytical error was that analysts and consumers failed to realize that this assumption could be disproved only when the unrest reached dangerous proportions, which meant that intelligence could not provide policymakers with more than an eleventh-hour warning. In the Iraq case, analysts explicitly noted their belief that they were seeing only a small fraction of the WMD activities, but they failed to understand that their belief that Saddam was running an extensive deception and denial operation was both crucial to their conclusions and essentially disconfirmable. These traps are of course much more visible in retrospect, but peer review and self-consciousness would at least increase the chances that they could be detected, subjected to scrutiny, and flagged for the consumers as potential vulnerabilities in the analysis.

The Iraq case also shows the need for more attention to basic social science methods.[101] All too often, the analysts (and the later critics) searched on the dependent variable, ignored relevant comparisons, overlooked significant negative evidence, and failed to employ the hypothetico-deductive method. These methodological shortcomings are not surprising because the appropriate ways of thinking do not come naturally, which is why professors pay so much attention to them in their teaching. Intelligence is not uniquely embarrassed in this regard, and most journalists, businessmen, and doctors are even less sophisticated.

As detailed in the previous chapter, analysts took as evidence of WMD programs some suspicious behavior, such as the use of convoluted procurement chains and the presence of special trucks at factories, that also characterized many legal activities. Making such comparisons probably seemed like a digression because their significance is apparent only when one thinks explicitly about how to go about confirming and disconfirming hypotheses, which in this case would have shown that the procurement patterns, while consistent with the proposition that Saddam was seeking WMD, did not provide added support to it. Even less intuitively obvious is the use of negative evidence, the "dogs that do not bark" discussed in the previous chapter. We tend to pass over things that have not occurred because they are not vivid, and we implicitly assume that only events that do occur call for explanations and can shed light on behavior. But this is not true: nonevents are highly relevant if important hypotheses or beliefs about the world imply that they *should* occur.

Analysts also generally neglect the hypothetico-deductive method. In part, this is because of bad experiences with what has been called "hypothesis-driven intelligence." In the IC, this means a paper written to muster all the relevant evidence for a proposition rather than to provide a balanced appreciation, and it has generally been employed as a politicized instrument to undermine IC views that are at variance with preferred policies. It is also unfortunately true that many intelligence errors have stemmed from the excessive role of deduction, with analysts (and policymakers) ignoring disturbing information on the grounds that they are sure that the other state would not act as the obvious reading of information indicates partly because, as noted earlier, such behavior would be self-defeating. But what social scientists mean is quite different. It is asking oneself, "If my proposition or belief is correct, what evidence would I expect to see or be able to gather?" Of course, this is not a panacea in either social science or intelligence, but if the IC had used this tool to probe the conclusion that Saddam had active WMD programs, it might have noticed startling lacunae and bits of negative evidence, especially with the nuclear program.

Similarly, analysts could ask themselves—and one another—what information could cast doubt on if not disconfirm their judgments. In addition to alerting them to places in which their thinking was not disconfirmable, this exercise could be useful in pointing to areas in which information should be sought and in maximizing the impact of discrepant information. For example, if they had been pressed to state their expectations before the results were known, analysts might have been more influenced by how little came of the attempt to draw out Iraqi WMD scientists. But, as usual, we should not expect too much from this technique. In the months before the Winter War with the USSR, Finnish diplomats pointed to the fact that the Soviets had issued threats only in private as evidence that they were bluffing, but did not change their judgments when the Soviets went public.[102]

Alternative interpretations and devil's advocates or red teams to provide critiques are also useful. Although they can easily become a rote exercise that would only leave the IC and consumers even more confident in the established views, these exercises should be a standard part of good practices. The fact that this prescription is made by every postmortem indicates how strongly the organization resists it, but it remains unclear whether the reason is that these techniques are impractical or that they could prove disruptive. The fact that on the important issue of Soviet military doctrine and intentions Team B was deployed as a political weapon rather than an analytical probe obviously makes the IC wary. Nevertheless, methods for making analysts consider alternatives should be sought.[103]

One useful parallel method would be a "premortem" in which analysts would do the thought experiment of contemplating a world in which their views turned out to be incorrect and then asking how this could have come about. For example, in 1978 analysts might have envisioned a world in which the Shah was overthrown and asked themselves how this might have happened; in 2002 analysts could have asked how they might explain the eventual discovery that Saddam did not have active WMD programs. Answers, especially the correct answer, would not appear automatically and even if they were found would not and should not necessarily be credited. Rather, the value of the exercise is in leading to the scrutiny of overlooked facts and possibilities. In the Iranian case, analysts would have had to think about reasons why the Shah might have refrained from using force, and they might have inventoried the powerful forces that could be arrayed against him, thought about how the Shah was weakened by being seen as an American puppet, and surfaced the role of religion in catalyzing dissent. In the Iraq case this approach might have led to a consideration of Saddam's fears of Iran and his own generals as well as focusing attention on how corruption could have explained many of the suspicious activities.[104]

Horses and Zebras

Intelligence is a form of diagnosis, and medical students are taught "When you hear hoofbeats, think horses, not zebras." In other words, the patient is likely to have a common disease, not an exotic one. Intelligence analysts too should pay attention to the frequency with which various kinds of behaviors, intentions, or situations exist in the world and realize that this is what they will usually face.[105] But there are four problems here. First, overall frequency is not a good starting point. If you are in Africa and hear hoofbeats, you *should* think of zebras. It is hard for the analyst to tell if he is in Africa, however. Usually he has enough information about the case to render the general frequencies less than compelling but not enough to establish the frequency that would be appropriate. In the case of Iraq, it was not particularly useful to know how often countries sought nuclear weapons. Iraq was not an ordinary country, and what could be said about the frequency of continuing programs in countries that had once sought (and used) WMD and had not cooperated with UN orders to cease these activities?

A second problem is that the universe of countries or situations for which one would like the frequency is not objectively given but depends in part on the observer's causal beliefs. To someone who believes that the nature of a state's regime is central to its behavior and its propensity for seeking WMD, the relevant universe is dictatorships. Someone who thinks that the external environment is central would look at cases of countries living in bad neighborhoods.

Third, analysts have to alert decision makers to possibilities that would be dangerous if they were to occur even if they are rare. Knowing that a terrorist group might have WMD can be more important than the judgment that it probably does not have them (this is linked to the costs of type 1 and type 2 errors discussed earlier and is something doctors have to contend with as well).

Finally, many of the cases of concern are exceptions to our generalizations. This was certainly true for the Iranian and most other revolutions. It is very hard to develop generalizations about when revolutions will occur, partly because if regimes expect them, they are likely to thwart them, and partly because they usually require odd concatenations of factors.[106] There also had to be several factors at work for Saddam to suspend his programs. The IC was right that it stood to reason that Saddam was pursuing WMD; under most circumstances this would have been normal, and here intelligence analysts thought of horses. Similarly, one reason why Great Britain was taken by surprise by the Nazi invasion of Norway in 1940 was that "conventional wisdom would seem to dictate that a weaker naval power should refrain from challenging a superior naval power in the latter's area of dominance," and indeed German leaders counted on this very factor to protect them by inducing complacency.[107] Inferences are guided by what our cognitive predispositions tell us is likely to be there, and most of the time, this will serve us well. But the exceptions are likely to produce intelligence failures.[108]

In other words, zebras *do* appear, and intelligence must be on the lookout for them. It helps that most come in one of four varieties. First, as we have discussed earlier, the other side may be driven by motivated biases. Its view of the world and behavior will seem strange and irrational to outside observers, who cannot feel the pressures that are bearing in on it. Because the behavior is not likely to succeed, perceivers are not likely to expect it. A second and related situation is that the other state may develop an unusual view of the world for any number of reasons, usually stemming from its domestic politics or the idiosyncratic views of its leader. As I discussed in the previous chapter, Saddam's outlook was odd, and it was not only American ethnocentrism and lack of empathy that led to the failure to understand it. Even in retrospect and with much fuller information, his ideas and policies are strange. A third kind of zebra appears when the other side does something new. Part of the reason why American and other observers were taken by surprise when the USSR put missiles into Cuba was that they believed that the Soviet Union had never allowed nuclear weapons to leave its soil.[109] We are prone to expect continuity, not change, especially in the absence of an obvious precipitating stimulus, which partly explains the failure to detect that Saddam had halted his WMD programs.[110] It takes particularly sharp and unambiguous evidence for us to detect a new kind of behavior.

Finally, particularly complex patterns are unusual, hard to comprehend, and likely to be seen in much simpler terms. Misunderstandings are likely not only when policies are incompetent but also when they are excessively creative. This was true for Bismarck's policy, which was dazzling in its diplomatic constructions that played off other countries' interests in a way that enabled Germany to make contradictory promises, keep the peace, and maintain significant leverage. It is not surprising that other countries never fully grasped what Bismarck was doing and constantly suspected him of trying to drag them into conflict. Indeed, even his own subordinates held oversimplified understandings of much of his reasoning and intent.[111]

The resulting prescription, which is not always easy to implement, is that while analysts should indeed think first of horses, they should not neglect zebras either. Knowing the four kinds of circumstances that are likely to produce unusual behavior tells observers a bit more, but by definition these cases will be hard to perceive correctly.

Empathy and Expertise

The two cases presented in this book show an unfortunate lack of empathy. We usually understand that others may have goals we find abhorrent, but we have more difficulty believing that they may see the world in ways that are foreign to us. Intelligence may have an advantage over decision makers here because being powerful seems to reduce empathy,[112] but in compensation decision makers often are particularly well attuned to what their opposite numbers need in order to survive politically. Both intelligence and decision makers are likely to have difficulty understanding the other's domestic and bureaucratic politics. Although analysts are fully aware of the powerful role these factors play in their own country, they are so hard to discern in adversaries, especially in closed societies, that they tend to be omitted from IC products. The problem is compounded by the fact that there are innumerable ways in which domestic and bureaucratic forces could play out. Nevertheless, analysts should be encouraged or even required to develop at least one alternative assessment that relies heavily on the other state's domestic and bureaucratic politics or political history.

This requires deep knowledge of the country. There are no quick fixes here, and again my suggestions are not original. The IC needs much greater competence in foreign languages, cultures, and histories. This means allowing some analysts to focus on a country or a region for extended periods of time, and perhaps for an entire career. INR does this more than the CIA, and the latter has too few people who are true experts on a country or region. During the cold war it cultivated specialists on the USSR and PRC who could hold their own with those in the universities, but this is no longer true because of the lack of a single adversary and the value placed on flexible generalists. Few analysts have research training or doctorates or can tap into the scholarly community.[113] Of course, it is now easy to say that the United States needs true experts on the Arab world, but it is harder to convince decision makers that we need analysts with a deep understanding of countries like Nigeria and Brazil, let alone Uruguay and Burma.

Investment

All these procedures and ways of thinking should be cultivated in a robust training program. New analysts are of course trained, but only briefly. With the great pressures to put analysts "on the line," training is seen as a luxury. It is not, and the time saved at the start will be purchased at the cost of lower-quality analysis over a lifetime. Additional training is needed throughout analysts' careers, as is understood by many business organizations and the American military. Officers spend a good deal of time in advanced education, but in the IC there is much less of this, and it is much less well thought out. The main reasons are that analysts are too readily seen by others—and themselves—as experts and, more important, they cannot be spared from their regular duties.[114] The war in Iraq may lead us to forget that the U.S. military rarely finds itself in combat, and so it can devote a good proportion of its time to advanced training and education. Since the IC is never "off-line," the natural tendency will be to stint on such programs.

Conclusion

The reforms I have discussed are feasible. But they are not cheap and will not eradicate intelligence failures. They are in the nature of investments and call for putting resources, time, and energy into the reforms. This would require sustained commitment throughout the IC, starting with its top leaders. Unfortunately this may not be forthcoming. Inducing new ways of thinking and interacting will be disruptive, the tasks are undramatic, and the benefits are uncertain and delayed. Logic and the history of the IC (and other organizations) give few grounds for optimism. Because intelligence is unpopular and better intelligence may be even more unpopular, political leaders are likely to be content with decrying intelligence's performance. Top leaders of the IC are understandably preoccupied with pressing tasks and are likely to have short time horizons, making it unreasonable to expect them to sustain these reforms. Analysts and middle-level officials who see the need for change are likely to become frustrated and isolated. We can then probably look forward to even more failures than are necessary and to more books like this.

Notes

1. Adventures in Intelligence

1. This causes problems for our theories as well as the states because many of the former rest on each side's having accurate expectations about what the other will do: David Kreps, *Game Theory and Economic Modelling* (New York: Oxford University Press, 1990).

2. The best general discussions of intelligence and policymaking are Michael Herman, *Intelligence Power in Peace and War* (Cambridge: Cambridge University Press, 1966), and Richard Betts, *Enemies of Intelligence* (New York: Columbia University Press, 2007).

3. For another discussion of the meaning of the concept, see Mark Lowenthal, "The Burdensome Concept of Failure," in *Intelligence: Policy and Process,* ed. Alfred Maurer, Marion Tunstall, and James Keagle (Boulder, CO: Westview, 1985), chap. 5.

4. Numbers 13:1–2, 31–32. The literature on surprise and errors is enormous: the best discussion is Richard Betts, *Surprise Attack* (Washington, DC: Brookings Institution, 1982); the classic study is Roberta Wohlstetter, *Pearl Harbor: Warning and Decision* (Stanford: Stanford University Press, 1962). Good historical studies are Ernest May, ed., *Knowing One's Enemies: Intelligence Assessment before the Two World Wars* (Princeton: Princeton University Press, 1984), and the special issue of *Journal of Strategic Studies,* vol. 13, Spring 1998, edited by Martin Alexander and entitled "Knowing Your Friends." Much of this work rests on analysis of how individuals process information and see the world, as I have discussed in *Perception and Misperception in International Politics* (Princeton: Princeton University Press, 1976). For an application of this approach to improving intelligence, see Richards Heuer, *Psychology of Intelligence Analysis* (Washington, DC: CIA Center for the Study of Intelligence, 1999). For a superb study of individual difference in accuracy of predictions and willingness to change one's mind, see Philip Tetlock, *Expert Political Judgment: How Good Is It? How Can We Know?* (Princeton: Princeton University Press, 2005). For a detailed study of the failure of American, Dutch, and United Nations (UN) intelligence to anticipate the capture of Srebrenica and the massacre of the men captured there, see Cees Wiebes, *Intelligence and the War in Bosnia, 1992–1995* (Munster, Germany: Lit Verlag, 2003). For all their weaknesses in this area, democracies probably do a better job of assessing their adversaries than do nondemocracies: Ralph White, "Why Aggressors Lose," *Political Psychology,* vol. 11, June 1990, pp. 227–42; Dan Reiter and Allan Stam, *Democracies at War* (Princeton: Princeton University Press, 2002).

5. An excellent study of deception is Thaddeus Holt, *The Deceivers: Allied Military Deception in the Second World War* (New York: Scribner, 2004).

6. Indeed, Eliot Cohen has labeled arguments like mine the "no fault" school. This is not entirely accurate because my account finds numerous errors, many of them avoidable. Eliot Cohen and John Gooch, *Military Misfortunes* (New York: Free Press, 1990), pp. 40–43; for a good rebuttal see Betts, *Enemies of Intelligence*, pp. 27, 185–86. For the cogent but politically unacceptable argument that "if the September 11 and Iraq failures teach us anything, it is that we need to lower our expectations of what intelligence analysis can . . . do," see Thomas Mahnken, "Spies and Bureaucrats: Getting Intelligence Right," *Public Interest*, no. 81, Spring 2005, p. 41. This would mean trying to design policies that are not likely to fail disastrously if the supporting intelligence is incorrect, as I will discuss in chapter 4.

7. Jervis, *Perception and Misperception in International Politics;* Jervis "Understanding Beliefs," *Political Psychology*, vol. 27, October 2006, pp. 641–63.

8. Betts, *Enemies of Intelligence*, chap. 3.

9. *The Logic of Images in International Relations* (Princeton: Princeton University Press, 1970; 2nd ed. with a new introduction, New York: Columbia University Press, 1989); *Perception and Misperception in International Politics*. The two topics are discussed in tandem in my "Signaling and Perception: Drawing Inferences and Projecting Images," in *Political Psychology*, ed. Kristen Monroe (Mahwah, NJ: Erlbaum, 2002), pp. 293–312.

10. Christopher Ford and David Rosenberg, "The Naval Intelligence Underpinnings of Reagan's Maritime Strategy," *Journal of Strategic Studies*, vol. 28, April 2005, pp. 379–410; Sherry Sontag, Christopher Drew, and Annette Lawrence Drew, *Blind Man's Bluff: The Untold Story of American Submarine Espionage* (New York: Harper Torch, 1999); Benjamin Weiser, *Secret Life: The Polish Officer, His Covert Mission, and the Price He Paid to Save His Country* (New York: Public Affairs, 2004). The information supplied by Kuklinski and the resulting finished intelligence is now being declassified.

11. A short and very sanitized version of this paper was published as "Evaluating U.S. Intelligence Estimates," in *Intelligence Requirements for the 1980s: Analysis and Estimates*, ed. Roy Godson, vol. 2 (New Brunswick, NJ: Transaction Books, 1980), pp. 49–73. A less dramatic and more focused intelligence community product was National Intelligence Estimate 11-6-65, "Soviet Capabilities for Concealing Strategic Weapons Programs," U.S. Department of State, *Foreign Relations of the United States, 1964–1968*, vol. 10, *National Security* (Washington, DC: Government Printing Office, 2002), pp. 250–53.

12. Department of State, "Estimate of Damage to U.S. Foreign Policy Interests," *Foreign Relations of the United States, 1964–1968*, vol. 14, The Soviet Union (Washington, DC: Government Printing Office, 2001), pp. 111–14.

13. This judgment now appears to have been closer to the truth than I had believed at the time, as least as far as the KGB was concerned. Christopher Andrew and Vasili Mitrokhin, *The World Was Going Our Way: The KGB and the Battle for the Third World* (New York: Basic Books, 2005).

14. "Why Nuclear Superiority Doesn't Matter," *Political Science Quarterly*, vol. 94, Winter 1979–80, pp. 617–34; *The Illogic of American Nuclear Strategy* (Ithaca: Cornell University Press, 1984); *The Meaning of the Nuclear Revolution* (Ithaca: Cornell University Press, 1989).

2. Failing to See That the Shah Was in Danger

1. Most if not all of the cables became publicly available in the wake of the seizure of the Tehran embassy. They had been shredded, but the students were able to laboriously

piece them together. The pasting of the narrow strips makes them a bit hard to read, however. For a time they were not available in the United States because it was illegal to import anything in Iran, but they can now be found in many libraries as *Documents from the Den of Espionage,* and more conveniently, in the National Security Archive microfiche collection *Iran: The Making of U.S. Policy, 1977–1980,* ed. Eric Hooglund (Alexandria, VA: Chadwyck-Healey, 1990). For analyses of the intellligence failure, see Charles-Philippe David, *Foreign Policy Failure in the White House: Reappraising the Fall of the Shah and the Iran-Contra Affair* (Lanham, MD: University Press of America, 1993); Gregory Treverton with James Klocke, "Iran, 1978–1979: Coping with the Unthinkable," in *Dealing with Dictators: Dilemmas of U.S. Diplomacy and Intelligence Analysis, 1945–1990,* ed. Ernest May and Philp Zelikow (Cambridge: MIT Press, 2006), chap. 4; Ofira Seliktar, *Failing the Crystal Ball Test: The Carter Administration and the Fundamentalist Revolution in Iran* (Westport, CT: Praeger, 2000); Janne Nolan and Douglas MacEachin with Kristine Tockman, *Discourse, Dissent, and Strategic Surprise: Formulating US Security Policy in an Age of Uncertainty* (Washington, DC: Georgetown University Institute for the Study of Diplomacy, 2006), pp. 12–28.

2. Several years later I was able to publish highly sanitized versions of the report: "Improving the Intelligence Process: Informal Norms and Incentives," in *Intelligence: Policy and Process,* ed. Alred Maurer, Marion Tunstall, and James Keagle (Boulder, CO: Westview, 1986), pp. 113–24, and "What's Wrong with the Intelligence Process?" *International Journal of Intelligence and CounterIntelligence,* vol. 1, Spring 1986, pp. 28–41. Bob Woodward also had a fairly accurate summary in *Veil: The Secret Wars of the CIA, 1981–1987* (New York: Simon & Schuster, 1987), pp. 108–11, and this triggered a request for the report from DCI William Webster for transmittal to Congress.

3. Loch Johnson, "Spymaster Richard Helms: An Interview with the Former US Director of Central Intelligence," *Intelligence and National Security,* vol. 18, Autumn 2003, p. 33.

4. This is the judgment of the best book on the Iranian revolution, Charles Kurzman, *The Unthinkable Revolution in Iran* (Cambridge: Harvard University Press, 2004). As Nikki Keddie puts it, "Neither of the two sides [among his advisers] that alternately influenced Carter had much chance of influencing the Revolution." *Modern Iran* (New Haven: Yale University Press, 2006), p. 236.

5. The best account of this period remains that by Gary Sick, who was the NSC staffer for the region: *All Fall Down: America's Tragic Encounter with Iran* (New York: Random House, 1985). In addition to the memoirs of Vance and Brezezinski, see Robert Huyser, *Mission to Tehran* (New York: Harper & Row, 1986). Ambassador Sullivan's version is in his *Mission to Iran* (New York: Norton, 1981).

6. The British ambassador recounts that the Shah frequently said that he would not use massive force: Anthony Parsons, *The Pride and the Fall: Iran 1974–1979* (London: Jonathan Cape, 1984). Although the British and American ambassadors often saw the Shah together, the latter did not report this. For the Shah's account of what he perceived as wavering American support, see Mohammed Reza Pahlavi, *Witness to History* (New York: Stein and Day, 1980), pp. 161–65.

7. For discussion of the origins and some of the operation of this principle, see Stansfield Turner, *Burn before Reading: Presidents, CIA Directors, and Secret Intelligence* (New York: Hyperion, 2005), pp. 43–45, 65.

8. It appears that State Department policy was strongly influenced by the desk officer, Henry Precht, who remains a controversial figure. See Seliktar, *Failing the Crystal Ball Test,* pp. 84–86; James Bill, *The Eagle and the Lion: The Tragedy American-Iranian Relations* (New Haven: Yale University Press, 1988), pp. 244–47; Sick, *All Fall Down,* chaps. 5–7.

9. The complete declassified text is available from CIA. Requesters should ask for the most recent and complete version declassified under Executive Order 12958.

10. For research papers on the USSR, the PRC, and their relationship with each other, see the Caesar, Esau, and Polo series on the CIA's website (http://www.foia.cia.gov).

11. Lack of communication also helps explain the disturbing fact that when CIA analysts said they expected the Shah to "act decisively," they meant that he would use force, while others in the government read and employed the phrase to mean continued liberalization.

12. For the argument that the decline in oil prices that created much distress in Iran was the product of American (and Saudi) policies adopted in 1976 over the objection of Secretary of State Kissinger, who warned that it might destabilize our ally, see Andrew Scott Cooper, "Showdown at Doha: The Secret Oil Deal That Helped Sink the Shah of Iran," *Middle East Journal,* vol. 62, Autumn 2008, pp. 567–91. Of course, intelligence was not asked to predict the consequences of this policy, although I have no confidence that it would have responded well if it had been.

13. The question of whether intelligence should be organized functionally or geographically arose when CIA was formed: Sherman Kent, *Strategic Intelligence for American World Policy* (Princeton: Princeton University Press, 1949), pp. 116–22.

14. For a general discussion, see Erik Gartzke, "War Is in the Error Term," *International Organization,* vol. 53, Summer 1999, pp. 567–87; Kurzman in *Unthinkable Revolution* makes a similar argument in the Iranian case.

15. Parsons, *The Pride and the Fall,* p. 134. This account is thoughtful and insightful throughout. Also valuable is the report by the primary political officer in the American embassy (and a graduate school classmate of mine), John Stempel, *Inside the Iranian Revolution* (Bloomington: Indiana University Press, 1981).

16. Robert Jervis, *System Effects: Complexity in Social and Political Life* (Princeton: Princeton University Press, 1997), pp. 150–55, 163; Kurzman, *Unthinkable Revolution,* chap. 7.

17. Students of intelligence often distinguish between secrets that are written down somewhere and can be stolen and mysteries that can only be unraveled, if not guessed at. Revolutions fit into the latter category. See Gregory Treverton, "Estimating beyond the Cold War," *Defense Intelligence Journal,* vol. 3, Fall 1994, pp. 5–20; Joseph Nye, "Peering into the Future," *Foreign Affairs,* vol. 74, July/August 1994, pp. 82–93.

18. Kurzman, *Unthinkable Revolution.*

19. Klaus Knorr, "Failures in National Intelligence Estimates: The Case of the Cuban Missiles," *World Politics,* vol. 16, April 1964, pp. 455–67.

20. For good treatments, in addition to Kurzman, *Unthinkable Revolution,* see Ervand Abrahamian, *Khomeinism: Essays on the Islamic Republic* (Berkeley: University of California Press, 1993); Cheryl Benard and Zalmay Khalilzad, *"The Government of God": Iran's Islamic Republic* (New York, Columbia University Press, 1984), chap. 3; Michael Fischer, *Iran: From Religious Dispute to Revolution* (Cambridge: Harvard University Press, 1980); Mansoor Moaddel, *Class, Politics, and Revolution in the Iranian Revolution* (New York: Columbia University Press, 1993).

21. Keddie, *Modern Iran,* pp. 216–17.

22. Pahlavi, *Witness to History,* p. 167; Sullivan, *Mission to Iran;* Parsons, *The Pride and the Fall.* Of course the Shah did use significant force, and what the consequences of an all-out assault would have been are uncertain.

23. Marvin Zonis, *Majestic Failure: The Fall of the Shah* (Chicago: University of Chicago Press, 1991). Turner, *Burn before Reading*, p. 181, regrets that CIA did not do a psychological profile of the Shah at the time. Ambassador Sullivan reports that the Shah was not arrogant, as he had been led to expect, but he does not seem to have fully grasped his weakness. *Mission to Iran*, pp. 54–57.

24. There are some rumors that the Shah's doctors did tell their government, and John Stempel reports that someone in the U.S. government was informed in October 1978 (*Inside the Iranian Revolution*, pp. 104, 289), but if this is correct, the information did not reach CIA or the NSC.

25. This is documented in Rose McDermott's important study *Presidential Leadership, Illness, and Decision Making* (New York: Cambridge University Press, 2007).

3. The Iraq WMD Intelligence Failure

1. *Review of Intelligence on Weapons of Mass Destruction*, a Report of a Committee of Privy Counsellors to the House of Commons, July 14, 2004 (hereafter the Butler report); Senate Select Committee on Intelligence, *Report on the U.S. Intelligence Community's Prewar Intelligence Assessments on Iraq*, July 7, 2004 (hereafter SSCI); Senate Select Committee on Intelligence, *Report on Postwar Findings about Iraq's WMD Programs and Links to Terrorism and How They Compare with Prewar Assessments*, September 8, 2006; Commission on the Intelligence Capabilities of the United States regarding Weapons of Mass Destruction, *Report to the President of the United States*, March 31, 2005 (hereafter WMD Commission). *The Report of the Inquiry into Australian Intelligence Agencies*, July 2004 (the Flood report) is not as detailed as the U.S. and U.K. reports, and I will say little about it. The U.K. House of Commons Foreign Affairs Committee and the Intelligence and Security Committee had investigations and reports, although what is of value in them for our purposes is subsumed by the Butler report. The United Kingdom also held a special investigation into the suicide of David Kelly and the related question of whether the British government had "sexed up" its public dossier on WMD (the Hutton report). Most of the massive documentation on which the official reports rest remains classified, and so we cannot tell whether they accurately characterize it. Ironically, while the reports all note that intelligence analysts lacked sufficient access to their sources and so should have exercised greater caution, they do not seem to realize that the same stricture must be applied to the documents they have produced.

The Butler report covers some issues of policy as well as intelligence, in part because in the United Kingdom the line between the two is not as sharply drawn as in the United States. Indeed, "assessment is really viewed in the UK as a *government* function and not specifically an *intelligence* function." Philip Davies, "A Critical Look at Britain's Spy Machinery," *Studies in Intelligence*, vol. 49, no. 4, 2005, pp. 41–54. For other analyses of the Butler report, see Davies, "Intelligence Culture and Intelligence Failure in Britain and the United States," *Cambridge Review of International Affairs*, vol. 17, October 2004, pp. 495–520; Nigel West, "The UK's Not Quite So Secret Services," *International Journal of Intelligence and CounterIntelligence*, vol. 18, Spring 2005, pp. 23–30; Alex Danchev, "The Reckoning: Official Inquiries and the Iraq War," *Intelligence and National Security*, vol. 19, Autumn 2004, pp. 436–66; Richard Aldrich, "Whitehall and the Iraq War: The UK's Four Intelligence Enquiries," *Irish Studies in International Relations*, vol. 16, 2005, pp. 73–88. Prime Minister Blair gave his response to the Butler report in a speech to the House of Commons on July 13, 2004. For comparison of the British and American reports, see Lawrence Lamanna, "Documenting the Differences between American and

British Intelligence Reports," *International Journal of Intelligence and CounterIntelligence,* vol. 20, Winter 2007, pp. 602–28; Robert Jervis, "Commentary: The Butler Report," in *Exploring Intelligence Archives: Enquiries into the Secret State,* ed. R. Gerald Hughes, Peter Jackson, and Len Scott (London: Routledge, 2008), pp. 309–13; Loch Johnson, "Commentary: The Butler Report: A US Perspective," in Hughes, Jackson, and Scott, *Exploring Intelligence Archives,* pp. 313–17. For a critical assessment of Australian intelligence and policymaking, see the account by a former intelligence official, Andrew Wilkie, *Axis of Deceit* (Melbourne: Black Inc. Agenda, 2004), which, while polemical, contains good analysis. Also see James Pfiffner and Mark Pythian, eds., *Intelligence and National Security Policymaking on Iraq: British and American Perspectives* (Manchester, UK: Manchester University Press, 2008).

For earlier discussions of the intelligence failures, see James Bamford, *A Pretext for War: 9/11, Iraq, and the Abuse of America's Intelligence Agencies* (New York: Doubleday, 2004); Michael Isikoff and David Corn, *Hubris: The Inside Story of Spin, Scandal, and the Selling of the Iraq War* (New York: Crown, 2006); John Prados, *Hoodwinked: The Documents that Reveal How Bush Sold Us a War* (New York: New Press, 2004); and Prados "A Necessary War?" *Bulletin of the Atomic Scientists,* vol. 59, May/June 2003, pp. 26–33. These accounts do little to explain the failures, however. Also see Mark Phythian, "The Perfect Intelligence Failure? U.S. Pre-War Intelligence on Iraqi Weapons of Mass Destruction," *Politics & Policy,* vol. 34, June 2006, pp. 400–424.

For the CIA responses to the failure, see "CIA Revising Pre-Invasion Iraq Arms Intel," *New York Times,* February 2, 2005; CIA Directorate of Intelligence, "Continuous Learning in the DI: May 2004 Review of Analytic Tradecraft Fundamentals," Sherman Kent School, CIA, *Tradecraft Review,* vol. 1, August 2004; Richard Kerr et al., "Issues for the US Intelligence Community," *Studies in Intelligence,* vol. 49, no. 3, 2005, pp. 47–54.

2. This may be the appropriate place to note that my views are influenced by having headed a small team of academics who studied the failure and advised CIA on remedies. This and other consulting I have done may have made me (unduly?) sympathetic to the organization. Furthermore, although everything here is supported by declassified sources, some of what I heard and read remains classified.

3. Martin Melosi, *In the Shadow of Pearl Harbor: Political Controversy over the Surprise Attack, 1941–46* (College Station, TX: Texas A&M Press, 1977); it took an unofficial (but government-sponsored) study that was done much later to shed real light on the problems in an analysis that remains central to our understanding not only of this case but of surprise attacks in general. See Roberta Wohlstetter, *Pearl Harbor: Warning and Decision* (Stanford: Stanford University Press, 1962).

4. SSCI strongly concurs with this judgment, the WMD Commission does as well but with many more qualifications, and the Butler report points to problems but does not render an overall judgment. In general the Butler report is not as critical as are the American reports, which may reflect British understatement and the belief that blaming intelligence would inappropriately excuse the political leadership.

5. For good arguments that intelligence mattered less in the cold war than is generally believed, see John Gaddis, "Intelligence, Espionage, and Cold War History," *Diplomatic History,* vol. 13, Spring 1989, pp. 191–212, and Richard Immerman, "Intelligence and Strategy: Historicizing Psychology, Policy, and Politics," *Diplomatic History,* vol. 32, January 2008, pp. 1–14. For the general (and overstated) claim that intelligence matters little in warfare, see John Keegan, *Intelligence in War* (London: Hutchinson, 2003). For a small but important case in which good intelligence derived from intercepted cables guided policy, see Ken Kotani, "Could Japan Read Allied Signal Traffic? Japanese

Codebreaking and the Advance into French Indo-China, September 1940," *Intelligence and National Security*, vol. 20, June 2005, pp. 304–20. Not only may policy be independent of intelligence, but good policy may rest on bad intelligence. In the most important case of this kind, Winston Churchill convinced his colleagues to continue fighting Nazi Germany in June 1940, by utilizing estimates of German strength that were even more faulty than the WMD estimates. David Reynolds, "Churchill and the British 'Decision' to Fight on in 1940: Right Policy, Wrong Reasons," in *Diplomacy and Intelligence during the Second World War*, ed. Richard Langhorne (Cambridge: Cambridge University Press, 1985), pp. 147–67.

6. The report, complete with rebuttals from several Republicans and counterrebuttals from Democrats, finally appeared in 2008. Senate Select Committee on Intelligence, *Report on Whether Public Statements regarding Iraq by U.S. Government Officials Were Substantiated by Intelligence Information*, June 2008.

7. See, for example, his explanation to Tim Russert on *Meet the Press* on February 8, 2004, quoted in Thomas Ricks, *Fiasco: The American Military Adventure in Iraq* (New York: Penguin, 2006), pp. 375–76. This is consistent with what Under Secretary of Defense Douglas Feith reports about the president's views in his *War and Decision: Inside the Pentagon at the Dawn of the War on Terrorism* (New York: HarperCollins, 2008).

8. Vice President Cheney went so far as to argue that if there was even a 1 percent chance of a danger's occurrence, it had to be treated as a certainty, and while he cannot have meant this literally, it does reflect his and the president's mind-set. Ron Suskind, *The One Percent Doctrine: Deep Inside America's Pursuit of Its Enemies since 9/11* (New York: Simon & Schuster, 2006), p. 123 and passim. For a more generous and I think plausible interpretation of what Cheney meant, see George Tenet with Bill Harlow, *At the Center of the Storm: My Years at the CIA* (New York: HarperCollins, 2007), pp. 264–65.

9. As Feith argued in criticizing the administration for resting much of its case on the state of Iraq's WMD programs, "[O]ne did not need secret information to understand or explain the threat from Saddam." Feith, *War and Decision* p. 520.

10. As he was leaving office, Bush did say that "the biggest regret of all the presidency has to have been the intelligence failure in Iraq" (transcript: Charlie Gibson Interviews President Bush," December 1, 2008, http://abcnews.go.com/print?id=6356046), but this ducked the question asked—which concerned things he wished he had done differently—and did not say that the error influenced his behavior.

11. For further discussion of whether the Bush administration would have wanted and been able to go to war had it known the true state of Saddam's programs, see Feith, *War and Decision*, esp. pp. 228, 331, 471; Isikoff and Corn, *Hubris*, pp. 15–17, 349; Robert Jervis, "War, Intelligence, and Honesty," *Political Science Quarterly*, vol. 123, Winter 2008–9, pp. 1–30.

12. Much of this literature is summarized in Timothy Wilson, *Strangers to Ourselves: Discovering the Adaptive Unconscious* (Cambridge, MA: Harvard University Press, 2002). For a further discussion of this and related issues about the sources and nature of beliefs, see Robert Jervis, "Understanding Beliefs," *Political Psychology*, vol. 26, October 2006, pp. 641–63.

13. It was Congress rather than the president who called for the NIE, and National Security Adviser Rice admitted to not having read it. For the argument that the president's failure to call for an NIE meant that the executive was proceeding without agreed-upon intelligence, see Anthony Glees and Philip H. J. Davies, "Intelligence, Iraq and the Limits of Legislative Accountability during Political Crisis," *Intelligence*

and National Security, vol. 21, October 2006, p. 872; for the claim that the NIE did affect the administration, see Ricks, *Fiasco,* p. 52, but this is unsupported by any other accounts.

14. INR "believes that Saddam continues to want nuclear weapons and that available evidence indicates that Baghdad is pursuing at least a limited effort to maintain and acquire nuclear weapons-related capabilities. The activities we have detected do not, however, add up to a compelling case that Iraq is currently pursuing what INR would consider to be an integrated and comprehensive approach to acquire nuclear weapons. Iraq may be doing so, but INR considers the available evidence inadequate to support such a judgment." SSCI, pp. 86–7.

15. For comparisons between the classified and public American reports, see SSCI, pp. 286–97; Jessica Mathews and Jeff Miller, "A Tale of Two Intelligence Estimates," Carnegie Endowment for International Peace, March 31, 2004; Donald Kennedy, "Intelligence Science: Reverse Peer Review?" *Science,* vol. 303, March 26, 2004, p. 1945; Center for American Progress, "Neglecting Intelligence, Ignoring Warnings," January 28, 2004, http://www.americanprogress.org/site/pp.asp?c=biJRJ8OVF&b=24889. One of the main recommendations of the Butler report was that the Joint Intelligence Committee (JIC) not issue public estimates, which, contrary to precedent, it did in this case. Unfortunately the United States has not been able to exercise such self-restraint.

16. Richard Betts, *Enemies of Intelligence: Knowledge and Power in American National Security* (New York: Columbia University Press, 2007), pp. 116, 121–23. George Tenet picks up this formulation in his judgment of the issue in *At the Center of the Storm,* p. 338. Also see Nassim Taleb, *The Black Swan: The Impact of the Highly Improbable* (New York: Random House, 2007). For the interesting but unconvincing argument that focusing on uncertainty could have come much closer to the right answer on Iraq, see Belinda Canton, "The Active Management of Uncertainty," *International Journal of Intelligence and CounterIntelligence,* vol. 21, Fall 2008, pp. 501–13. As Jack Davis has noted, administrations tend to require a higher level of proof from intelligence when the evidence cuts against their desired policy. Davis, "Intelligence Analysts and Policymakers: Benefits and Dangers of Tensions in the Relationship," *Intelligence and National Security,* vol. 21, December 2006, pp. 1004–6.

17. WMD Commission, p. 50; see the next chapter for further discussion of problems caused by the rush to put items into the PDB.

18. Bob Woodward, *Plan of Attack* (New York: Simon & Schuster, 2004), pp. 196–97.

19. George Tenet, "The Text of C.I.A. Director George J. Tenet's Speech at Georgetown University," February 5, 2004, http://www.freerepublic.com/focus/f-news/1072070/posts; Tenet, *At the Center of the Storm,* pp. 229–30. For conflicting reports on what Sabri said, see Senate Select Commission on Intelligence, *Postwar Findings about Iraq's WMD Programs,* pp. 142–43; WMD Commission, p. 117; Tyler Drumheller, *On the Brink: An Insider's Account of How the White House Compromised American Intelligence* (New York: Carroll & Graf, 2006), chap. 5; Scott Shane, "Iraqi Official, Paid by C.I.A, Gave Account of Weapons," *New York Times,* March 22, 2006; Aram Reston, Lisa Myers, and the NBC Investigative Unit, "Iraqi Diplomat Gave U.S. Prewar WMD Details," MSNBC, March 21, 2006, http://www.commondreams.org/cgi-bin/print.cgi?file=/headlines06/03; Isokoff and Corn, *Hubris,* pp. 62–63, 350–51; Ron Suskind, *The Way of the World: A Story of Truth and Hope in an Age of Extremism* (New York: Harper, 2008), pp. 179–81. It is also possible that Sabri's reports were in error. Most senior Iraqi officials believed that their country had WMD, which points to a potential danger of good intelligence in that to the extent that the United States or United Kingdom had tapped

into what these people were saying, any lingering doubts would have been dispelled. The ICs rarely paid much attention to the possibility of what is known as Red-on-Red deception in which some members of the other country deceive their colleagues. As Tenet notes, "We failed . . . to factor in how the regime's harsh treatment of its citizens would make truthful reporting to superiors on the status of weapons programs less likely." *At the Center of the Storm,* p. 331.

20. Butler report, p. 13; for general discussions, see Charles Weiss, "Communicating Uncertainty in Intelligence and Other Professions," *International Journal of Intelligence and CounterIntelligence,* vol. 21, Spring 2008, pp. 57–85; Joab Rosenberg, "The Interpretation of Probability in Intelligence Estimation and Strategic Assessment," *Intelligence and National Security,* vol. 23, April 2008, pp. 139–52; Betts, *Enemies of Intelligence,* p. 33.

21. Israeli intelligence did employ red team to make the case that Saddam had destroyed his WMD, but its arguments were found to be unpersuasive: Ephraim Kahana, "Analyzing Israel's Intelligence Failures," *International Journal of Intelligence and Counter-Intelligence,* vol. 18, Summer 2005, pp. 273–74. In fact, academic research casts doubt on the efficacy of this approach. See Charlan Nemeth, Keith Brown, and John Rogers, "Devil's Advocate versus Authentic Dissent: Stimulating Quantity and Quality," *European Journal of Social Psychology,* vol. 31, November/December 2001, pp. 707–20. Within CIA, the best work is on the related approach of alternative analysis: see especially the exposition of how this method could have been used before the Soviet missiles were discovered in Cuba in Jack Davis, "Alternative Analysis and the Perils of Estimating: Analyst-Friendly Approaches" (unpublished manuscript, October 6, 2003).

22. WMD Commission, p. 155.

23. A lack of imagination may have been shown by the IC's unwillingness to think about puzzling aspects of Iraq's behavior. Had the IC asked why Saddam was not doing all he could to avoid war, it might have been led in an interesting and highly policy-relevant direction. After the war, there were scattered reports that France and Russia had told Saddam that they would restrain the United States, and this may have played a role in his decision (and if these countries did believe that the United States would back down, this was the most consequential of the intelligence failures). Working backwards from his recalcitrance and combining it with any intelligence on what French and Russian diplomats were saying could have led the IC to flag this possibility. The obvious policy would have been for the United States and United Kingdom to tell France and Russia in the strongest possible terms that their opposition would not deter the United States and that those countries could best contribute to peace by making this clear to Saddam. Of course they might not have been willing to comply, and it might not have made a difference, but imagination does seem to have been absent here.

24. SSCI, p. 18.

25. Irving Janis, *Victims of Groupthink* (Boston: Houghton Mifflin, 1972); for later research in this area see Paul't Hart, Eric Stern, and Bengt Sundelius, eds., *Beyond Groupthink: Political Group Dynamics and Foreign Policy-Making* (Ann Arbor: University of Michigan Press, 1997); Robert Baron, "So Right It's Wrong: Groupthink and the Ubiquitous Nature of Polarized Group Decision-Making," *Advances in Experimental Social Psychology,* vol. 37, 2005, pp. 219–53. I think it is fair to say that groupthink has a stronger following in the general public than among researchers, perhaps because of its catchy name. For the report of a plausible example, however, see "The Performance of the Intelligence Community before the Arab-Israeli War of October 1973: A Preliminary Post-Mortem Report," December 1973, p. 18 (http://www.faqs.org/cia/docs/53/0001331429/THE-

PERFORMANCE-OF-THE-INTELLIGENCE-COMMUNITY-BEFORE-THE-ARAB-ISRAELI-WAR-OF-OC.html).

26. For reports of pressures to conform within CIA, see WMD Commission, pp. 191–94; for the argument that INR has developed a culture that encourages dissent and the CIA has not, see Justin Rood, "Analyze This," *Washington Monthly,* January/February 2005, pp. 18–21.

27. SSCI, p. 22. In the mid-1980s CIA's Senior Review Panel reached a similar conclusion based on examining a number of cases from 1945 to 1978. Willis Armstrong et al., "The Hazards of Single-Outcome Forecasting," originally in *Studies in Intelligence,* vol. 28, Fall 1984, pp. 57–70, and published in declassified form in H. Bradford Westerfield, ed., *Inside CIA's Private World: Declassified Articles from the Agency's Internal Journal, 1955–1992* (New Haven: Yale University Press, 1995), pp. 238–54. Political psychologists have similarly argued that much information is ordinarily processed "online"—that as new information is received, it is melded with the person's standing judgment on the subject, with the person's not being aware of how this judgment was formed. See, for example, Kathleen McGraw and Milton Lodge, "Review Essay: Political Information Processing," *Political Communication,* vol. 13, January–March 1996, pp. 131–38; also see Charles Taber, "Information Processing and Public Opinion," in *Oxford Handbook of Political Psychology,* eds. David Sears, Leonie Huddy, and Robert Jervis (New York: Oxford University Press, 2003), pp. 433–76. An interesting possible case is the CIA's overestimate of the length of time it would take the USSR to produce an atomic bomb. The Agency was so sure that the USSR suffered from a great shortage of uranium that it missed the signs that large-scale enrichment was under way. Donald Steury, "Dissecting Soviet Analysis, 1946–50: How the CIA Missed Stalin's Bomb," *Studies in Intelligence,* vol. 49, no. 1, 2005, pp. 24–25.

28. CIA, *Comprehensive Report of the Special Advisor to the DCI on Iraq's WMD,* September 30, 2004 (hereafter Duelfer report). There is some tension between this report and the views of Duelfer's predecessor, David Kay, as stated in "Iraq's Weapons of Mass Destruction," *Miller Center Report,* vol. 20, Spring/Summer 2004, pp. 6–14. In many ways the best study is Kevin Woods, et al., *The Iraqi Perspectives Report: Saddam's Senior Leadership on Operation Iraqi Freedom from the Official U.S. Joint Forces Command Report* (Annapolis: Naval Institute Press, 2006) (a shorter version appears as Kevin Woods, James Lacey, and Williamson Murray, "Saddam's Delusions: The View From the Inside," *Foreign Affairs,* vol. 85, May/June 2006, pp. 2–26). Also see James Risen, "The Struggle for Iraq: Intelligence; Ex-Inspector Says CIA Missed Disarray in Iraqi Arms Program," *New York Times,* January 26, 2004.

29. Kay, "Iraq's Weapons of Mass Destruction," p. 8; also see his quote in Bob Woodward, *State of Denial: Bush at War, Part III* (New York: Simon & Schuster, 2006), p. 278. It also does not help when a CIA analyst newly assigned to a case starts by "reading into" not the field reports but the finished intelligence that gives the office's established views.

30. Robert Jervis, *Perception and Misperception in International Politics* (Princeton: Princeton University Press, 1976), chap. 4.

31. On politicization in general, see H. Bradford Westerfield, "Inside Ivory Bunkers: CIA Analysts Resist Managers' 'Pandering'—Part I," *International Journal of Intelligence and CounterIntelligence,* vol. 9, Winter 1996/97, pp. 407–24; Westerfield, "Inside Ivory Bunkers: CIA Analysts Resist Managers' 'Pandering'—Part II," *International Journal of Intelligence and CounterIntelligence,* vol. 10, Spring 1997, pp. 19–56; Betts, *Enemies of Intelligence,* chap. 4; a personal account of some bitterness but also persuasiveness is John Gentry, *Lost Promise: How CIA Analysis Misserves the Nation* (Lantham, MD: University Press of America, 1993).

32. This point is strongly made in James Risen, *State of War: The Secret History of the CIA and the Bush Administration* (New York: Free Press, 2006), pp. 20, 76, and is strongly rejected by Tenet in *At the Center of the Storm*, pp. 409–10.

33. Douglas Jehl, "C.I.A. Chief Says He's Corrected Cheney Privately," *New York Times*, March 10, 2004; for further discussion see Tenet, *At the Center of the Storm*, pp. 315–17, 341. Tenet reports one occasion on which the vice president canceled a speech because he told the president it distorted intelligence. Ibid, pp. 356–57. For a compilation of relevant statements by policymakers and intelligence—and a partisan but informative debate about what they mean—see Senate Select Committee on Intelligence, *Report on Whether Public Statements Regarding Iraq by U.S. Government Officials Were Substantiated.*

34. For further discussion, see Josua Rovner, *Fixing the Facts* (Ithaca: Cornell University Press, forthcoming).

35. Butler report, pp. 125–27, which concludes that the Joint Intelligence Committee (JIC) "should not have included the '45 minute' report in its assessment and in the Government's [public] dossier without stating what it was believed to refer to"; for related U.S. intelligence, see SSCI, pp. 251–52.

36. July 23 memo from Matthew Rycroft to David Manning, which is printed in many places, for example, *New York Review of Books*, June 9, 2005, p. 71. Tenet reports that Dearlove later told him that the memo had misquoted him. *At the Center of the Storm*, p. 310.

37. SSCI, pp. 484–85; also see Risen, *State of War*, p. 111; Isikoff and Corn, *Hubris*, pp. 135–36, 140.

38. Kerr et al., "Issues for the US Intelligence Community."

39. WMD Commission, pp. 191–94.

40. Quoted in Gentry, *Lost Promise*, p. 243.

41. Wesley Wark, *The Ultimate Enemy: British Intelligence and Nazi Germany, 1933–1939* (Ithaca: Cornell University Press, 1985). The literature on motivated bias is discussed and applied to international politics in Robert Jervis, Richard Ned Lebow, and Janice Gross Stein, *Psychology and Deterrence* (Baltimore: Johns Hopkins University Press, 1985). Lord Hutton's report clearing the Blair government of the BBC's charges that it distorted intelligence notes the possibility that analysts were "sub-consciously influenced" by their knowledge of what the government wanted to hear. Quoted in Brian Urquhart, "Hidden Truths," *New York Review of Books*, March 25, 2004, p. 44. For a fascinating case of motivated bias in science, see Frank Close, *Too Hot to Handle: The Race for Cold Fusion* (Princeton: Princeton University Press, 1991).

42. One point on the other side is that the United States did not allocate sufficient forces to the mission of safeguarding the expected WMD sites. But this is probably explained by the small size of the force and the general incompetence of the planning for the postwar environment. For discussions, see Michael Gordon and Bernard Trainor, *Cobra II: The Inside Story of the Invasion and Occupation of Iraq* (New York: Pantheon, 2006), pp. 78–83, 156; Richard Shuster, "The Iraq Survey Group," *Journal of Strategic Studies*, vol. 31, April 2008, pp. 231–33. The military was more concerned with seeing that WMD were not used against the soldiers than with securing them from theft, and General Franks seems to have thought that once American troops moved into Iraq, people would simply direct them to the sites. Ricks, *Fiasco*, p. 100.

43. For the claim that French intelligence was skeptical, see Brigitte Rossigneux, "French Intelligence Lectures the Yankees," *Le Canard Enchaine*, September 25, 2002, although if this story is correct the contrast was achieved in part by distorting what the American

and British ICs believed. There also are some indications that Canadian officials were skeptical. "PM Wants Proof before Backing Attack on Iraq," CBC News, September 6, 2002, http://cbc.ca/story/news/national/2002/09/05iraq_pm020905.html. The Germans and Russians may also have doubted that Saddam had restarted his nuclear program. A few scattered individuals dissented. According to Hans Blix, France's president Jacques Chirac was one of them, remarking on the propensity of intelligence services to "intoxicate each other" (a claim that implicitly denies that French intelligence was much different from the American judgment). Blix, *Disarming Iraq* (New York: Pantheon, 2004), p. 129. The former UN weapons inspector also dissented, and with better reasons than he was credited with at the time. William Rivers Pitt with Scott Ritter, *War in Iraq: What Team Bush Doesn't Want You to Know* (New York: Context Books, 2002). Comparing the views of different national intelligence services can shed light on other cases as well. Thus the common claim that Stalin was taken by surprise by Hitler's attack because of the particular infirmities of his intelligence system, although partly correct, needs to be reconsidered in light of the fact that Soviet and British estimates were closely parallel until the last weeks. Gabriel Gorodetsky, *Grand Delusion: Stalin and the German Invasion of Russia* (New Haven: Yale University Press, 1999), esp. pp. 264–65, 281.

44. Senate Select Committee on Intelligence, *Report of the Select Committee on Intelligence on Prewar Intelligence Assessments about Postwar Iraq*, May 2007; also see Richard Best, Jr., "What the Intelligence Community Got Right About Iraq," *Intelligence and National Security*, vol. 23, June 2008, pp. 289–302.

45. Letter from George Tenet to Senator Robert Graham, *Congressional Record*, October 9, 2002, p. S10154; for some evidence about pressure on Iraq's links to terrorism but a muddy interpretation, see SSCI, pp. 357–65; for more detailed discussion of what the IC said and how this compares with what we now believe, see SSCI, *Postwar Findings about Iraq's WMD Programs*. For a discussion of the background to the establishment of a Pentagon office that was designed to show links between Saddam's regime and al Qaeda, see Maria Ryan, "Filling in the 'Unknowns': Hypothesis-Based Intelligence and the Rumsfeld Commission," *Intelligence and National Security*, vol. 21, April 2006, pp. 286–315. The Department of Defense's Inspector General report on this operation can be found at http://www.fas.org/irp/agency/dod/ig020907-decl.pdf.

46. Robert Drogin, *Curveball: Spies, Lies, and the Con Man Who Caused a War* (New York: Random House, 2007), p. 53.

47. Paul Pillar, "Intelligence, Policy, and the War in Iraq," *Foreign Affairs*, vol. 85, March/April 2006, pp. 15–27.

48. Ricks, *Fiasco*, p. 51.

49. Butler report, p. 91; SSCI, pp. 404–422.

50. Butler report, p. 92, also see p. 87; Tenet, *At the Center of the Storm*. Also see Suskind, *Way of the World*, pp. 262–67; Isikoff and Corn, *Hubris*, pp. 165–66, 205–6; David Barstow, William Broad, and Jeff Gerth, "The Nuclear Card: The Aluminum Tube Story," *New York Times*, October 3, 2004.

51. Drogin, *Curveball*, pp. 166–77, 182; Barton Gellman, *Angler: The Cheney Vice Presidency* (New York: Penguin, 2008), pp. 220–21.

52. In a break from this pattern, in the fall of 2002 new evidence did lead CIA to pull back from its previous position that the software package purchased for Iraq's UAVs indicated an intent to develop the ability to strike the United States. WMD Commission, pp. 139–41. Perhaps the fact that this issue was less important than others explains the willingness to change, but I can only speculate.

53. SSCI, p. 249; also see WMD Commission, pp. 189–91. Drumheller's firsthand reports of CIA's dismissal of doubts about Curveball similarly come from December 2002. *On the Brink,* pp. 82–83, 260–64.

54. See, for example, Risen, *State of War,* pp. 79–80.

55. See, for example, National Intelligence Council, *How the Intelligence Community Arrived at the Judgments in the October 2002 NIE on Iraq's WMD Programs,* cited in WMD Commission, p. 197, note 3.

56. WMD Commission, p. 173; Drogin, *Curveball,* p. 127.

57. Spencer Weart, *The Discovery of Global Warming* (Cambridge, MA: Harvard University Press, 2003), p. 89.

58. For a brief but trenchant discussion, see the Butler report, p. 11; for discussion of a similar issue in judging the evidence of the existence of a bird long believed to be extinct, see James Gorman, "Ivory-Bill or Not? Proof Flits Tantalizingly Out of Sight," *New York Times,* August 30, 2005, sec. F.

59. For brief mentions of Kamel's testimony, see SSCI, p. 218; Butler report, pp. 47–48, 51. For better but still brief discussions, see Richard Russell, *Sharpening Strategic Intelligence: Why the CIA Gets It Wrong and What Needs to Be Done to Get It Right* (New York: Cambridge University Press, 2007), p. 82, John Diamond, *The CIA and the Culture of Failure* (Stanford: Stanford University Press, 2008), pp. 395–96.

60. Good summaries are Prados, *Hoodwinked,* chap. 6, and SSCI, chaps. 7 and 15; for Tenet's discussion see *At the Center of the Storm,* pp. 371–75; for Powell's views see Karen DeYoung, *Soldier: The Life of Colin Powell* (New York: Knopf, 2006), pp. 440–47. Also see the brief but interesting comment on the inability of CIA's technical analysts to convey information in a way busy nonspecialists can use in Russell, *Sharpening Strategic Intelligence,* p. 78.

61. Drumheller, *On the Brink;* Drogin, *Curveball.*

62. Tenet, *At the Center of the Storm,* pp. 321–23, 373–74.

63. Jervis, *Perception and Misperception,* chap. 6. Overlearning in the IC is a theme of Diamond, *CIA and the Culture of Failure.*

64. As a reaction to the Iraq errors, assessments apparently now shy away from claims of great certainty, and the IC's inability to declare that it was more than 80 percent certain that it had located the hideout of bin Laden or his top associate in late 2005 contributed to Rumsfeld's refusal to authorize a raid. Evan Thomas et al., "Into Thin Air," *Newsweek,* September 3, 2007, pp. 30–32.

65. WMD Commission, p. 92.

66. For Tenet's retrospective understanding of this, see *At the Center of the Storm,* pp. 328–31. Other estimates have been built on beliefs that cannot be disconfirmed, and in most of these cases analysts and consumers failed to realize this. As I explained in the last chapter, CIA's belief that the Shah would crack down if the situation became really serious was immune from contradicting evidence and led to the conclusion that his rule was not threatened. In 1941 both Stalin and most British officials believed that Hitler would not attack without making demands first and that some of the alarming signs emanated from the bellicose military rather than Hitler, beliefs that only the attack itself could dispel. Gorodetsky, *Grand Delusion,* esp. pp. 180–86.

67. WMD Commission, pp. 93, 150; also see Woods et al., *Iraqi Perspectives Report;* Drumheller, *On the Brink,* p. 77.

68. Prados, *Hoodwinked*, pp. 229–30. But British intelligence did in fact study and believe in Iraq's deception program. Butler report, p. 89.

69. See, for example, WMD Commission, pp. 22–178, 285–86, 320–21, 367, 437. Even before this failure, many people were claiming that the United States was slighting HUMINT, but for a dissent see Stansfield Turner, "Intelligence for a New World Order," *Foreign Affairs*, vol. 70, Fall 1991, pp. 154–56.

70. Butler report, pp. 99–103.

71. Woodward, *Plan of Attack*.

72. The most thorough account is Drogin, *Curveball*, although it uncritically accepts the version propounded by some members of DO.

73. The most thorough study (although not completely unbiased) is Senate Select Committee on Intelligence, *The Use by the Intelligence Community of Information Provided by the Iraqi National Congress*, September 8, 2006. Although some uncertainty remains about whether Curveball was an INC plant, this appears to be unlikely. For what became of Curveball, see John Goetz and Bob Drogin, "'Curveball' Speaks, and a Reputation as a Disinformation Agent Remains Intact," *Los Angeles Times*, June 18, 2008.

74. For a similar error by the British after World War I, see Gill Bennett, *Churchill's Man of Mystery: Desmond Morton and the World of Intelligence* (London: Routledge, 2007), p. 39.

75. SSCI, *Use by the Intelligence Community of Information Provided by the Iraqi National Congress*, pp. 62–64. In another case analysts missed the fabricator notice. Ibid, p. 64. Also see Tenet, *At the Center of the Storm*, p. 329; Drogin, *Curveball*, p. 155. Even if they had received the notices, there might have been a problem because if people form an impression on the basis of certain information and then are told that the information is false, the impression remains. See Lee Ross, Mark Lepper, and Michael Hubbard, "Perseverance in Self-Perception and Social Perception: Biased Attribution Processes in the Debriefing Paradigm," *Journal of Personality and Social Psychology*, vol. 32, November 1975, pp. 880–92; for how to correct for this, see Charles Lord, Mark Lepper, and Elizabeth Preston, "Considering the Opposite: A Corrective Strategy for Social Judgment," *Journal of Personality and Social Psychology*, vol. 47, December 1984, pp. 1231–43.

76. SSCI, p. 43; also see p. 46.

77. Quoted in Bennett, *Churchill's Man of Mystery*, p. 44; also see pp. 193–94.

78. Intelligence services are generally loath to fully share their sources, but there seems to have been unusual friction between CIA and the German service. Drogin, *Curveball*, pp. 30–36; for an intriguing but far-fetched claim, see Suskind, *Way of the World*, pp. 176–78. Much remains unclear about the timing, extent, and depth of the doubts about Curveball and how far up the chain of command they were conveyed. Drogin, *Curveball;* Drumheller, *On the Brink*, pp. 81–87; Tenet, *At the Center of the Storm*, pp. 376–83; statement of John E. McLaughlin, former director of Central Intelligence, April 1, 2005, http://www.fas.org/irp/offdocs/wmd_mclaughlin.html. Ironically, if McLaughlin (then Deputy DCI) was informed (which he denies), then information flowed more appropriately and fewer corrections are within reach.

79. Drogin, *Curveball*, pp. 87, 96.

80. For a discussion of similar weaknesses in the British system, see Butler report, pp. 102–4, and Davies, "SIS, Requirements, and Iraq." The praise for the DO for sounding the alarm in December (Drumheller, *On the Brink;* Drogin, *Curveball;* WMD Commission, pp. 95–98) overlooks the passivity of the directorate at earlier times when crucial

judgments were being formed. DO might have acted sooner if it had realized the extent to which analysts were relying on the source. WMD Commission, p. 179.

81. WMD Commission, p. 103 (quoting a DO officer); Drogin, *Curveball*, p. 137. For another case in which evidence from a source deemed unreliable was accepted because it fit with what was believed, see WMD Commission, p. 127.

82. An excellent treatment is Barstow, Broad, and Gerth, "The Nuclear Card."

83. WMD Commission, pp. 49, 56; SSCI, pp. 85–119. The same problem appeared in the United Kingdom. Butler report, pp. 130–34. Some of the discussions of chemical weapons and UAVs also displayed this ambiguity. SSCI, pp. 204, 221–30. For postwar explanations for the suspicious way in which Iraq procured the tubes, see the Duelfer report, vol. 2, pp. 21–30, and Woodward, *State of Denial*, pp. 278–79.

84. Tenet sees this as part of the explanation. *At the Center of the Storm*, p. 232.

85. WMD Commission, p. 55; also see pp. 67–68 and SSCI, pp. 93–94, 100–102; also see Senate Select Committee on Intelligence, *Report on Whether Public Statements regarding Iraq by U.S. Government Officials Were Substantiated*, pp. 8, 93, 118.

86. Part of the reason probably was that NGIC had concentrated on Soviet (and then Russian) weapons. WMD Commission, p. 172.

87. Tenet, *At the Center of the Storm*, p. 325; Barstow, Broad, and Gerth, "The Nuclear Card"; WMD Commission, pp. 58–59, 75, 183.

88. SSCI, pp. 88–119. Woodward reports that Tenet's deputy, John McLaughlin, took a great interest in the tubes from the beginning and became wedded to his position, but there is no other evidence that this was true. Woodward, *State of Denial*, p. 282. The influence of an individual analyst may also have played a large role in the CIA's error in underestimating the flow of supplies that came through Sihanoukville during the Vietnam War: Lewis Sorley, *A Better War: The Unexamined Victories and Final Tragedy of America's Last Years in Vietnam* (New York: Harcourt, Brace, 1999), p. 102.

89. A common source of false convictions is the tendency of the police to jump to the conclusion that they have found the criminal. See, for example, Fernanda Santos, "Playing Down DNA Evidence Contributed to Wrongful Conviction, Review Finds," *New York Times*, July 3, 2007. For a further discussion of processes that are appropriate but impossible to adopt for political and psychological reasons, see Robert Jervis, "Bridges, Barriers, and Gaps: Research and Policy," *Political Psychology*, vol. 29, August 2008, pp. 571–92.

90. For discussion of the role of the forged documents, see Carlo Bonini and Guiseppe D'Avanzo, *Collusion: International Espionage and the War on Terror*, trans. James Marcus (Hoboken, NJ: Melvillehouse, 2007), and especially the documents reprinted on pp. 203, 211. Also see Richard Aldrich, "Global Intelligence Co-operation versus Accountability: New Facets to an Old Problem," *Intelligence and National Security*, vol. 24, February 2009, pp. 38–40. A good general discussion of the Wilson mission and subsequent controversy is Isikoff and Corn, *Hubris*, pp. 252–92. SSCI, *Prewar Intelligence Assessments about Postwar Iraq*, pp. 205–22, has new details but is highly partisan. Tenet's scars are displayed in *At the Center of the Storm*, chap. 24.

91. Tenet, *At the Center of the Storm*, p. 454.

92. WMD Commission, p. 173; apparently this was also true in Australian intelligence. Flood report, p. 26.

93. Douglas Ford, "Planning for an Unpredictable War: British Intelligence Assessments and the War Against Japan, 1937–1945," *Journal of Strategic Studies*, vol. 27, March 2004,

p. 148; for other examples, see Gorodetsky, *Grand Delusion*, p. 233; Stephen Budiansky, *Her Majesty's Spymaster* (New York: Viking, 2005), p. 203.

94. SSCI, pp. 161–62; also see Drogin, *Curveball*, p. 52. The plausibility of Iraq's mobile facilities may account for the CIA's being especially slow to change its views as new information came in after the war, although stubbornness and idiosyncratic factors may have been at work as well.

95. SSCI, pp. 38, 228.

96. WMD Commission, pp. 144–45.

97. Feith, *War and Decision*, p 265; Isikoff and Corn, *Hubris*, p. 114.

98. Tenet, *At the Center of the Storm*, pp. 344–45.

99. Duelfer report, pp. 29, 32, 55, 62 (this and subsequent references are to volume 1 unless otherwise noted); vol. 3, "Biological Warfare," p. 56; vol. 1, "Regime Strategic Intent," p. 32; Woods et al., *Iraqi Perspectives Report.*

100. Duelfer report, p. 64. John Mueller had earlier speculated that Saddam's limitations on the inspectors were motivated by his fear of assassination. "Letters to the Editor: Understanding Saddam," *Foreign Affairs*, vol. 83, July/August 2004, p. 151.

101. SSCI, pp. 102–3; Isikoff and Corn, *Hubris*, p. 307.

102. SSCI, *Postwar Findings about Iraq's WMD Programs*, p. 67.

103. Duelfer report, p. 34; also see p. 57. Ending economic sanctions and ending inspections would not necessarily have coincided, and it is not clear which of them was viewed as most troublesome and why. With some reason, by the late 1990s Saddam seems to have concluded that showing that he had no WMD programs would not have been sufficient to end the sanctions, and so cooperating with the inspectors was pointless. Indeed, the UN resolutions provided for sanctions to continue even after inspections ended, and Saddam had terminated inspections in 1998. This presents a puzzle because if inspections had been the main barrier, Saddam should have resumed his programs at that point, as most observers expected. But it is hard to see how the sanctions were inhibiting him because after the institution of the Oil for Food program and extensive oil smuggling, the regime had sufficient cash to procure what it needed.

104. INR in fact had this insight in the spring of 1973, but it dropped out of subsequent analysis: "The Performance of the Intelligence Community before the Arab-Israeli War of October 1973," pp. 15–16.

105. This is the view of a former high IC official. Mark Lowenthal, "Towards a Reasonable Standard for Analysis: How Right, How Often on Which Issues?" *Intelligence and National Security*, vol. 23, June 2008, p. 311.

106. For a related argument, see WMD Commission, pp. 10, 12, 173, 175.

107. SSCI, e.g., pp. 187, 192, 194, 204, 213. The Butler report, pp. 73, 75, makes a similar point about some instances of British intelligence but without implying that this was illegitimate.

108. Woods et al., *Iraqi Perspectives Report*, pp. 93–95. This is why an experienced military intelligence analyst argues that "the perception of the adversary's fundamental goals and priorities is the sine qua non of warning. It constitutes the most significant difference between those who 'have warning' and those who do not." Cynthia Grabo, *Anticipating Surprise: Analysis for Strategic Warning* (Washington, DC: Center for Strategic Intelligence Research, Joint Military Intelligence College, 2002), p. 81.

109. Jervis, *Perception and Misperception*, pp. 156–61. This also recasts the argument that a common inference error is to under-weight base-rate data about the frequency of phenomena: Jervis, "Representativeness in Foreign Policy Judgments," *Political Psychology*, vol. 7, September 1986, pp. 483–506.

110. Betts, "Warning Dilemmas: Normal Theory vs. Exceptional Theory," *Orbis*, vol. 26, Winter 1983, pp. 828–33; Betts, *Enemies of Intelligence*, chap. 3; Mark Lowenthal, "Intelligence Epistemology: Dealing with the Unbelievable," *International Journal of Intelligence and CounterIntelligence*, vol. 6, Fall 1993, pp. 319–26.

111. Drogin, *Curveball*, p. 82; also see p. 73.

112. For a summary, see Ziva Kunda, *Social Cognition: Making Sense of People* (Cambridge, MA: MIT Press, 1999), pp. 112–20.

113. SSCI, p. 21; also see p. 268. CIA apparently also declined to ask for the specifications of the Italian rocket that some (correctly) thought in modified form was the intended use of the aluminum tubes on the grounds that it was firmly established that the tubes were part of an enrichment program. WMD Commission, p. 68.

114. The phrase apparently originated with Carl Sagan and was used by DCI William Casey when he was disputing the significance of the lack of evidence for Soviet involvement with terrorism. Davis, "Intelligence Analysts and Policymakers," p. 1004. It should be noted that while Casey was wrong in some of his specific allegations, we now know that the Soviets did indeed train and support many terrorist movements.

115. Thomas Mahnken, "Spies and Bureaucrats: Getting Intelligence Right," *Public Interest*, no. 81, Spring 2005, p. 37.

116. Iran's president reacted to the fact that lack of hard evidence that Iran was seeking nuclear weapons had not dispelled Western suspicions by declaring, "Usually, you cannot prove that sort of thing [i.e., that a country is not seeking weapons]. How can you prove that you are not a bad person?" Quoted in Steven Weisman and Warren Hoge, "Iranian Leader Promises New Proposals to End Nuclear Impasse," *New York Times*, September 16, 2005. As I will discuss in the next section, the paucity of evidence sometimes can be explained by the other's deception and denial activities, an argument made by the United States in this case as well as about Iraq. Bill Gertz, "U.S. Report Says Iran Seeks to Acquire Nuclear Weapons," *Washington Times*, September 16, 2005.

117. WMD Commission, p. 93; also see James Risen, "C.I.A Held Back Iraqi Arms Data, U.S. Officials Say," *New York Times*, July 6, 2004; Risen, *State of War*, chap. 4; and Isikoff and Corn, *Hubris*, p 167. Jami Miscik, the head of DI, did express surprise at the paucity of signals intelligence pointing to WMD programs. Tenet, *At the Center of the Storm*, p. 364. For the dismissal of negative evidence that was received in another case, see Gorodetsky, *Grand Delusion*, p. 282.

118. After the war, former deputy prime minister Tariq Aziz pointed this out to his interrogators. SSCI, *Postwar Findings about Iraq's WMD Programs*, p. 67.

119. SSCI, p. 3.

120. For a fascinating discussion of the ignoring of negative evidence from signals intelligence in the Gulf of Tonkin incident, see Robert Hanyok, "Skunks, Bogies, Silent Hounds, and Flying Fish: The Gulf of Tonkin Mystery, 2–4 August 1964," *Crypotologic Quarterly*, vols. 19–20, Winter 2000–Spring 2001, esp. pp. 31–32, 41, 43–44, available at http://www.gwu.edu~nsaarchiv/NSAEBB/NSAEBB132/relea00012.pdf. Negative evidence apparently also was ignored by those in the IC who argued that the "yellow rain" in Cambodia was caused by the Vietnamese use of toxic agents presumably supplied by the USSR. Merle Pribbenow, "'Yellow Rain': Lessons from an Earlier WMD

Controversy," *International Journal of Intelligence and CounterIntelligence*, vol. 19, Winter 2006/2007, pp. 737–45. For other examples from intelligence, see Matthew Aid, *The Secret Sentry: The Untold Story of the National Security Agency* (New York: Bloomsbury Press, 2009), p. 78 and Eduard Mark, "*In Re* Alger Hiss: A Final Verdict from the Archives of the KGB," *Journal of Cold War Studies*, vol. 11, Summer 2009, p. 65.

121. Quoted in SSCI, p. 184.

122. Ibid., p. 107.

123. Ibid., pp. 20–21, 106.

124. Ibid., pp. 199–200; WMD Commission, pp. 122–26. Part of the problem may have been the reorganization that moved imagery analysis out of CIA and into a larger unit controlled by the military. Russell, *Sharpening Strategic Intelligence*, pp. 80–81; also see Diamond, *CIA and the Culture of Failure*, pp. 379–85.

125. The Australian Flood report is unusual in acknowledging that "it is doubtful that a better process would have changed the fundamental judgment about the existence of WMD" (p. 27). In places the WMD Commission comes close to seeing this, and the Butler report can be read in this way as well, although it is artfully ambiguous.

126. Woodward, *Plan of Attack*, p. 249. Tenet says that he was explaining that more information could be declassified (*At the Center of the Storm*, pp. 360–63), but by this point an additional bias may have come from his knowledge that CIA had a string of sources in Iraq whose lives (and those of their families) would be sacrificed if the United States did not invade. Jake Blood, *The Tet Effect: Intelligence and the Public Perception of War* (London: Routledge, 2005), p. 176.

4. The Politics and Psychology of Intelligence and Intelligence Reform

1. Quoted in Rhodri Jeffreys-Jones, *The CIA and American Democracy*, 2nd ed. (New Haven: Yale University Press, 1998), p. 177. For excellent discussions of intelligence and its role in policymaking, see Michael Herman, *Intelligence Power in Peace and War* (Cambridge: Cambridge University Press, 1966); Gregory Treverton, *Reshaping National Intelligence in an Age of Information* (New York: Cambridge University Press, 2001), chap. 6; Mark Lowenthal, "Tribal Tongues: Intelligence Producers, Intelligence Consumers," in *Strategic Intelligence*, ed. Loch Johnson and James Wirtz (Los Angeles: Roxbury Press, 2004), pp. 234–41; Hans Heyman, "Intelligence/Policy Relationships," in *Intelligence: Policy and Process*, ed. Alfred Maurer, Marion Tunstal, and James Keagle (Boulder, CO: Westview, 1985), pp. 57–66; Roger George and Robert Kline, eds., *Intelligence and the National Security Strategist* (Lanham, MD: Rowman and Littlefield, 2006); Roger George and James Bruce, eds., *Analyzing Intelligence: Origins, Obstacles, and Innovations* (Washington, DC: Georgetown University Press, 2008); William Odom, "Intelligence Analysis," *Intelligence and National Security*, vol. 23, June 2008, pp. 316–32. For the perspective of a former head of Israeli intelligence, see Efraim Halevy, *Man in the Shadows: Inside the Middle East Crisis with a Man Who Led the Mossad* (New York: St. Martin's, 2006), chap. 14. Older but still excellent treatments are Sherman Kent, *Strategic Intelligence for American World Policy* (Princeton: Princeton University Press, 1949), chap. 11; Harry Howe Ransom, *Central Intelligence and National Security* (Cambridge: Harvard University Press, 1965); Roger Hilsman, *Strategic Intelligence and National Decisions* (Glencoe, IL: Free Press, 1956).

2. I owe this simile to Martin Peterson, who heard it from a colleague.

3. Quoted in Trudi Osborne, "The (Really) Quiet American: Richard McGarrah Helms," *Washington Post*, May 20, 1973.

4. Quoted in Nina Easton, "The Last Hawk: James Woolsey Wants Iraq's Saddam Hussein Brought to Justice," *Washington Post*, December 27, 2001.

5. The secretary's staff meeting, October 8, 1975, pp. 42–43, http://www.gwu.edu/~nsarchiv/NSAEBB/NSAEBB193/HAK-10-8-75.pdf. According to one authority, the Germans, at least in World War I, made better use of intelligence because they did not expect too much of it. Terence Zuber, "The German Intelligence Estimates in the West, 1885–1914," *Intelligence and National Security*, vol. 21, April 2006, pp. 198–99.

6. For discussion of German military doctrine that was shaped by the knowledge of the limits of intelligence, see Samir Puri, "The Role of Intelligence in Deciding the Battle of Britain," *Intelligence and National Security*, vol. 21, June 2006, p. 420.

7. The classic statement is Theodore Lowi, *The End of Liberalism* (New York: Norton, 1969), chap. 6. For further discussion of overselling in the overthrow of Saddam, see chapter 3 of this book.

8. Dean Acheson, *Present at the Creation: My Years at the State Department* (New York: Norton, 1969), p. 375.

9. Douglas Jehl, "New C.I.A. Chief Tells Workers to Back Administration Policies," *New York Times*, November 17, 2004.

10. Richard Immerman, "Intelligence and Strategy: Historicizing Psychology, Policy, and Politics," *Diplomatic History*, vol. 32, January 2008, p. 12.

11. John Bolton, often accused of putting illegitimate pressure on intelligence, apparently believed that the problem instead was that members of the IC were overreaching and trying to censor his "political judgment as to how to interpret this data," in the words of one of his top aides. Douglas Jehl, "Released E-Mail Exchanges Reveal More Bolton Battles," *New York Times*, April 24, 2005, and Jehl, "Bolton Asserts Independence On Intelligence," *New York Times*, May 12, 2005. Unfortunately, it is much harder for anyone below the level of the president or perhaps the cabinet to make clear that what he or she is giving is a judgment different from that of the IC because it would invite the obvious question of whether the president agreed.

12. Where to draw the line and whether Bush administration officials crossed it is debated by Democratic and Republican Senators in Senate Select Committee on Intelligence, *Report on Whether Public Statements regarding Iraq by U.S. Government Officials Were Substantiated by Intelligence Information*, June 2008. This problem is not unique to intelligence but also comes up in areas in which policy is supposed to be based on science, and the years of the Bush administration were filled with controversy on this score.

13. For further discussion, see Robert Jervis, "Understanding Beliefs," *Political Psychology*, vol. 27, October 2006, pp. 641–64.

14. For the argument that Saddam could have been deterred even if he had developed nuclear weapons, see Robert Jervis, *American Foreign Policy in a New Era* (New York: Routledge, 2005), chap. 3.

15. Senate Select Committee on Intelligence, *Report of the Select Committee on Intelligence on Postwar Findings about Iraq's WMD Programs and Links to Terrorism and How They Compare with Prewar Assessments*, September 8, 2006.

16. Senate Select Committee on Intelligence, *Report of the Select Committee on Intelligence on Prewar Intelligence Assessments about Postwar Iraq*, May 2007.

17. Steven Holmes, "Administration Is Fighting Itself On Haiti Policy," *New York Times*, October 23, 1993. The title of this article shows the problem: intelligence is part of the administration but is committed to independent analysis. Treverton argues that given the sensitivity of the subject and the softness of the evidence, the assessment should not have been written but rather orally briefed to policymakers. Treverton, *Reshaping National Intelligence*, pp. 188–89. When President Truman felt that he had to withdraw troops from Korea in 1948–49, he ignored estimates that this would "probably in time be followed by an invasion." Michael Warner, ed., *CIA Cold War Records: The CIA under Harry Truman* (Washington, DC: CIA Center for the Study of Intelligence, 1994), p. 268.

18. Philip Tetlock, "Cognitive Style and Political Ideology," *Journal of Personality and Social Psychology: Personality Processes and Individual Differences*, vol. 45, 1983, pp. 118–26; Tetlock, "A Value Pluralism Model of Ideological Reasoning," *Journal of Personality and Social Psychology: Personality Processes and Individual Differences*, vol. 50, 1986, pp. 819–27.

19. "Implications of an Unfavorable Outcome in Vietnam," September 11, 1967, in *Estimative Products on Vietnam, 1948–1975* (Washington, DC: National Intelligence Council, 2005), pp. 394–426; Richard Helms, with William Hood, *A Look over My Shoulder: A Life in the Central Intelligence Agency* (New York: Random House, 2003), pp. 314–15; Robert McNamara, with Brian VanDeMark, *In Retrospect: The Tragedy and Lessons of Vietnam* (New York: Random House, 1995), pp. 292–93.

20. Senate Select Committee on Intelligence, *Intelligence on Prewar Intelligence Assessments about Postwar Iraq;* Norah Bensahel, "Mission Not Accomplished: What Went Wrong with Iraqi Reconstruction," *Journal of Strategic Studies*, vol. 29, June 2006, pp. 453–74.

21. Lady Gwendolen Cecil, *Life of Robert, Marquis of Salisbury*, vol. 2 (London: Hodder and Stoughton, 1921), p. 145. Of course there is a selection effect at work here: if the country changes its policy, we will never know if continuing it would have yielded success. For example, although the current consensus is that the Vietnam War was lost to the United States from the start, some argue that more perseverance (perhaps coupled with changes in tactics) would have produced victory. The latest such claim is Mark Moyar, *Triumph Forsaken: The Vietnam War, 1954–65* (New York: Cambridge University Press, 2006).

22. Quoted in Todd Purdum, "Prisoner of Conscience," *Vanity Fair*, February 2007, p. 14; quoted in David Sanger, "Bush Adds Troops in Bid to Secure Iraq," *New York Times*, January 10, 2007.

23. George Downs and David Rocke, "Gambling for Resurrection," in *Optimal Imperfection? Domestic Uncertainty and Institutions in International Relations* (Princeton: Princeton University Press, 1995); Hein Goemans, *War and Punishment: The Causes of War Termination and the First World War* (Princeton: Princeton University Press, 2000).

24. See, for example, Kim Rutenberg, "Parts of Iraq Report Grim Where Bush Was Upbeat," *New York Times*, July 15, 2007.

25. A good summary by a former high-ranking CIA official is Harold Ford, *CIA and Vietnam Policymakers: Three Episodes, 1962–1968* (Washington, DC: CIA Center for the Study of Intelligence, 1998); also see Thomas Ahern, Jr., *Good Questions, Wrong Answers: CIA's Estimates of Arms Traffic through Sihanoukville, Cambodia, during the Vietnam War*, February 2004, http://www.foia.cia.gov/vietnam/4_GOOD_QUESTIONS_WRONG_ANSWERS.pdf. The pattern in Iraq seems similar.

26. David Reynolds, "Churchill and the British 'Decision' to Fight on in 1940: Right Policy, Wrong Reasons," in *Diplomacy and Intelligence during the Second World War*, ed.

Richard Langhorne (New York: Cambridge University Press, 1985), pp. 147–67, quoted in Harold Evans, "His Finest Hour," *New York Times Book Review*, November 11, 2001. DCI McCone's insight that Khrushchev was deploying offensive missiles in Cuba was similarly grounded in part on incorrect reasoning. James Blight and David Welch, "What Can Intelligence Tell Us about the Cuban Missile Crisis, and What Can the Cuban Missile Crisis Tell Us about Intelligence?" *Intelligence and National Security.* vol. 13, Autumn 1998, p. 5. We like to think that good intelligence leads to good policy, but sometimes ignorance is bliss. When Eisenhower became president, he sought to withdraw American forces from Europe and give the European states nuclear weapons, either individually or collectively. Marc Trachtenberg, *A Construction Peace: The Making of the European Settlement, 1945–1963* (Princeton: Princeton University Press, 1999). Although the Europeans and the Soviets had their suspicions, the Americans were able to keep their plans secret. They were never fully implemented, and the secrecy proved invaluable not only to the United States but to the Europeans. If they had had better intelligence, they would have triggered a bitter intra-alliance dispute with unpredictable ramifications.

27. Nicholas Wade, *The Nobel Duel: Two Scientists' 21-Year Race to Win the World's Most Coveted Research Prize* (Garden City, NY: Doubleday, 1981).

28. Albert Hirschman, "The Principle of the Hiding Hand," *Public Interest*, no. 13, 1967, pp. 10–23. That is why we often celebrate those who persevere in the pursuit of worthy but apparently lost causes: for a recent example see Peter Appelbaum, "Not a D.N.A. Case, but Many Supporters Who Say a Convicted Murderer is Innocent," *New York Times*, July 15, 2007. But the dark side of this is the "psychological trap" by which people can be drawn deeper into activities harmful to themselves or others. Joel Brockner and Jeffrey Rubin, *Entrapment in Escalating Conflicts* (New York: Spring-Verlag, 1985).

29. Julian Robinson, Jeanne Guillemin, and Matthew Meselson, "Yellow Rain: The Story Collapses," *Foreign Policy*, no. 68, Autumn 1987, pp. 100–117.

30. For a summary of the literature, see Richard Nisbett and Lee Ross, *Human Inference: Strategies and Shortcomings of Social Judgment* (Englewood Cliffs, NJ: Prentice-Hall, 1980), pp. 113–15, 119–20, 150–51, 292–93.

31. Shelley Taylor and J. Brown, "Illusion and Well-Being: A Social Psychological Perspective on Mental Illness," *Psychological Bulletin*, vol. 103, March 1998, pp. 193–210; Taylor, *Positive Illusions: Creative Self-Deception and the Healthy Mind* (New York: Basic Books, 1989). Also see Dominic Johnson, *Overconfidence and War: The Havoc and Glory of Positive Illusions* (Cambridge: Harvard University Press, 2004).

32. Henry Kissinger, *White House Years* (Boston: Little, Brown, 1979), p. 483.

33. Quoted in John Steinbruner, *The Cybernetic Theory of Decision* (Princeton: Princeton University Press, 1974), p. 332.

34. Quoted in Bob Woodward, *State of Denial: Bush at War, Part III* (New York: Simon and Schuster, 2006), pp. 325–26; also see p. 371 and Robert Draper, *Dead Certain: The Presidency of George W. Bush* (New York: Free Press, 2007). But interestingly enough, Secretary of State Powell and his deputy, Richard Armitage, believed that self-doubt was essential to doing a good job: Woodward, *State of Denial*, p. 325.

35. Richard Russell, "CIA's Strategic Intelligence in Iraq," *Political Science Quarterly*, vol. 117, Summer 2002, pp. 201–7.

36. Kennedy did make a private commitment to Khrushchev to remove the missiles in the near future, but news of it arrived in Moscow only after Khrushchev had decided to withdraw the missiles in return for Kennedy's pledge not to invade Cuba. For

another case in which intelligence increased confidence, see David Easter, "GCHQ and British External Policy in the 1960s," *Intelligence and National Security,* vol. 23, October 2008, p. 699.

37. Michael Barnhart, *Japan Prepares for Total War: The Search for Economic Security, 1919–1941* (Ithaca: Cornell University Press, 1987), pp. 170–75. It is not only intelligence that can be in the position of bringing unwanted news and advice, and in these circumstances other agencies also face the choice between adjusting their views and losing influence with the leadership. Although there were some exceptions, it appears that the Joint Chiefs of Staff largely chose the former alternative during Vietnam. Knowing that their views that the war could be won only if it was fought with many fewer restrictions was unacceptable and hoping to get more of their way by being "realistic," they gave the civilian leaders doses of a much weaker medicine. H. R. McMaster, *Dereliction of Duty: Johnson, McNamara, the Joint Chiefs of Staff, and the Lies That Led to Vietnam* (New York: HarperCollins, 1997). Much the same seems to have occurred in Iraq.

38. Thomas Hughes, "Experiencing McNamara," *Foreign Policy,* no. 100, Fall 1995, pp. 154–57; Louis Sarris, "McNamara's War, and Mine," *New York Times,* September 5, 1995.

39. Ashley Schiff, *Fire and Water: Scientific Heresy in the Forest Service* (Cambridge, MA: Harvard University Press, 1962).

40. For a similar argument, see Treverton, *Reshaping National Intelligence,* pp. 183–85. In the Iranian case, furthermore, by the time CIA (and the ambassador in Tehran) understood the seriousness of the crisis in early November when extensive rioting led to the installation of a military government, I doubt that the United States could have done anything to stop Khomeini from coming to power. Charles Kurzman, *The Unthinkable Revolution in Iran* (Cambridge, MA: Harvard University Press, 2004), p. 137.

41. Harold Deutsch, "Commanding Generals and the Uses of Intelligence," *Intelligence and National Security,* vol. 3, July 1988, p. 245; for cases see Brian Loring Villa, *Unauthorized Action: Mountbatten and the Dieppe Raid* (New York: Oxford University Press, 1989), and Guy Vanderpool, "COMINT and the PRC Intervention in the Korean War," *Cryptologic Quarterly,* vol. 15, summer 1996, pp. 1–26, declassified and available as document 21 at http://www.gwu.edu/~nsarchiv/NSAEBB/NSAEBB278/index.htm.

42. Deutsch, "Commanding Generals and the Uses of Intelligence," pp 206–7; Stansfield Turner, *Burn before Reading: Presidents, CIA Directors, and Secret Intelligence* (New York: Hyperion, 2005), p. 128.

43. Both politics and psychology make this very difficult to overcome: Robert Jervis "Bridges, Barriers, and Gaps: Research and Policy," *Political Psychology,* vol. 29, August 2006, pp. 578–81. For a parallel discussion in medical diagnosis, see Jerome Groopman, *How Doctors Think* (Boston: Houghton Mifflin, 2007).

44. As magicians well understand, the power of expectations and predispositions is so strong that deception works best and may work only when it fits with what the perceiver already thinks the state will do. Hitler's deception program leading up to his attack on the USSR in June 1941 would not have succeeded if from the start Stalin had not been expecting him to exert pressure and issue an ultimatum before resorting to overt warfare. The extensive and skillful Allied efforts to mislead Hitler as to where they were going to land in Europe in June 1944 similarly worked only because Hitler was convinced that Calais was the best landing place. This also means that an important role for intelligence in facilitating deception is learning what the other side expects.

45. David Evans, "USS Vincennes Case Study," http://www.owlnet.rice.edu/~nava 201/VCS/vincennes.pdf. Ironically, this tragic incident helped end the war because Iranian leaders believed the United States had done this on purpose as part of its anti-Iranian campaign, and they inferred that even worse punishment would likely be forthcoming unless the war was settled.

46. See, for example, George Tenet with Bill Harlow, *At the Center of the Storm: My Years at the CIA* (New York: HarperCollins, 2007), pp. 317, 348.

47. Risen, *State of War,* p. 130. For a general discussion of the importance of analysts' worldviews, see David Muller, Jr., "Intelligence in Red and Blue," *International Journal of Intelligence and CounterIntelligence,* vol. 21, Spring 2008, pp. 1–12; also see Huw Dylan, "Britain and the Missile Gap: British Estimates on the Soviet Ballistic Missile Threat, 1957–61," *Intelligence and National Security,* vol. 23, December 2008, pp. 794–96.

48. Personality may play a large role as well, although this is difficult to determine. See, for example, Lloyd Etheredge, *A World of Men: The Private Sources of American Foreign Policy* (Cambridge, MA: MIT Press, 1978); Saul Friedlander and Raymond Cohen, "The Personality Correlates of Belligerence in International Conflict," *Comparative Politics,* vol. 7, January 1975, pp. 155–86.

49. Quoted in Donald Cameron Watt, "British Intelligence and the Coming of the Second World War in Europe," in *Knowing One's Enemies: Intelligence Assessment before the Two World Wars,* ed. Ernest May (Princeton: Princeton University Press, 1984), p. 268.

50. For meticulous research showing that those who are less theory-driven tend to make more accurate predictions and to better adjust their views in the face of discrepant evidence, see Philip Tetlock, *Expert Political Judgment: How Good Is It? How Can We Know?* (Princeton: Princeton University Press, 2005); also see Milton Rokeach, *The Open and Closed Mind: Investigations into the Nature of Belief Systems and Personality Systems* (New York: Basic Books, 1960).

51. John Gentry, *Lost Promise: How CIA Analysis Misserves the Nation* (Lanham, MD.: University Press of America, 1993), pp. 35–37. The best general analysis of varieties of politicization is Joshua Rovner, *Fixing the Facts* (Ithaca: Cornell University Press, forthcoming).

52. Quoted in Ralph Weber, ed., *Spymaster: Ten CIA Officers in Their Own Words* (Wilmington: DE: Scholarly Resources Books, 1999), p. 251. It is not clear, however, whether Johnson was dictating the subjects to be covered or the conclusions to be reached. There also is some ambiguity in the incident Helms described in *A Look over My Shoulder,* pp. 339–40. For his discussion of political pressures in the later controversy over estimating the size of enemy forces in Vietnam, see pp. 324–29. For DCI Tenet's views of the pressures by policymakers to conclude that there were significant links between al Qaeda and Iraq, see *At the Center of the Storm,* pp. 349–50. For the claim that analysts at the World Bank are required to produce papers that support bank policy and specific projects, see Michael Goldman, *Imperial Nature: The World Bank and Struggles for Social Justice in the Age of Globalization* (New Haven: Yale University Press, 2005), p. 127.

53. Stansfield Turner, *Burn before Reading,* pp. 130–32; also see John Prados, *The Soviet Estimate: U.S. Intelligence Analysis and Russian Military Strength* (New York: Dial Press, 1982), pp. 218–24, and Helms, *A Look over My Shoulder,* pp. 386–88. For the (plausible) claim that political consideration led to the withholding of information on the status of Iran's "moderates" during the period when the Reagan White House was trading arms for hostages, see the memorandum from an Iranian analyst to the deputy Director of Intelligence, December 2, 1986, printed in Gentry, *Lost Promise,* pp. 276–81.

54. For an attempt to draw such lines, see the speech that Robert Gates gave to analysts when he became DCI after deeply contentious confirmation hearings pivoting on whether he had politicized intelligence when he was deputy to William Casey. Gates, "Guarding against Politicization," *Studies in Intelligence,* vol. 36, no. 5, 1992, pp. 5–13. Also see Jack Davis, "Intelligence Analysts and Policy-Makers: Benefits and Dangers of Tensions in the Relationship," *Intelligence and National Security,* vol. 21, December 2006, pp. 999–1021. Richard Betts, *Enemies of Intelligence* (New York: Columbia University Press, 2007), chap. 4, points out that the IC has two models—one based on the philosophy of one of its founding analysts, Sherman Kent, that stresses the need for distance from policymakers, and the other developed by Robert Gates when he was DCI, which stresses the need for intelligence close to them to be able to speak to their concerns. The first runs the danger of irrelevance, the second of politicization. Betts also points out that for important issues "any relevant analysis will perforce be politically charged because it will point at least implicitly to a conclusion about policy" (p. 75). Also see Gregory Treverton, "Intelligence Analysis: Between 'Politicization' and Irrelevance," in George and Bruce, *Analyzing Intelligence,* pp. 91–104, and Jack Davis, "The Kent-Kendall Debate of 1949," *Studies in Intelligence,* vol. 36, no. 5, 1992, pp. 91–103.

55. Turner, *Burn before Reading,* p. 132.

56. For good discussions, see the sources in note 31 in chapter 3. Furthermore, when intelligence is most thoroughly politicized, evidence for this no longer appears. In an application of the familiar dynamic that power is most effective when it does not need to be applied openly, if an intelligence agency is filled with people who know and share the leader's views, intelligence will be supportive without leaving any fingerprints. Richard Russell, *Sharpening Strategic Intelligence: Why the CIA Gets It Wrong and What Needs to Be Done to Get It Right* (New York: Cambridge University Press, 2007), p. 121; John Diamond, *The CIA and the Culture of Failure* (Stanford: Stanford University Press, 2008), p. 43. Self-censorship by the analysts is also impossible to detect. Diamond, p. 19.

57. For a discussion of the later case by the national intelligence officer in charge, see Paul Pillar, "Intelligence, Policy, and the War in Iraq," *Foreign Affairs,* vol. 85, March/April 2006, pp. 15–28.

58. It is the job of top IC officials to shield their subordinates from political pressures. But if there is any chance that intelligence will be listened to, they must also scrutinize unpopular assessments with great care, trying to see that all objections have been met and that excessive claims have been avoided. To subordinates, this scrutiny may appear as illegitimate political pressure, and indeed in one sense it is.

59. Douglas Feith, *War and Decision: Inside the Pentagon at the Dawn of the War on Terrorism* (New York: HarperCollins, 2008).

60. "Once when an analyst averred that reliable evidence had become available that indicated a suspected development that undermined an administration initiative was 'almost certainly taking place,' a policy critic retorted that the analyst 'couldn't get a murder-one conviction in an American court with [his] evidence.'" Jack Davis, "Intelligence Analysts and Policymakers: Benefits and Dangers of Tensions in the Relationship," *Intelligence and National Security,* vol. 21, December 2006, p. 1004. Years earlier Paul Wolfowitz had argued that when analysts denied uncertainty on a contentious issue, this often would be used as a weapon in the policy arena, and yet I think it is likely that he would have viewed any expression of doubt on the WMD issue as aimed at aiding opponents of the war. Davis, p. 1006.

61. See, for example, Richard Betts, "Analysis, War, and Decisions: Why Intelligence Failures are Inevitable," *World Politics,* vol. 31, October 1978, pp. 61–89. Eliot Cohen

has labeled the arguments like this the "no fault" school. Eliot Cohen and John Gooch, *Military Misfortunes* (New York: Free Press, 1990), pp. 40–43; for a good rebuttal see Betts, *Enemies of Intelligence*, pp. 27, 185–86. The previous chapters of this book showed numerous errors, many of them avoidable. For a good commentary on the dispute, see Or Arthur Honig, "A New Direction for Theory-Building in Intelligence Studies," *International Journal of Intelligence and CounterIntelligence*, vol. 20, Winter 2007, pp. 699–716. For a parallel discussion in another field, see Orrin Pilkey and Linda Pilkey-Jarvis, *Useless Arithmetic: Why Environmental Scientists Can't Predict the Future* (New York: Columbia University Press, 2007).

62. For further discussion and examples, see Robert Jervis, *System Effects: Complexity in Political and Social Life* (Princeton: Princeton University Press, 1997).

63. See, for example, Groopman, *How Doctors Think;* Jack Dowie and Arthur Elstein, eds., *Professional Judgment: A Reader in Clinical Decision Making* (New York: Cambridge University Press, 1988); Arthur Elstein, Lee Shulman, and Sarah Sprafka, *Medical Problem Solving: An Analysis of Clinical Reasoning* (Cambridge, MA: Harvard University Press, 1978); Lester King, *Medical Thinking: An Historical Preface* (Princeton: Princeton University Press, 1982); Pat Croskerry, "Achieving Quality in Clinical Decision Making: Cognitive Strategies and Detection of Bias," *Academic Emergency Medicine*, vol. 9, November 2002, pp. 1184–1204; Stephen Marrin and Jonathan Clemente, "Modeling an Intelligence Analysis Profession on Medicine," *International Journal of Intelligence and CounterIntelligence*, vol. 19, Winter 2006–2007, pp. 642–65.

64. I discussed theoretical aspects of deception and gave numerous examples in *The Logic of Images in International Relations* (Princeton: Princeton University Press, 1970); 2nd ed. (New York: Columbia University Press 1989). Also see J. Barton Bowyer (pseudonym for J. Boyer Bell and Barton Whaley), *Cheating* (New York: St. Martin's, 1980); Charles Cruickshank, *Deception in World War II* (New York: Oxford University Press, 1980); Michael Howard, *British Intelligence in the Second World War*, vol. 5, *Strategic Deception* (Norwich, UK: Her Majesty's Stationery Office, 1990); and esp. Thaddeus Holt, *The Deceivers: Allied Military Deception in the Second World War* (New York: Scribner, 2004). The classic text on surprise attack to which we are all indebted is Roberta Wohlstetter, *Pearl Harbor: Warning and Decision* (Stanford: Stanford University Press, 1962); the best general study is Richard Betts, *Surprise Attack* (Washington DC: Brookings Institution 1982). For the claim (overstated, I believe, if true in many cases) that watching for the adversary's mobilization is key, see Cynthia Grabo, *Anticipating Surprise: Analysis for Strategic Warning* (Washington, DC: Center for Strategic Intelligence Research, Joint Military Intelligence College, 2002).

65. Peter Calvocoressi, *Top Secret Ultra* (New York: Ballantine Books, 1980) p. 124. For another example, see Matthew Aid, *The Secret Sentry: The Untold Story of the National Security Agency* (New York: Bloomsbury Press, 2009), p. 30.

66. A study of the related question of why people miss signals of an impending breakup is relevant to intelligence. Diane Vaughan, *Uncoupling: Turning Points in Intimate Relationships* (New York: Oxford University Press, 1986).

67. The most complete account is David Murphy, *What Stalin Knew: The Enigma of Barbarossa* (New Haven: Yale University Press, 2005); also see Geoffrey Roberts, *Stalin's Wars* (New Haven: Yale University Press, 2007), chap. 3.

68. The classic study is Richard Neustadt, *Alliance Politics* (New York: Columbia University Press, 1970).

69. Raymond Garthoff, *Detente and Confrontation: American-Soviet Relations from Nixon to Reagan* (Washington, DC: Brookings Institution, 1985), pp. 964–65.

70. Lawrence Freedman, *The Official History of the Falklands Campaign*, vol. 1, *The Origins of the Falklands War* (London: Routledge, 2005), p. 225.

71. Douglas MacEachin, *Predicting the Soviet Invasion of Afghanistan: The Intelligence Community's Record* (Washington, DC: CIA Center for the Study of Intelligence, 2002), p. 46; Diamond, *CIA and the Culture of Failure*, p. 29; William Odom, "How Far Can Soviet Reform Go?" *Problems of Communism*, vol. 36, November–December 1987, p. 30. As MacEachin notes in connection with another case, "when analysts did try to make the case for the dumb move, they were also categorized as dumb." *U.S. Intelligence and the Confrontation in Poland, 1980–1981* (University Park: Pennsylvania State University Press, 2002), p. 231.

72. Quoted in Gabriel Gorodetsky, *Grand Delusion: Stalin and the German Invasion of Russia* (New Haven: Yale University Press, 1999), pp. 305, 308. Shortly before he was overthrown, Archbishop Makarios of Cyprus dismissed this possibility because a coup would lead to an invasion by Turkey and so "would not make sense, it would not be reasonable." Quoted in Lawrence Stern, *The Wrong Horse* (New York: New York Times Books, 1977), p. 106. In parallel, the American chief of intelligence in Vietnam looked back at the Tet offensive and declared, "Even had I known exactly what was to take place, it was so preposterous that I probably would have been unable to sell it to anybody. Why would the enemy give away his major advantage, which was his ability to be elusive and avoid heavy casualties?" Quoted in William Westmoreland, *A Soldier Reports* (Garden City, NY: Doubleday, 1976), p. 321.

73. Treverton, *Reshaping National Intelligence*, pp. 4–5.

74. Sherman Kent, "A Crucial Estimate Relived," *Studies in Intelligence*, vol. 8, Spring 1964, pp. 1–18; also see Klaus Knorr, "Failures in National Intelligence Estimates: The Case of the Cuban Missiles," *World Politics*, vol. 16, April 1964, pp. 455–67.

75. This is a topic I have revisited several times, most recently in "Understanding Beliefs," pp. 641–63. Robert Trivers argues that this kind of self-deception is functional and has evolved because it facilitates the actor's deception of others. *Natural Selection and Social Theory* (New York: Oxford University Press, 2002), pp. 55–93. Although there is something to this, as I will explain below, it also makes it easier for people to live with themselves.

76. For further discussion, see Jervis, *American Foreign Policy in a New Era*, pp. 125–29.

77. In fact, it is clear that much of the fragmentation and many of the gaps and inefficiencies in the IC stem from the desire to serve multiple political and bureaucratic objectives, combined with the fear of an excessively powerful intelligence service. Amy Zegart, *Flawed by Design: The Evolution of the CIA, JCS and NSC* (Stanford: Stanford University Press, 1999); also see the classic analysis by Herbert Kaufman, *Red Tape: Its Origins, Uses, and Abuses* (Washington, DC: Brookings Institution, 1977). But it does not seem that any country's intelligence system has produced markedly better results than the American one, and in the wake of the 1973 war Israel's Agranat commission urged reforms that amounted to copying much of the U.S. system, despite that the fact that the United States too had been taken by surprise. Betts, *Enemies of Intelligence*, p. 35.

78. For IC organization, a valuable study is Michael Warner and J. Kenneth McDonald, *U.S. Intelligence Community Reform Studies Since 1947* (Washington, DC: CIA Center for the Study of Intelligence, 2005).

79. Diane Vaughan, *The Challenger Launch Decision: Risky Technology, Culture, and Deviance at NASA* (Chicago: University of Chicago Press, 1996). Vaughan draws in part on

Charles Perrow, *Normal Accidents: Living with High Risk Technologies* (New York: Basic Books, 1984). For another superb analysis of this type see Scott Snook, *Friendly Fire: The Accidental Shootdown of U.S. Black Hawks Over Northern Iraq* (Princeton: Princeton University Press, 2000). For a report on the Army Corps of Engineers errors that led to the failures of the New Orleans levees in 2005, see Douglas Woolley and Leonard Shabman, "Decision-Making Chronology for the Lake Pontchartrain & Vicinity Hurricane Protection Project," June 2007, http://www.iwr.usace.army.mil/inside/products/pub/hpdc/DraftFinalHPDC3.pdf.

80. For related treatments, see Herman, *Intelligence Power,* pp. 224–28; Mark Lowenthal, "The Burdensome Concept of Failure," in Maurer, Tunstal, and Keagle, eds., *Intelligence,* pp. 43–56; Lowenthal, "Towards a Reasonable Standard for Analysis: How Right, How Often on Which Issues?" *Intelligence and National Security,* vol. 23, June 2008, pp. 303–15; Treverton, *Reshaping National Intelligence,* chap. 6; Betts, *Enemies of Intelligence,* pp. 21, 64–65, 187–90. Also see Steve Chan, *American Political Science Review,* vol. 73, March 1979, pp. 171–80. For a parallel discussion in terms of judgment, see Tetlock, *Expert Political Judgment,* pp. 10–13.

81. For further discussion, see Paul Pillar, "Predictive Intelligence: Policy Support or Spectator Sport?" *SAIS Review,* vol. 28, Winter–Spring 2008, pp. 25–35.

82. This largely but not completely parallels the distinction between secrets and mysteries. Gregory Treverton, "Estimating beyond the Cold War," *Defense Intelligence Journal,* vol. 3, Fall 1994, pp. 5–20; Joseph Nye, "Peering into the Future," *Foreign Affairs,* vol. 74, July/August 1994, pp. 82–93.

83. *U.S. Department of State, Foreign Relations of the United States, 1964–1968,* vol. 10, *National Security Policy* (Washington, DC: Government Printing Office, 2002), pp. 461–62.

84. For reforms in intelligence structure, see Betts, *Enemies of Intelligence,* pp. 142–58. For justly critical reviews of the 9/11 Commission report, see Richard Posner, "The 9/11 Report: A Dissent," *New York Times Books Review,* August 29, 2004; Richard Falkenrath, "The 9/11 Commission Report: A Review Essay," *International Security,* vol. 29, Winter 2004–5, pp. 170–90; Joshua Rovner and Austin Long, "The Perils of Shallow Theory: Intelligence Reform and the 9/11 Commission," *Journal of Intelligence and CounterIntelligence,* vol. 18, Winter 2005–6, pp. 609–37; Paul Pillar, "Good Literature and Bad History: The 9/11 Commission's Tale of Strategic Intelligence," *Intelligence and National Security,* vol. 21, December 2006, pp. 1022–44. For more of an explanation than a defense, see Ernest May and Philip Zelikow, "Sins of Commission?" *International Security,* vol. 29, Spring 2005, pp. 208–9. For good discussions of the 9/11 case, see Charles Parker and Eric Stern, "Blindsided? September 11 and the Origins of Strategic Surprise," *Political Psychology,* vol. 23, September 2002, pp. 601–30; Parker and Stern, "Bolt from the Blue or Avoidable Failure? Revisiting September 11 and the Origins of Strategic Surprise," *Foreign Policy Analysis,* vol. 1, November 2005, pp. 301–31.

85. Michael Cohen, James March, and Johan Olsen, "A Garbage Can Model of Organizational Choice," *Administrative Science Quarterly,* vol. 17, March 1972, pp. 1–25; James March and Johan Olsen, *Ambiguity and Choice in Organizations* (Bergen, Norway: Universitetsforlaget, 1976).

86. For a good discussion, see Turner, *Burn before Reading;* for a parallel argument about reform of the Department of Defense, see Charles Reis, *The Management of Defense: Organization and Control of the U.S. Armed Services* (Baltimore: Johns Hopkins University Press, 1964).

87. For a good discussion, see Elbridge Colby, "Making Intelligence Smarter," *Policy Review,* no. 144, August–September 2007, pp. 71–82.

88. It still is, with the fate of the original plan to move it to the new DNI facilities now unclear.

89. For a related discussion, see Betts, *Enemies of Intelligence,* pp. 152–54.

90. John Diamond shows, however, that most of the failures of communication were within each agency rather than between agencies. *CIA and the Culture of Failure,* chap. 8.

91. Pat Roberts, "Comments & Responses: Intelligence Reform," *National Interest,* no. 81, Fall 2005, p. 8; Commission on the Intelligence Capabilities of the United States regarding Weapons of Mass Destruction, *Report to the President of the United States,* March 31, 2005, p. 321 (hereafter WMD Commission). For a good discussion, see Calvert Jones, "Intelligence Reform: The Logic of Information Sharing," *Intelligence and National Security,* vol. 22, June 2007, pp. 384–401. The recently instituted requirement that a necessary condition for promotion within the IC is serving a tour in another intelligence unit, a reform modeled on the Goldwater-Nichols act of 1986 regulating the military, is not as subject to these criticisms, but whether the advantages outweigh the disruptions is not yet apparent.

92. WMD Commission, pp. 125–26; Senate Select Committee on Intelligence, *Report on the U.S. Intelligence Community's Prewar Intelligence Assessments on Iraq,* July 7, 2004, pp. 267–68. Also see James Bruce, "The Missing Link: The Analyst-Collector Relationship," in George and Bruce, *Analyzing Intelligence,* pp. 191–210; for some of the dangers of close contact between analysts and collectors, see Garrett Jones, "It's a Cultural Thing: Thoughts on a Troubled CIA," part 1, June 28, 2005, Foreign Policy Research Institute, http://www.fpri.org/endnotes/20050628.americawar.jones.ciaculture.html.

93. This not only was recommended by the WMD Commission (p. 412) but had been urged by a CIA analyst in 1964. John Alexander, "An Intelligence Role for the Footnote," *Studies in Intelligence,* vol. 8, no. 3, 1964, reprinted in *Studies in Intelligence,* vol. 52, June 2008, pp. 59–66. For an earlier advocacy of footnotes, see Kent, *Strategic Intelligence,* pp. 178–79.

94. Many of these ideas grow out of the ones I proposed on the basis of my Iran postmortem, which indicates both how little has changed and how little I have learned. In addition to chapters 1 and 2 of this book, see my "What's Wrong with the Intelligence Process?" *International Journal of Intelligence and CounterIntelligence,* vol. 1, Spring 1986, pp. 42–56. For discussions of reforms that have some overlap with mine, see William Odom, *Fixing Intelligence: For a More Secure America* (New Haven: Yale University Press, 2003); Russell, *Sharpening Strategic Intelligence;* Jeffrey Cooper, *Curing Analytic Pathologies: Pathways to Improved Intelligence Analysis* (Washington, DC: CIA Center for the Study of Intelligence, 2005); Rob Johnston, *Analytic Culture in the U.S. Intelligence Community* (Washington, DC: CIA Center for the Study of Intelligence, 2005); Bruce Berkowitz and Allan Goodman, *Best Truth: Intelligence in the Information Age* (New Haven: Yale University Press, 2000); Jennifer Sims and Burton Gerber, eds., *Transforming U.S. Intelligence* (Washington, DC: Georgetown University Press, 2005). For reports on recent government efforts, see the testimony of Michael Hayden, Deputy Director of National Intelligence, http://intelligence.house.gov/Reports.aspx?Section=122; "A Tradecraft Primer: Structured Analytic Techniques for Improving Intelligence Analysis," published by CIA's Sherman Kent School, *Tradecraft Review* 2 (June 2005); Walter Pincus, "Estimates to Undergo More Scrutiny," *Washington Post,* March 26, 2008; National Intelligence Estimate, "Prospects for Iraq's Stability: A Challenging Road Ahead," January 2009, pp. 3–5; John Kringen, "How We've Improved Intelligence," *Washington Post,* April 3, 2006; Director of National Intelligence, Intelligence Community Directive No. 203, "Analytic Standards," June 21, 2007; Mike McConnell, "Overhauling

Intelligence," *Foreign Affairs,* vol. 86, July/August 2007, pp. 49–58. For discussions of some of the barriers to reform, see Richard Russell, "A Weak Pillar for American National Security: The CIA's Dismal Performance against WMD Threats," *Intelligence and National Security* vol. 20, September 2005, pp. 466–85; Gentry, *Lost Promise,* esp. pp. 93–107, 184; Thomas Mahnken, "Spies and Bureaucrats: Getting Intell Right," *Public Interest,* no. 159 (Spring 2005), pp. 22–42; Jones, "It's a Cultural Thing: Thoughts on a Troubled CIA," part 1 and part 2, August 19, 2005, Foreign Policy Research Institute, http://www.fpri.org/endnotes/20050819.americawar.jones.culturetroubledcia.html.

95. For a discussion of an intelligence success, see David Robarge, "Getting It Right: CIA Analysis of the 1967 Arab-Israeli War," *Studies in Intelligence,* vol. 49, no. 1, 2005, pp. 1–8. For a discussion of some of the earlier CIA postmortems, see Richard Shyrock, "The Intelligence Community Post-Mortem Program, 1973–1975," *Studies in Intelligence,* vol. 21, Fall 1997, pp. 15–22; also see Woodrow Kuhns, "Intelligence Failures: Forecasting and the Lessons of Epistemology," in *Paradoxes of Strategic Intelligence,* ed. Richard Betts and Thomas Mahnken (London: Cass, 2003), pp. 80–100; John Hedley, "Learning from Intelligence Failures," *International Journal of Intelligence and CounterIntelligence,* vol. 18, Fall 2005, pp. 435–50; Betts, *Enemies of Intelligence,* pp. 187–89. Douglas MacEachin, a former career CIA official, has done a series of excellent postmortems: *Predicting the Soviet Invasion of Afghanistan; U.S. Intelligence and the Confrontation in Poland; The Final Months of War With Japan: Signals Intelligence, U.S. Invasion Planning, and the A-Bomb Decision* (Washington, DC: CIA Center for the Study of Intelligence, 1998). Also see Janne Nolan and Douglas MacEachin with Kristine Tockman, *Discourse, Dissent, and Strategic Surprise: Formulating U.S. Security Policy in an Age of Uncertainty* (Washington, DC: Institute for the Study of Diplomacy, Georgetown University, 2006), and Loch Johnson, "Glimpses into the Gems of American Intelligence: The *President's Daily Brief* and the National Intelligence Estimate," *Intelligence and National Security,* vol. 23, June 2008, pp. 333–70. For the British experience, see "The Dog That Didn't Bark: The Joint Intelligence Committee and Warning of Aggression," *Cold War History,* vol. 7, November 2007, pp. 529–51. Of course postmortems are often highly politicized, as was true for several official studies of Iraq and 9/11; for an earlier example, see Max Holland, "The Politics of Intelligence Postmortems: Cuba 1962–1963," *International Journal of Intelligence and CounterIntelligence,* vol. 20, Fall 2007, pp. 415–52. The Iraq intelligence failure led to unusually serious self-examination within CIA and resulted in significant changes, some of which are noted in this chapter.

96. For an erroneous prediction of the collapse of a country, see Mark Mazzetti, "In '97, U.S. Panel Predicted a North Korea Collapse in 5 Years," *New York Times,* October 27, 2006. Of course one reason for the neglect of cases like this is that it usually takes years before one can be sure that they were wrong.

97. Liam Sarsfield et al., *Safety in the Skies: Personnel and Parties in NTSB Aviation Accident Investigations—Master Volume* (Santa Monica, CA: RAND, 2000).

98. For strong criticisms of CIA's managers, see Russell, *Sharpening Strategic Intelligence,* pp. 66–67, 90–93.

99. Jack Davis, personal communication. There is more peer review in NIEs because of the use of outside experts and the fact that the NIC itself constitutes a group of peers. Exactly how well this functions is not clear, however.

100. One does not have to believe in psychoanalysis to see that the evidence on this point is overwhelming. For a good summary, see Timothy Wilson, *Strangers to Ourselves: Discovering the Adaptive Unconscious* (Cambridge, MA: Harvard University Press, 2002).

101. For a good overview of existing and desirable analytic practices, see Mark Lowenthal, *Intelligence: From Secrets to Policy,* 3rd ed. (Washington, DC: CQ Press, 2006), chap. 6. For a general discussion of how cognitive biases apply to intelligence and might be counteracted, see Richards Heuer, *Psychology of Intelligence Analysis* (Washington, DC: CIA Center for the Study of Intelligence, 1999); also see David Moore, "Critical Thinking and Intelligence Analysis" (Joint Military Intelligence College Occasional Paper No. 14, May 2006).

102. Max Jacobson, *The Diplomacy of the Winter War* (Cambridge, MA: Harvard University Press, 1961), pp. 132–34.

103. For an excellent discussion of how alternative analysis can be developed, see Jack Davis, "Alternatives Analysis and the Perils of Estimating" (unpublished paper, October 6, 2003); also see Roger George, "Fixing the Problem of Analytical Mind-Sets: Alternative Analysis," *International Journal of Intelligence and CounterIntelligence,* vol. 17, Fall 2004, pp. 385–404. It is particularly important to examine alternatives that, even if unlikely, could have important policy consequences.

104. I owe this paragraph to discussion by Richard Smoke, although unfortunately I cannot locate the publication.

105. Quite a bit of psychology indicates that people tend to pay insufficient attention to these base rates, but it is not clear that this applies to foreign policy inferences. Robert Jervis, "Representativeness in Foreign Policy Judgments," *Political Psychology,* vol. 7, September 1986, pp. 483–506; for examples from medical diagnosis, see Groopman, *How Doctors Think,* pp. 126–28.

106. For a good discussion in the Iranian case, see Kurzman, *Unthinkable Revolution in Iran;* for the general problem of expectations being self-disconfirming, see Erik Gartzke, "War Is in the Error Term," *International Organization,* vol. 53, Summer 1999, pp. 567–87.

107. Olav Riste, "Intelligence and the 'Mindset': The German Invasion of Norway in 1940," *Intelligence and National Security,* vol. 22, February 2007, pp. 533–34.

108. For more on this point, see Richard Betts, "Warning Dilemmas: Normal Theory vs. Exceptional Theory," *Orbis,* vol. 26, Winter 1983, pp. 828–33; Betts, *Enemies of Intelligence,* chap. 3; Mark Lowenthal, "Intelligence Epistemology: Dealing with the Unbelievable," *International Journal of Intelligence and CounterIntelligence,* vol. 6, Fall 1993, pp. 319–26. The same phenomenon complicates doctors' diagnoses: Groopman, *How Doctors Think,* chaps. 2, 5.

109. In fact, the USSR had briefly put nuclear missiles into East Germany in 1959 but had taken them out again quite quickly. Although American intelligence had learned of this (ironically the Soviets were so concerned to keep this secret that they evicted Germans from the area and brought in Soviet laborers to do the work, and the resulting disturbances led analysts to discover what was happening), this episode had little impact and was not known to the analysts in 1962. Matthias Uhl and Vladimir Ivkin, "'Operation Atom': The Soviet Union's Stationing of Nuclear Missiles in the German Democratic Republic, 1959," *Cold War International History Bulletin,* no. 12/13, Fall/Winter 2001, pp. 299–307.

110. David Kay, "Iraq's Weapons of Mass Destruction," *Miller Center Report,* vol. 20, Spring/Summer 2004, p. 8. Ironically, the NIO in charge had led the postmortem on CIA's failure to realize that a facility the United States had destroyed in the Gulf War contained chemical weapons and had concluded that the basic flaw was that analysts assumed that Iraq would continue its pattern of storing these materials in buildings with a distinctive shape. Treverton, *Reshaping National Intelligence,* pp. 210–11.

111. Norman Rich, *Friedrich von Holstein: Politics and Diplomacy in the Era of Bismarck and Wilhelm II,* vol. 1 (London: Cambridge University Press, 1965); for an example of a state's incompetence leading to its being misperceived, see p. 366. As Rich says, "stupidity is of all political factors one of the most difficult for both friend and foe to evaluate and may lead to totally mistaken conclusions about the motives of a particular state."

112. Adam Galinsky, Joe Magee, M. Ena Inesi, and Deborah Gruenfeld, "Power and Perspectives Not Taken," *Psychological Science,* vol. 17, December 2006, pp. 1068–74.

113. For a harsh but I fear justified critique on this score, see Russell, *Sharpening Strategic Intelligence,* chap. 6.

114. William Nolte, "Rethinking War and Intelligence," in *Rethinking Principles of War,* ed. Anthony McIvor (Annapolis, MD: Naval Institute Press, 2005), chap. 13; Betts, *Enemies of Intelligence,* p. 127. In 1999 Deputy DCI John McLaughlin proudly noted that one out of seventy DI analysts was studying on a college campus, twice the number of the year before. Vernon Loeb, "Inside Information," *Washington Post,* December 13, 1999. This is not enough, however. A general discussion of how the IC can do better at attracting and retaining talent is Adrian Martin and Michael Tanji, "Farm Teams and Free Agents: The Sporting Way to Solve the Intelligence Community's Talent Woes," *International Journal of Intelligence and CounterIntelligence,* vol. 21, Winter 2008–2009, pp. 748–67.

Index